Setting Limits

How to Order:

Quantity discounts are available from the publisher, Prima Publishing, P.O. Box 1260BK, Rocklin, CA 95677; telephone (916) 632-4400. On your letterhead include information concerning the intended use of the books and the number of the books you wish to purchase.

▼

Setting Limits

How to Raise Responsible, Independent Children by Providing Reasonable Boundaries

Robert J. Mac Kenzie, Ed.D.

Prima Publishing
P.O. Box 1260BK
Rocklin, CA 95677
(916) 632-4400.

Library of Congress Cataloging-in-Publication Data
Mac Kenzie, Robert.
    Setting limits / Robert Mac Kenzie.
      p.   cm.
    Includes index.
    ISBN 1-55958-220-0
    1. Discipline of children. 2. Child rearing. 3. Parenting.
I. Title.
HQ770.4.M34   1992
649'.64—dc20   92-26210
                                      CIP

97 98 99 AA 10 9 8

Printed in the United States of America

To Jeanne, Scott, and Ian for their patience, love, and support. Without it, this book never would have been possible.

▼
___

Contents

Acknowledgments			ix
Introduction			xi
Chapter	1	How Parents Teach Their Rules	1
Chapter	2	How Children Learn Your Rules	33
Chapter	3	The Family Dance	47
Chapter	4	Are Your Limits Firm or Soft?	77
Chapter	5	Getting Off the Dance Floor	105
Chapter	6	Encouragement: The Language of Cooperation	121
Chapter	7	Teaching Problem-Solving Skills	139
Chapter	8	Supporting Your Rules with Consequences	157
Chapter	9	Setting Limits with Teens	201
Chapter	10	Handling Chores	241
Chapter	11	The Homework Dance	267
Chapter	12	Preparing for Change	297
Appendix		Starting a Parent Study Group	321
Suggested Reading			325
Index			327

▼

Acknowledgments

This book began as a workshop—actually two workshops, one for teachers and one for parents—titled TRIC: Training Responsible Independent Children. My appreciation goes to all who participated in these workshops over the last eight years. Your experiences, and your willingness to share them, helped to refine and improve many of the methods in this book. In many ways, you helped write this book.

Special thanks also goes to those who supported my workshops in major ways and to those who contributed to the writing of this book.

To Bob Trigg, superintendent of Elk Grove Unified School District, for funding and supporting my TRIC workshops for teachers over the last eight years.

To Chris Weber-Johnson, community services program coordinator, Davis, California, for supporting my TRIC parent workshops in the Davis community.

To Benzion Dominitz, publisher; Jennifer Basye, editor; and all the other good folks at Prima Publishing for believing in my project.

To Duane Newcomb, literary consultant, for teaching me nearly everything I know about writing a book of this type and for helping me get started.

To Karen Newcomb, my agent, for your patience, enthusiasm, and support.

To Barbara Wilhelm, Debbie Horowitz, staff, and parents at David Parent Nursery School for your suggestions on chores for preschoolers.

To Dr. Jonathan Sandoval, professor of Education, University of California, Davis, for your technical expertise with portions of the book.

To Dr. David Vollmar for your helpful editorial suggestions and willingness to be a sounding board when I needed to test out new ideas.

To Jean Seay and Dr. Curt Acredalo for your assistance with the many charts and diagrams.

To all the parents and children I've seen over the years in my counseling work. Your experiences helped many of the ideas and methods in this book take shape.

Introduction

This book was written for parents, but the concepts and methods it presents can be useful for anyone who wants to improve the way they communicate and set limits with children. The methods can be applied in many different settings.

Setting Limits provides the methods you need to stop misbehavior and to teach your rules in the clearest and most understandable way. You can say good-bye to lectures, threats, punishment, and persuasion. You won't need them anymore. No more arguments or power struggles, either. Your children will understand what you mean when you learn to set firm limits and support your words with effective action. This book will show you how to do that. The methods should be a welcome alternative to the ineffective extremes of punishment and permissiveness.

In the chapters that follow, you'll learn a complete and integrated approach to child guidance that is clear, systematic, and developmentally appropriate for your children, one that has been tested and used successfully by thousands of teachers and parents. The methods work,

and you can use them throughout your child's development, from age two through the teenage years.

As a family counselor and parent educator for a large
Northern California school district, and also in private
practice, I see hundreds of parents each year who have
become frustrated and discouraged by their children's
misbehavior. The vast majority of these parents are sincerely motivated to be effective in their child training.
They want their children to cooperate and be responsible,
but they don't know what to do to get that message across.
They've tried yelling, threatening, lecturing, reasoning,
bribing, spanking, grounding, and removing nearly every
favorite toy or privilege for long periods of time, all without success.

Their methods range from extreme permissiveness
to harsh punishment, but these parents all share at least
one thing in common. They are having problems setting
limits. They are doing the best they can with the skills they
have, but their methods aren't working for them, and
they don't know what else to do. They need more effective methods.

Setting limits is a process parents use to teach their
rules and expectations for acceptable behavior. The process is universal. All parents do it. It's the way we teach the
rules of our family, our society, and, ultimately, our culture.

How do we do it? Some parents do it with harsh
reprimands and punishment. Others do it with gentle
reminders and persuasion. Some shift back and forth between these two extremes. Still others do it by stating their
rules clearly and firmly and by holding children accountable for their choices.

Our methods may differ, but we all use the same basic
tools to get our message across: our words and our actions. Both send a message about our rules, but most of us
are more aware of our words than our actions. Communi-

cation can break down, and often does, when either of these messages are unclear or ineffective.

For example, when our words ("Clean up your room before playing") do not match our actions (child goes out to play, and mom cleans up the room), children receive a mixed message or unclear signal about our rules and expectations. Our words say "Clean it up," but our actions say "You really don't have to." What's the actual rule then about cleaning the room before playing? Of course, it's not really required. If your desire was to go out and play, which message would you follow?

Or consider the nine-year-old who is sent home from school for hitting. When his father finds out, the boy receives a stern lecture about cooperation and a spanking for violating school rules. What did this boy really learn about his father's rules? His father's words said "Cooperate at school," but the spanking conveyed a different message: "Hitting is the way we solve problems and get cooperation." What is this child most likely to do the next time he has an argument on the playground? Sure, he'll continue to use the methods he's really being taught.

Many parents today are holding up the wrong signals to stop misbehavior and teach their rules. They don't realize that their stop signs do not really require stopping or that their spoken rules are different from the rules they actually practice. They are teaching their rules with mixed messages.

These mixed messages, which I refer to as *soft limits* in the book, achieve the opposite of their intended effect. They invite testing and resistance and set up both parents and children for conflict. The toll on children, families, our schools, and our culture is enormous—behavior problems at home and in the classroom, power struggles, damaged relationships, and children poorly prepared to follow rules or handle freedom responsibly.

The tragedy is that many of these problems are

avoidable. They begin in our families, and they are the result of miscommunication about limits. Throughout the book, I refer to this pattern of miscommunication as the *family dance,* because nearly every family that operates on unclear or ineffective limits has its own special dance that it performs over and over again in conflict situations. Helping you to break free from these dances is a major goal of this book.

The first step toward breaking old patterns is to recognize the things that aren't working for you. Without this awareness, it will be difficult, if not impossible, to avoid repeating your old mistakes because most of them are made unconsciously. The first three chapters of the book are devoted to this purpose. You'll discover your current training approach, how children learn your rules, and the type of family dance you may be using to get your children to cooperate.

With an understanding of what hasn't worked for you, you'll be ready to learn new skills. Chapters 4 through 8 form the core of the skill-training program. In these chapters, you'll learn how to give clear messages about your rules, how to stop your family dances, how to encourage cooperation and better problem solving, and how to hold your children accountable with instructive consequences that won't injure their feelings or bodies.

In Chapter 9, you'll learn how to apply these methods with your teenager, who requires slightly different handling. In Chapters 10 and 11, you will see how these methods can be used to handle problems with chores and homework.

At the end of each chapter, you'll find a series of study group questions and topics for discussion as well as recommended skill-training exercises for the periods between meetings. Use them even if you are not participating in an organized study group. The questions should stimulate your thinking and help you become more involved with the material. The Appendix includes further information for scheduling and conducting parent study group meetings.

Learning the methods in this book will be the easiest part of your training. Most are fairly straightforward. The hardest part, for many of you, will be overcoming your strong desire to revert back to your old habits and do things the way you always have.

You may recognize intellectually that the methods will lead to the type of change you desire, but the methods and the changes they bring may not feel comfortable to you or your children in the beginning. You will likely encounter pressure and resistance to change, not only from your children, but from within yourself.

Chapter 12 will help you cope with the resistance you're likely to encounter and prepare you for the change that lies ahead. You'll learn how to overcome discouragement by developing realistic expectations and how to keep yourself on track by developing support systems when you need them.

You'll probably be tempted to try out the methods as you go, but I encourage you to read the entire book before using them with your children. The methods fit together and complement each other. Some require words; others require actions. Your total skills package will not be complete until you learn to use both of these steps together.

When you finish the book, refer to the suggestions for getting started immediately following Chapter 12. These tips will help you start off with the skills you need most and provide you with a comfortable schedule for adding new skills to your repertoire.

You should expect to make mistakes when you begin practicing your new skills. That's OK. Mistakes are part of learning. Your goal should be improvement, not perfection, and you will improve the more you practice. If you encounter unexpected problems with any of the methods, refer back to the pertinent chapters for assistance. Note the specific language that is used to carry out these techniques in the various examples. Chapter 12 should be particularly helpful to you during the critical first eight weeks.

The more consistency you can achieve between your methods and the methods used by other important people in your child's life, the faster your child's behavior will improve. Share your methods with your child's teacher, day-care provider, relatives, or friends who help out with child care. Their support will pay off.

Finally, many of the examples in this book reflect actual cases from my counseling work. In all of these examples, the names have been changed to protect the privacy of those involved.

The methods in this book have helped many parents and teachers enjoy more satisfying and cooperative relationships with children. If you are willing to invest the time and energy needed to learn the skills, you too can share the rewards. Enjoy *Setting Limits*.

How Parents Teach Their Rules

Years ago, when I first started giving workshops for parents, I didn't ask them what methods they already used. I just jumped in at the first session and showed them the methods I knew would be effective. As it turned out, this mistake led me to an important discovery.

I started getting calls and letters from parents thanking me for the helpful workshop. They would make comments such as: "Setting firm limits works great! I only have to yell once now and my kids do what I ask." "I like limited choices. When my son refuses to clean his room now, I tell him he has a choice—he can do it or get spanked." Perhaps my favorite came from a parent who said, "Now that I'm using firm limits I don't have to remind my kids more than two or three times to do what I ask."

Were we at the same workshop? I wondered. How is it possible that someone could so misinterpret the methods I was sharing? Then it occurred to me that we were view-

1

ing the methods from very different reference points. These parents were interpreting new methods through old beliefs and applying them the way they always had. Punitive parents were using them punitively, and permissive parents were using them permissively. They all thought they were doing things differently, but they were just repeating their old mistakes with new methods. I could see this was not a conscious process.

When I give workshops today, my first task is to help parents become acquainted with their current training methods so they can avoid repeating their old mistakes. I usually begin by demonstrating how a typical discipline problem can be handled in three different ways: punitively, permissively, and democratically. Then we examine the teaching and learning process that accompanies each approach. Most parents find this helpful.

My preference would be, if time permitted, to do the same thing I do in my counseling work to help parents understand their approach. I ask them to pick a typical misbehavior that occurs in their home. Then I ask each parent to describe, in a step-by-step manner, exactly what they say and do when their children behave this way. As each parent describes what happens, I diagram out on a blackboard each step in the interactional sequence. A visual picture of each parent's methods begins to emerge.

Unfortunately, we cannot draw your diagram together in a book, but we can do the next best thing. We can examine the experiences and diagrams of other parents who use similar methods to help you discover your approach. Let's begin by looking at how three parents handle a common playground problem.

Three parents are sitting on a park bench watching their children on a large play structure. One mother notices that the play is getting out of hand. The children are pushing each other at the top of the spiral slide.

"Meg, that looks a little dangerous to me," says the

2

mother. "I'm afraid one of you is going to get hurt. I'd feel more comfortable if you didn't do that."

"I'll be careful, Mommy," says Meg.

"I know you will, honey," says her mother, "but what you're doing worries me. I really wish you would stop." But Meg and the other children continue to push each other down the top of the slide.

Jeff's father also thinks the pushing looks dangerous. "Jeff!" he shouts. "Did you hear what Meg's mother just said? Now cut it out unless you want to get spanked."

"OK," says Jeff, but after a couple of minutes he and the other two children are back at it again. This catches the attention of the third parent, Patrick's mom.

"Patrick, would you come here please?" she asks. When Patrick arrives, his mother says, in a matter-of-fact voice, "You can play on the slide without pushing or play somewhere else. What would you like to do?"

"I won't push," Patrick says.

"Thanks," says his mom, and Patrick heads back up the play structure and no longer pushes. The children continue playing.

After a few minutes, the parents hear a sharp thud and a scream at the top of the slide. When they investigate, they discover that Jeff pushed Meg, and Meg conked her head on the side of the slide.

"What does it take to get through to you?" shouts Jeff's father as he applies several swats to Jeff's backside. "I hope you've learned something from this." With a disgusted look on his face, Jeff's dad returns to his seat on the bench. Jeff, still rubbing his backside, heads back to the slide.

With a bump on her head, Meg joins the boys once again. The play continues, but not more than a minute goes by before Meg lets out a second scream. "He pushed me again," she cries, holding her knee this time and pointing an accusing finger at Jeff.

"Why, you little brat!" shouts Jeff's father angrily. "I've had it with you!" He gives Jeff two more swats, much harder than before, grabs him by the collar, and marches him off for home.

Each of the parents tried to set limits on their child's behavior, but only one enjoyed much success. Jeff's father used the punitive approach. His limits were firm, but his methods were harsh and not very respectful. Jeff ended up rebelling.

Meg's mother used permissiveness. Her methods were respectful, but her limits lacked firmness. Meg ignored her mother's requests.

Patrick's mother used the democratic approach. Her limits were firm, and her methods were respectful. Unlike his playmates, Patrick ended up cooperating.

Most parents discipline primarily from one of these three basic training models (Figure 1A). Some switch back and forth between the ineffective extremes — the punitive and permissive models. Each model is premised on a different set of beliefs about how children learn, the parent's role in the training process, and the proper distribution of power and responsibility between parents and children. Each model also teaches a different set of lessons about cooperation, responsibility, and your rules for acceptable behavior.

Figure 1A. Three training models

Permissive Approach	Democratic Approach	Punitive/Autocratic Approach
Freedom without limits	Freedom within limits	Limits without freedom
Problem Solving by Persuasion	Problem Solving through Cooperation and Accountability	Problem Solving by Force

4

The Punitive or Autocratic Approach (Limits Without Freedom)

Let's look at how a typical behavior problem, a sibling quarrel, is handled from each of these three training models. We'll begin with the punitive approach. As the parent arrives on the scene, her two sons are pushing and yelling and struggling over a toy. An argument is about to become a fight.

Parent: (in a loud voice, almost yelling) "What's going on here? Can't you two play quietly without acting like wild animals?"

Sibling 1: "I had it first, and he took it away from me."

Sibling 2: "No, I had it first! Make him give it back to me."

Parent: (clearly angered) "Both of you couldn't have had it first, so one of you must be lying. Tell me the truth. Who really had it first?"

Sibling 1: "I did."

Sibling 2: "He's lying! I had it first."

Parent: "I knew I couldn't trust you two to tell me the truth. I've had enough of this squabbling and lying! Nobody is going to play with the toy because I'm putting it away. Now if I hear any more arguing or fighting from you two, you're going to spend the rest of the evening in your rooms. Do you understand? (yelling now) So, knock it off!"

Sibling 1: "The wicked witch strikes again."

Sibling 2: (Laughs at the comment.)

Parent: "That's not funny, and I won't tolerate anybody talking to me like that. You both just earned yourselves an evening in your rooms."

Sibling 1: "I bet you enjoy making life miserable for others."

Sibling 2: "Yeah!"

Parent: (yelling) "Get to your rooms now!" (Gives each child a swat on the behind as they head for their rooms.)

Sound familiar? If it does, you're not alone. The punitive approach remains one of the most widely used training models.

Parents who use punishment find themselves in the roles of police detective, judge, jailer, and probation officer. Their job is to investigate their children's misdeeds, determine guilt, assign blame, impose penalties, and carry out sentences. Parents direct and control the problem-solving process, which is often adversarial. Penalties tend to be severe.

Let's examine a diagram of the interaction of the two boys and their mother so we can get a better idea of what's going on (Figure 1B). We'll place the parent's behavior on the left side of the diagram and the children's behavior on the right.

At point A, the parent arrives on the scene already annoyed and intervenes with detective work. The tone is adversarial. The focus is on right and wrong, guilt and blame, good guys and bad guys.

The kids pick up on this dynamic quickly and appeal to the parent while accusing each other of lying. The detective work only leads to more blaming and accusations. The parent becomes more frustrated.

By midpoint in the interaction, the parent's anger and frustration takes over. She has completely personalized the conflict. The original sibling quarrel is now secondary to the parent-child conflict that dominates the interaction. What started off as problem solving has deteriorated into a hurtful and escalating power struggle.

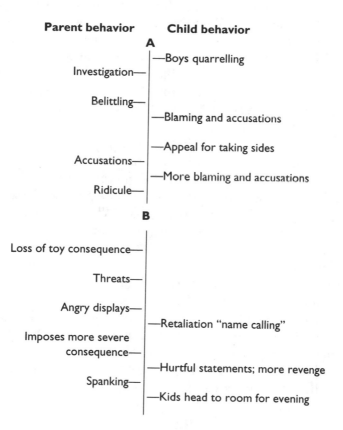

Figure 1B. Diagram of punitive interaction

Parent behavior | Child behavior

A
—Boys quarrelling

Investigation—

Belittling—
—Blaming and accusations

—Appeal for taking sides

Accusations—
—More blaming and accusations

Ridicule—

B

Loss of toy consequence—

Threats—

Angry displays—
—Retaliation "name calling"

Imposes more severe
consequence—
—Hurtful statements; more revenge

Spanking—
—Kids head to room for evening

The parent attempts next to end the quarrel at point B by applying a consequence. She removes the toy and threatens more severe consequences if the boys don't cooperate. But it's too late. The interaction won't end that easily. Sharing the toy is no longer the central issue. Feelings have been hurt, and the kids want revenge. They launch into a new round of name calling and disrespectful statements.

7

So the parent plays her final power card. She gives each child a swat and sends them to their rooms for the evening. The interaction ends, but what was really accomplished?

The parent did stop the misbehavior eventually, but did the kids learn any new skills for resolving conflicts on their own? Did they receive any positive object lessons in cooperation or responsibility? And what did they learn about problem solving?

As a training model, the punitive approach only partially accomplishes our basic training goals. It usually does stop unwanted behavior, but it doesn't teach independent problem solving, and it doesn't teach positive lessons about responsibility or self-control. Why not? Because parents make all the decisions, and parents do all the problem solving. Parents have all the power and control, and the kids are left out of the process. In effect, the punitive approach takes responsibility and learning opportunities away from children.

What do you think will happen the next time the two brothers have a conflict? Sure, one of them will scream for mom or dad to come solve the problem for them. If mom or dad doesn't show up in time, the boys will battle it out with the methods they know best—yelling, threatening, blaming, name calling, and hitting.

Some may think that my example proves that punishment works. After all, the parent did stop her children's misbehavior. I agree. If your definition of effectiveness is limited to stopping misbehavior in an immediate situation, then punishment works. But the cooperation punishment achieves often comes at a high price: injured feelings, damaged relationships, and angry power struggles.

Punishment is humiliating to children. It hurts their feelings, makes them angry, and incites their resistance or withdrawal. The harsh methods prevent our getting

8

across the message of cooperation.

Imagine that your supervisor tries to exhort you on to better performance by criticizing and degrading you in front of others. Would your response be to say, "Thanks, I needed that. I understand your point, and I'll do a much better job now." Probably not. Would you feel like cooperating with this person? Again, probably not.

More likely, you would feel like inflicting back some of the hurt and pain that was inflicted upon you. Or you might choose instead to be overly compliant and avoid contact with this person altogether. When it comes to being humiliated, children respond much like adults. They get angry. They rebel and seek revenge, and, sometimes, they withdraw in fearful submission.

If punishment has so many limitations, why then do so many parents continue to use it? Most parents use punishment because they were trained that way. It feels natural, and they don't question its effectiveness. When things break down, they assume the problem is with their children, not their methods.

I recall one parent who arrived at my office with his ten-year-old son, Kyle. "He's going through some kind of a rebellious stage," his father announced. "He won't do anything he's told."

Kyle and his father had been locked in a power struggle for some time. Both sides were so angry with one another that they hadn't spoken for nearly a week.

The problem began when Kyle arrived home nearly two hours late from school one day. He told his parents he was playing basketball and simply lost track of the time. Kyle's father was determined to see that the problem didn't happen again. He suspended Kyle's afterschool play privileges for two weeks.

When Kyle tried to protest the decision, his father sent him to his room. Kyle got mad. "You're a tyrant!" he

9

shouted, and he kicked a hole in his door. His father shouted back and informed Kyle he was grounded until further notice and that his allowance would be withheld for two months to pay for the door. Kyle refused to do his chores.

After three weeks, they were still stuck. No chores had been done, and Kyle spent most of his time sulking around the house. His parents were miserable too. Both sides blamed the other, and neither side was willing to budge. It was hard to tell who was being punished most, Kyle or his parents.

"How would your father have handled this problem?" I asked the father, hoping to take some of the pressure off Kyle.

"I would have been spanked as soon as I got home, and then I would have been grounded, probably for a couple of weeks," he replied.

"Did that kind of punishment ever seem excessive to you?" I asked.

"Sometimes it did, but that was my father's way of teaching me a lesson. Lots of parents did that when I was young, and their kids learned from it too," he replied.

Like many parents raised with punishment, Kyle's father was taught that consequences had to be painful for children to learn. He was applying this same belief with his son.

"Did your father's lessons ever make you angry?" I asked.

"Frequently," he replied. "I can remember thinking he was a real tyrant at times. We had our share of quarrels too." Kyle began to perk up and get interested.

"So punishment made you angry and rebellious too," I observed. "Were your quarrels with your father anything like the one you're having now with Kyle?"

He looked at Kyle and smiled. He was beginning to see that rebellion was not the problem. His methods were

Figure 1C. The autocratic or punitive approach

Parents' beliefs	If it doesn't hurt, children won't learn
	Children won't respect your rules unless they fear your methods
	It's my job to control my children
	It's my job to solve my children's problems
Power and control	All for parents
Problem-solving process	Problem solving by force
	Adversarial
	Win-lose (parents win)
	Parents do all the problem solving and make all the decisions
	Parents direct and control the process
What children learn	Parents are responsible for solving children's problems
	Hurtful methods of communication and problem solving
How children respond	Anger, stubbornness
	Revenge, rebellion
	Withdrawal, fearful submission

(see Figure 1C). He was ready to learn some better ways to get his message across.

The Permissive Approach (Freedom Without Limits)

Permissiveness emerged prominently in the 1960s and 1970s as a reaction against the rigidity and autocratic nature of the punitive approach. Many parents were

11

looking for a new and more democratic method of raising children based on principles of freedom, equality, and mutual respect.

Putting these principles into practice, however, was not as easy as it sounded. This was uncharted territory for those of us who grew up with the punitive model. How do you do it? Was it a simple matter of relaxing your rules and expectations and giving your children more freedom and control? That's what many parents tried, but the experiment often backfired because a vital ingredient was left out — firm limits.

Freedom without limits is not democracy. It's anarchy, and children trained with anarchy do not learn respect for rules or authority or how to handle their freedom responsibly. They tend to think primarily of themselves and have an exaggerated sense of their own power and control.

Let's return now to our example of the sibling conflict and see how this problem is handled from the permissive approach.

Parent: "Hey guys, I don't like all this yelling and arguing. It sounds like a battle zone around here." (Walks out of the room, but quarrel continues.)

Parent: (entering the room again, annoyed) "Did you two hear what I just said? Would you keep it down and stop all the hassling? OK?" (Leaves again, but quarrel continues.)

Parent: (entering the room a third time) "How many times do I have to tell you guys? Do you think I enjoy repeating myself? Can't you two just be nice to one another for a change? I can't stand living in a house where people shout and argue with each other all the time! Someday, you'll regret the way you're treating each other. Now please, try to get along!" (Quarrel continues.)

Sibling 1: "I had it first, and he took it away from me."

Sibling 2: "No I didn't. He set it down and wasn't playing with it, so I started playing with it."

Parent: "Why don't you guys just take turns with it?"

Sibling 1: "OK, I get it first." (Grabs the toy.)

Sibling 2: "No, I get it first." (Also tugs at it.)

Parent: (exasperated and yelling) "I've had it with you guys! (grabs the toy away from both of them) Now, nobody is going to have it!"

Sibling 1: "That's not fair!"

Sibling 2: "Yeah, we were playing with it!"

Parent: "Will you both promise not to fight over it any more?"

Sibling 1: "I promise."

Sibling 2: "I promise too."

Parent: "OK, you can have it back, but no more fighting. I really mean it." (Hands toy back to sibling 1.)

Sibling 2: (protesting and tugging again at the toy) "He already had a turn. It's my turn."

Sibling 1: "No I didn't!"

Parent: "You guys are incorrigible! I've had it. Go ahead and fight it out if you want, but do it quietly." (Leaves the room exasperated.)

Permissive parents, like the one in our example, are constantly shifting gears and trying different tactics to convince their children to cooperate. They do a lot of repeating, reminding, pleading, cajoling, bargaining, lecturing, reasoning, debating, and other forms of persuasion. Consequences, if they are used at all, are typically late and ineffective. By the time everything is said and done, parents usually end up compromising away their

13

limits or giving in altogether, and children end up getting their own way. Permissiveness is humiliating to parents.

As a training approach, permissiveness is certainly much worse than punishment for both parents and children. It doesn't accomplish any of our basic goals. It doesn't stop misbehavior. It doesn't teach responsibility, and it doesn't teach the lessons we intend about our rules or our authority.

Let's become better acquainted with this approach by examining a diagram of the interaction in our example (Figure 1D).

The first thing you probably notice is the length of this diagram. Permissive parents invest a great deal of time and energy in methods that aren't working for them. This parent is no exception. She begins at point A with a lot of repeating and reminding. The children respond by ignoring her. So she tries lecturing and pleading, but that doesn't work either. The kids continue to ignore her.

So the parent suggests a reasonable solution — taking turns — but neither child is willing to cooperate if the solution means not getting his own way. The parent becomes frustrated.

She shifts gears again and tries something different. She removes the toy but is quickly confronted with a chorus of protests. Her kids are upset. She feels guilty and gives in.

She makes a final attempt at bargaining for their cooperation. Promises are made, then broken, and she finally gives up and leaves the scene discouraged. She never did succeed in stopping their misbehavior or teaching them a better way to resolve disputes.

Why didn't the boys cooperate? The reason is simple. They didn't have to. Cooperation was optional, not required. There was nothing holding them accountable for their behavior because their mother was unwilling to sup-

Figure 1D. Diagram of permissive interaction

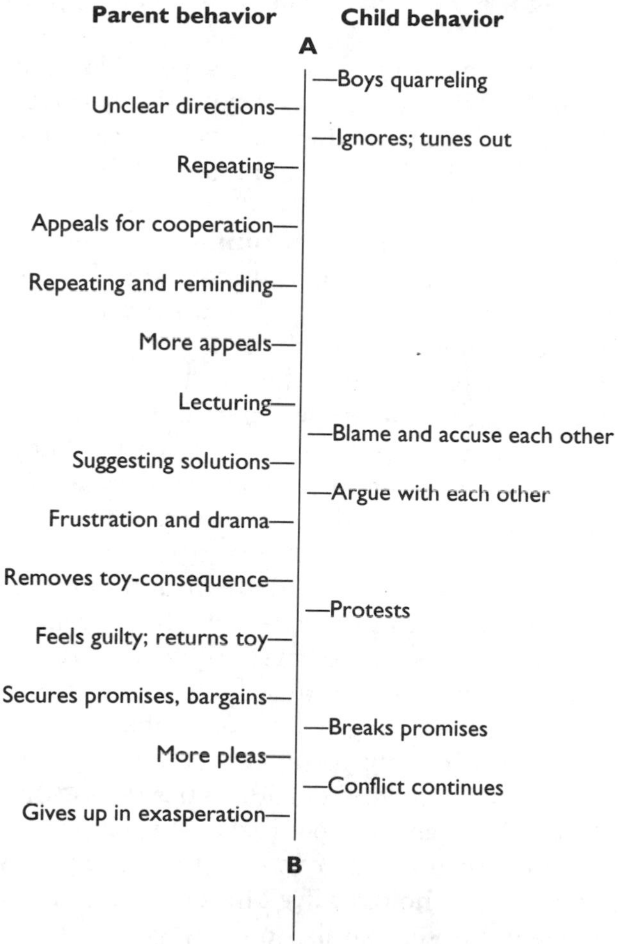

Parent behavior	Child behavior
	A
	—Boys quarreling
Unclear directions—	
	—Ignores; tunes out
Repeating—	
Appeals for cooperation—	
Repeating and reminding—	
More appeals—	
Lecturing—	
	—Blame and accuse each other
Suggesting solutions—	
	—Argue with each other
Frustration and drama—	
Removes toy-consequence—	
	—Protests
Feels guilty; returns toy—	
Secures promises, bargains—	
	—Breaks promises
More pleas—	
	—Conflict continues
Gives up in exasperation—	
	B

port her words with effective action (consequences). She relied instead on persuasion to get her message across.

Can you imagine what things would be like if traffic laws were enforced in this way? There you are, on your way home. The traffic is light, and each time you ap proach an intersection with no other cars around you run the stop sign. Eventually, a cop sees you and pulls you over.

"You ran four stop signs," he says. "That's against the law, and the laws are there for your safety and protection. Please try to follow them in the future." Then he gets in his car and drives off, and that's all that ever happens.

Would this stop you from running stop signs in the future? Do you think it would stop others? If all of our traffic laws were enforced like this, do you think people would take them very seriously? Not likely.

Permissive parents are a lot like the cop. They give lots of warnings, reminders, and persuasive reasons when their kids fail to stop at their stop signs. They may threaten to write tickets, and sometimes they actually follow through, but most of the time their kids talk their way out of it and things pass with just a warning. Without tickets (consequences) to hold them accountable, kids have little cause to take their parents' rules seriously.

Why are permissive parents so reluctant to use consequences in their training? Most have the best of intentions. They're not trying to be vague about their rules. They're simply looking for a way to get their message across without causing their children frustration or upsetting them. These parents believe that the temporary frustration that accompanies consequences might damage their children psychologically. Therefore, when children act sufficiently upset, parents quickly give in to protect their children from emotional injury. A set-up for tantrums? You bet!

Let's do a little reality testing. Are you accustomed to always getting your own way out in the world? When you don't, do you feel good about it? Aren't we supposed to feel a little frustrated when we don't get what we want? Isn't that how we learn to adjust to reality? When we prevent children from experiencing the consequences of their actions, we also prevent much of their learning.

If consequences play such a minor role in the training process, then what stops misbehavior? How do children learn our rules? Permissive parents believe that children will stop misbehaving when they realize that stopping is the right thing to do. The parents' job, therefore, is to convince children to accept this belief.

When we test this assumption against our actual experiences, we see how it begins to break down. Sometimes children do cooperate because they realize that cooperation is the right thing to do. Other times, the only reason they cooperate is because they have to.

Imagine that it's time for dinner in your house. You've prepared a nice meal, and you're ready to serve it. Your children are watching their favorite TV show in the other room. When you ask them to come to the table, you hear in chorus, "We will, Mom." But five minutes go by and still nobody shows up. The food is getting cold. You're getting annoyed.

So you try again, "Guys, I said it's time for dinner." And you hear, "Please Mom, this is the best part. We'll be there in just a minute." You say, "OK, but only a minute," and another five minutes go by. Now, you're very annoyed.

So you walk into the other room, stand between your children and the set, and say, "It's time to come to the table now!" And you hear, "Oh please Mom, it's almost over! Please. . . . " But you've had enough. You turn off the set, and the children head for the table.

Why did the children come to the table? Was it because that was the right thing to do? No. They came because they had to. The set was turned off, and they could no longer watch their program. They finally got a clear message about your expectations.

When our words are supported by our actions, children get a clear message about our rules and expectations. They know that our spoken rules are the rules we practice, and they learn to take our words seriously.

When our words are not supported by our actions, however, children learn to ignore our words and to continue to do what they want. The message they receive sounds something like this: "I don't like what you're doing, but I'm not going to insist that you stop, at least not for awhile."

How do they know when they really are expected to stop? They don't. The only way they will know is by testing our limits to see how far they can go.

James, age five, is a good example. He was getting off to a rough start in kindergarten when I first met him. The note his teacher sent said "James is very disruptive and uncooperative in class. He pushes everything to the limit. When I ask him to join an activity, he usually ignores me and does what he wants. When I insist, he cries or has a tantrum. He seems to think the classroom rules don't apply to him."

James's mother, a single parent, also was very frustrated. "He's the same way at home," she complained. "He refuses to get dressed in the morning. He won't come in when I call him for dinner and getting him to bed at night is a nightmare by itself. I have to ask him over and over again, and most of the time he just ignores me and does what he wants."

Like many children trained with permissiveness, James was accustomed to getting his own way, and he had learned a full repertoire of skills to make that happen. He was an expert at tuning out, ignoring, resisting, avoiding, arguing, debating, bargaining, challenging, and defying. If those tactics didn't work, James played his power card. He threw a tantrum. His mother usually felt guilty and gave in.

James's intentions were not malicious. He did it because it worked. His experiences had taught him that "Rules are for others, not me. I make my own rules, and I do what I want." James operated on these beliefs both at home and in the classroom.

It wasn't hard to understand why James had such an exaggerated perception of his own power and authority and why he was doing so much testing. At home, his stop signs did not require stopping, and no really meant yes most of the time. When he misbehaved, he knew he would hear a lot of repeating, reminding, lecturing, and empty threats, but none of those methods required stopping. His training had not prepared him for the real stop signs he was encountering out in the world. (See Figure 1E.)

The Democratic Approach (Freedom Within Limits)

We've seen that effective child training requires a balance between firmness and respect. The punitive approach is firm but not respectful. The permissive approach, on the other extreme, is respectful but lacks firmness. Both extremes are based on win-lose methods of problem solving and faulty beliefs about learning. Neither extreme teaches responsibility or accomplishes our basic training goals. What, then, is the alternative?

Fortunately, there is an alternative to the extremes of punishment and permissiveness. The democratic approach is a win-win method of problem solving that combines firmness with respect and accomplishes all of our basic training goals. It stops misbehavior. It teaches responsibility. And it conveys, in the clearest way, the lessons we want to teach about our rules for behaving acceptably. Best of all, this approach achieves our goals with less

Figure 1E. The permissive approach

Parents' beliefs	Children will cooperate when they understand that cooperation is the right thing to do
	My job is to serve my children and keep them happy
	Consequences that upset my children cannot be effective
Power and control	All for children
Problem-solving process	Problem solving by persuasion
	Win-lose (children win)
	Parents do most of the problem solving
What children learn	"Rules are for others, not me. I do as I wish."
	Parents serve children
	Parents are responsible for solving children's problems
	Dependency, disrespect, self-centeredness
How children respond	Limit testing
	Challenge and defy rules and authority
	Ignore and tune out words
	Wear parents down with words

time and energy and without injuring feelings, damaging relationships, or provoking angry power struggles in the process.

The democratic approach succeeds where others fail because the process is cooperative, not adversarial. It focuses on what child training is all about — teaching and

20

learning. Parents guide, not direct, the problem-solving process by providing children with clearly defined limits, acceptable choices, and instructive consequences that hold them accountable for their actions (Figure 1F).

Let's return once again to our now-familiar sibling conflict and see how this problem is handled from the democratic approach.

Figure 1F. The democratic approach

Parents' beliefs	Children are capable of solving problems on their own
	Children should be given choices and allowed to learn from the consequences of their choices
	Encouragement is an effective way to motivate cooperation
Power and control	Children are given only as much power and control as they can handle responsibly
Problem-solving process	Cooperative
	Win-win
	Based on mutual respect
	Children are active participants in the problem solving process
What children learn	Responsibility
	Cooperation
	Independence
	Respect for rules and authority
	Self-control
How children respond	More cooperation
	Less limit testing
	Resolve problems on their own
	Regard parents' words seriously

21

Parent: (in a matter-of-fact voice) "Guys, stop the yelling and arguing. I'm sure we can find a way to share that toy without fighting over it. Do you guys need a little time to cool off first before we talk?"

Sibling 1: "I can talk."

Sibling 2: "Me too."

Parent: "What would be another way to handle this problem without yelling and arguing about it?"

Sibling 1: "I don't know, but I had it first, and he took it from me."

Sibling 2: "No, he put it down, so I started playing with it."

Parent: "Well, you guys can either share the toy for ten minutes each, or I can put the toy away. What would you like to do?"

Sibling 1: "I'll share."

Sibling 2: "So will I, but I get it first."

Parent: "Good choice guys, and we'll flip a coin to see who gets it first. I'll go set the timer."

Unlike the previous examples, this parent succeeds at stopping her children's misbehavior and teaching the lessons she intends. She accomplishes all of this without conflicts or power struggles. Let's take a closer look at how she does this by examining a diagram of the interaction (Figure 1G).

Notice how short this diagram is. Effective teaching requires much less time and energy. This parent is working with a plan. She knows what she's going to do, and she's prepared for whatever resistance she may encounter. No time is wasted on ineffective lobbying or detective work.

Her first step is to give a clear message about the behavior she wants to stop. She requests her children, in a

Figure IG. Diagram of democratic interaction

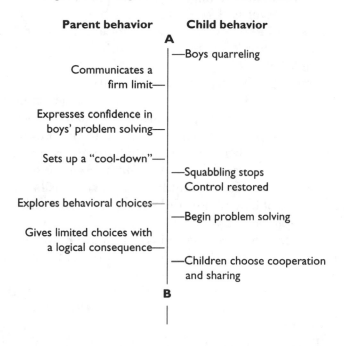

matter-of-fact voice, to stop the yelling and arguing. Then she gets right to work creating a climate of cooperation by using "we" messages and expressing confidence in their ability to work things out. Her words are encouraging. Her message is clear and direct. In two brief sentences, she establishes an atmosphere of cooperation and mutual respect.

This parent understands that successful problem solving rarely occurs in an atmosphere of anger and upset, so she provides her sons with the skills they need to manage their angry feelings. She asks if they need a cool-off period before talking.

The cool-off period, in this instance, is presented as a choice, and the exercise of that choice teaches children to be responsible for managing their angry feelings. If the frustration level had been greater, the cool-off period would have been presented as mandatory rather than optional (such as "We need to cool off for five minutes, then we'll talk.").

When she is sure emotional control has been restored, she checks in with her children to determine if they have the skills and information needed to resolve the quarrel on their own. Their responses indicate they don't, so she suggests several solutions that are presented, once again, in the form of limited choices. By choosing the solution themselves, the children learn responsibility for their own problem solving and acquire a tool for resolving future disputes on their own.

The training exercise ends at point B the way it began — in an atmosphere of cooperation and mutual respect. All goals were accomplished. The misbehavior stopped. The children received the skill training they needed, and no feelings were injured in the process. Everyone emerged a winner.

This parent was so effective at setting limits and teaching problem solving that consequences were not even needed. If consequences had been needed, she would have applied them like Amanda's father in the next example.

Three-year-old Amanda is blowing bubbles in her cup at the dinner table. In a firm but matter-of-fact voice, her father says, "Amanda, we don't blow bubbles at the table. I know you can use the cup the right way, but if you don't I'll have to take it away."

Amanda gives her father a defiant look, puts the cup back to her lips, and blows some more bubbles. Without any words, her father reaches over and takes the cup away. "You can have it back when the buzzer goes off," he says. He sets the timer for ten minutes. No reminding, no threats, no angry lectures or power struggles. All he needed was a clear message, a little encouragement, and an instructive consequence to get his message across.

Amanda cannot avoid learning responsibility for her behavior. She has all the information she needs to cooperate. Whether she chooses to stop or continues blowing bubbles, either way, she is accountable for her behavior, and she will learn the desired lesson about her family's rules. Her father is teaching effectively.

Can you see yourself handling problems like these two parents? Can you imagine how much more rewarding your parenting would be without all the arguments and power struggles? If you're shaking your head, you're not alone.

Mike's parents were feeling very defeated and discouraged when I first met them. They had read books, attended parenting classes, and had even consulted a pediatrician to see if there was a medical reason for their eight-year-old's misbehavior. Nothing had helped. They were desperate, and, to add to their distress, Mike's four-year-old brother was beginning to act the same way.

"Everything turns into a power struggle," his mother said as she described the problems they were having. "We talk to him until we're blue in the face, but he still does exactly what he wants. He ignores our rules, refuses to do chores, and takes things without asking. When we try to put our foot down, he becomes argumentative and disrespectful."

I asked each parent to describe what they said and did when Mike misbehaved. As they spoke, I drew a diagram of the interaction (Figure 1H). Their methods were very similar.

"Look familiar?" I asked, as we examined the diagram.

"That's it!" said his mother. "I'll bet we go through that routine half a dozen times a day."

I handed each parent a short description of the three

Figure 1H. A mixed approach—permissive and punitive

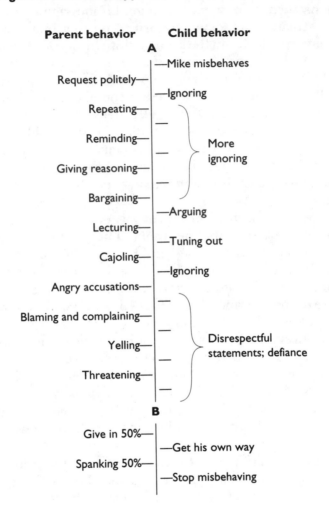

training models we've discussed thus far and gave them a few minutes to read it over. I could see by their raised eyebrows that they were beginning to recognize their approach.

"We're permissive!" said Mike's father with a surprised look on his face. "And I thought we were too hard on him. We're always yelling and complaining and lecturing him about one thing or another."

"No, I think we're punitive," Mike's mom corrected. "We sometimes use spankings too."

"Actually, you're both right," I said. Mike's parents were using what I call a mixed approach. They start off permissively, but half the time they become so angry with Mike's defiance that they end up using punitive methods. That's usually when the yelling and angry drama begins. Sometimes, they feel guilty at how tyrannical they sound and give in. Other times, they follow through with spankings. Mike doesn't know from one time to the next what will happen, so he usually tests the limits.

We spent the first part of our session examining the punitive and permissive training models and the responses these approaches evoke from children. It didn't take long for the parents to see why their message wasn't getting across. Their limits lacked firmness and consistency, and their consequences, if they occurred at all, were late or hurtful. Their methods were actually inspiring Mike's testing and revenge.

We got right to work practicing the skills you will learn in the upcoming chapters. They caught on quickly. In two brief sessions, they learned how to give clear messages, use the check-in procedure, limited choices, logical consequences, and time-out. They were eager to try the methods at home. That evening, before dinner, the parents sat down with their two sons and explained what they would do when the boys misbehaved.

Mike tested right away. After dinner, he was asked to clear his dishes from the table, a chore he was expected to do every night. He pretended not to hear. He walked into the other room, turned on the TV, and started watching a show.

27

His mother followed him. "Mike, did you understand what I just asked you to do?" she said in a matter-of-fact voice.

"Yeah, I heard you," he said. "I'll do it later."

Mike's mother turned off the TV and replied calmly, "You can do it in the next two minutes or you can spend the next ten minutes in your room getting ready to do it. What would you like to do? I'll set the timer."

What is this? thought Mike. *She's never done this before!* He crossed his arms defiantly and continued testing. The buzzer went off.

"Well, Mike," said his mother matter-of-factly, "you need to head to your room now. You'll have a chance to try it again in ten minutes."

Mike looked at her incredulously and so did his younger brother. *What? No reminders or lectures? No arguing or debating? What's going on?* he thought. So he shouted defiantly, "I'm not going, and you can't make me!"

His mother remained calm and continued to use her new skills. "You can go on your own for ten minutes or I can take you there for fifteen. What would you like to do?" she asked. Mike dug in his heels, so she carried him back, and he stayed there the full fifteen minutes.

When the buzzer went off, his mother invited him back. She didn't even seem annoyed. "Ready to clear your place now?" she asked. Mike glared at her defiantly, but he went to the table and cleared his dishes.

Over the next several weeks, Mike and his parents went through many more encounters like this, but the results were always the same. No lectures. No spankings. No angry power struggles. Mike either decided to cooperate or he experienced the consequences of his decision not to. Either way, Mike learned the lessons his parents were trying to teach.

Four weeks after we started, I got a call from Mike's dad. "I wanted you to know that things have really improved. Mike still tests from time to time, but he's cooperating much better than before. He's even doing his homework. This is sure a lot easier than battling with him.''

Mike and his parents were well on their way to improvement. It would be awhile before the changes would become part of their normal way of doing things, but their message was finally getting across.

In the chapters that follow, you and I will go through much the same experience as Mike's parents. First, we will examine your training methods and the ways that teaching and learning break down. You'll discover the type of limits you use and why your children respond to you the way they do. With an awareness of what hasn't worked for you, you'll be ready to learn new methods.

Parent Study Group Questions

1. What roles do parents frequently play when using each of the three training models?

2. Discuss the beliefs held by parents who use punishment with regard to problem solving, how children learn, and why children cooperate. Were you raised with these beliefs? Are you comfortable with them?

3. Discuss the beliefs held by parents who use permissiveness with regard to problem solving, how children learn, and why children cooperate. Were you raised with these beliefs? Are you comfortable with them?

4. Colin, age six, is asked to get ready for his bath but tries to talk his way out of it. "Do what I said!" shouts his dad, "and don't give me any arguments or you're going to get paddled." Two minutes pass and Colin doesn't move toward the bathroom. His dad walks over, gives him a swat, and threatens to do it again if Colin doesn't head to the bathroom quickly. In tears, Colin heads off to take his bath.

   What approach is Colin's father using? What lessons is he teaching Colin about problem solving, cooperation, responsibility, and power and authority? If these methods are used consistently, how do you think Colin will handle conflicts with his siblings or peers?

5. Jenny, age ten, knows she's not supposed to get into her mother's purse without asking, but when she hears the ice cream truck coming down the street she takes out a dollar and heads for the truck. When she returns, her mother notices the ice cream. "Where

did you get the money for that?" asks her mother. Jenny shrugs her shoulders without answering. "Did you take it out of my purse?" asks her mother. Again, Jenny shrugs and tries to look innocent.

"I really wish you wouldn't get into my purse without asking," her mother admonishes. "Will you ask next time? Please?" Jenny nods.

What approach is Jenny's mother using? What lessons did Jenny learn about asking before she gets into her mother's purse? What do you think she'll do next time? What is the actual rule about asking?

6. Sid, age seven, is asked to put on his helmet before he rides his bike to school. "I don't want to. Helmets look dumb!" he protests.

   "You can wear the helmet or you won't be riding your bike to school," replies his father. "It's up to you. What would you like to do?" Reluctantly, Sid puts the helmet on and heads off to school.

   What approach is Sid's father using? What lessons is he teaching Sid about responsibility, cooperation, and problem solving? Is his rule clear?

7. What approach are you using now? Are your children responding as you expect them to? Does their behavior make more sense to you? What lessons are you teaching about cooperation? Responsibility? Problem solving? Your rules for acceptable behavior?

8. Why do punitive and permissive training approaches fail to teach our intended lessons about responsibility?

9. Describe the methods your parents used? Can you identify their training approach? Is that approach similar to the approach you're using now?

10. Are you confident that you've identified your approach? If not, ask other group members for assistance. Describe the things you do when your children misbehave. Then describe how your children respond to what you do. Your descriptions should provide important clues about your approach.

How Children Learn
Your Rules

Wouldn't the task of parenting be easier if children were born with an understanding of our rules and all we had to do was bring them home and enjoy them as they grew up? Can you imagine what it would feel like to sip your coffee in the morning knowing that your children would do everything you expected—get dressed and ready for school, use good table manners, put away their dirty clothes, do all their chores and homework, and go to bed without dawdling or arguments? An appealing thought, but not reality.

Children are not born with an inherent understanding of our rules for acceptable behavior. These must be acquired over time through a teaching and learning process. We are the teachers. It's our job to get our rules across in the clearest and most understandable way.

Our job gets off to a fast start as soon as our children become toddlers. Toddlers love to explore, and some of their favorite items to investigate are stereos, televisions, and videocassette recorders. All those buttons and dials and colorful lights are irresistible. What do we do when our toddler begins to play with these items? We rush over and begin teaching our rules.

Those of us who use punishment do it with a sharp no, a look of disapproval, and a slap on the hand before moving the child away. If we're permissive, we do it with many no's, persuasive reasons, and long explanations before relocating our youngster. If we're democratic, we say no clearly and firmly and support our message by moving our child away.

After we go through this routine ten or twelve times, a curious thing begins to happen. Just as our toddlers arrive at their target and reach out to touch, they stop and look at us for a reaction. Why? They are beginning to understand our rule. But they still need more time to test it out.

So what do we do when our toddlers begin to test? If our approach is punitive, we get a stern look on our face, hold up our hand in slapping position, and issue a warning: "You better not!" If we're permissive, we launch into a new wave of reasons and explanations. If our approach is democratic, we do the same thing we did before. We say no clearly and firmly and wait to see how our toddler responds before moving on to our action step.

All the parents in the example above are trying to teach their rules for acceptable behavior, but only those using the democratic method are actually teaching the lesson they all intend. In this chapter, you'll discover why. You'll understand how children learn your rules and why the teaching and learning process often breaks down. By the time you're done, you'll be a step closer to getting your message across in the clearest and most understandable way. Let's take a look at how Simon's parent does it.

Simon, three years old, is swinging his plastic telephone over his head like a lariat and nearly misses a lamp. His father intervenes.

"Simon, it's not OK to swing your telephone like that in the house," he says matter-of-factly. "You can play with it the right way, or I'll have to take it away."

"But it's fun," says Simon, as he swings the phone even harder than before.

His father reaches over and takes the phone away. "You can have it back later this afternoon," he says, "if you play with it the right way."

Simon is in the process of learning his family's rules about playing with toys in the house. He and his parents may need to repeat this lesson several more times before he finally masters the rule, but his father's methods will surely lead to the desired outcome.

Simon's father is teaching his rules very effectively. His words say stop, and his actions convey the same message when he takes the phone away. When our words are consistent with our actions, we don't need a lot of words or harsh consequences to get our message across. The message is clear, and so is our rule behind it.

Children Learn Concretely

Jean Piaget's research on children's intellectual development has shown that the thinking and learning of most children is qualitatively different from that of adults. Children think and learn concretely. For the young child, immediate sensory experience plays an even greater role in shaping their reality than for older children or adults.

What does this mean in everyday terms? It means that what children experience with their senses (what they see, hear, touch, smell, and feel) determines how they think things really are. Their beliefs and perceptions about the way the world works are based primarily on their concrete experiences.

Piaget's findings have important implications for how we go about teaching our rules to children. We do this in two basic ways—with our words and with our actions. Both teach a lesson, but only our actions are concrete. Actions, not words, define our rules.

For example, if I tell my nine-year-old son that his bedtime is 8:30, but he regularly goes to bed at 9:00, what would he be learning about my rule for his bedtime? Of course, he'd be learning that my actual rule is 9:00. If I asked him to be in bed by 8:30, do you think he would take me very seriously?

If, on the other hand, I had told him that his bedtime was 8:30 and I made sure he was in bed at that time regularly, he and I would probably share the same belief about my rule—his bedtime is 8:30. If I asked him to go to bed at that time, he would know that I meant what I said.

When our words match our actions consistently, children learn to take our words seriously and to recognize the rules behind them. When our words do not match our actions, however, children learn to ignore our words and to base their beliefs on what they experience. In effect, we are teaching two different rules: a rule in theory versus a rule in practice.

This essential miscommunication is the source of most breakdowns in the teaching and learning process. Most of us are not even aware it's happening. We just continue to teach our rules with our words while our children learn by our actions. Here's a typical example:

Five-year-old Sarah is sitting on the sofa and drawing pictures with colored marker pens. Her mother enters the room and recognizes the perilous situation for the sofa.

"Sarah, that doesn't look like a very good idea," her mother says. "You might mark the sofa."

"I'll be careful, Mommy," Sarah says convincingly.

"I know you will, honey," says her mother, "but I really wish you would work on the table where you can't stain anything."

"I will," says Sarah, "but I want to finish this one part first."

"After you finish, you'll move to the table, OK?" says her mother as she leaves the room satisfied that her message got across.

"OK," says Sarah, but ten minutes later she's still sitting on the sofa drawing her pictures.

"Sarah, I thought I asked you to do your artwork at the table," her mother says with concern in her voice. "Your father and I would be very upset if any marks got on the sofa. I really wish you would do what you were asked."

"I will, Mommy," says Sarah, "but I just want to finish this one picture and then I'll move. I'm almost done."

"You better finish it quickly then," says her mother. "I'm starting to get mad." She waits, tapping her foot impatiently, but Sarah keeps on drawing.

"Sarah!" her mother finally shouts. "I've had enough of this, young lady! Do you understand?"

"OK, I'm finished with it anyway," Sarah says as she puts her work away and leaves the sofa.

Sarah's mother sincerely believes she's communicating a message that says stop when she points out the hazards of using marker pens on the sofa. She becomes quite frustrated and annoyed when Sarah does not respond as expected. In actuality, Sarah's mother is communicating two messages, but she is aware of only one.

With her words, she is saying something that resembles stop, but what does Sarah experience? It isn't stopping. Instead, she hears more talking. Her mother's action message is really saying, "Go ahead and do what you want. I don't like it, but I'm not going to do anything about it, at least not for awhile."

Sarah responds to this type of mixed message like many children do. She ignores the words and learns from what she experiences. What is Sarah's interpretation about her mother's rule for using marker pens on the sofa? Yes, it's OK as long as she can tolerate her mother's reminding.

Let's not overlook another, even more subtle, lesson Sarah is learning about communication. What does she say each time she is asked to move to the table? She says, "I will," but what does she do? It isn't moving. This isn't really lying. What she really means is, "I will if I have to."

Sarah is learning to communicate with mixed messages more skillfully than her mother. Parents who use stop messages that don't mean stop often have children who use I will or in a minute messages that really mean I won't and maybe never.

Punitive Rules

Those of us who use punishment rely heavily on our actions to teach our rules, but our actions often teach a different lesson than we intend. This is what happened to Steven's parents. When I first met them, their fourth-grader had already been suspended from school four times for hitting, and it was still October. The year had barely begun.

"Living with Steven is like being around a bomb waiting to explode," said his frustrated mother. "He knows that hitting is not OK, but he does it anyway. He hits his younger brother; he hits other kids in the neighborhood; and he hits kids at school. We've talked to him over and over again, but it doesn't seem to sink in."

"What exactly do you say to him when he hits his brother?" I asked, curious about their verbal messages.

"Well, I get a little loud," confessed Steven's father. "It makes me very angry to see Steven mistreating his little brother. So I let him know very clearly that I'm not going to tolerate it."

"What do you do to get that point across?" I asked.

"We paddle him when he needs it," said his father. "We don't believe in all the permissive stuff that's going on today. Kids need to know that you mean business."

"How many times a week does Steven need that kind of reminder?" I asked.

"Two or three times, and sometimes more, like this week when he got suspended. He needs to know when he's gone too far," replied his mother.

"With that many reminders, why do you think Steven is having such a difficult time learning your rules?" I asked.

"We suspect he has some kind of a learning problem," she said. "We're thinking about having him tested."

As I got to know Steven, I could see he didn't need testing. The problem wasn't learning. It was teaching. In fact, Steven was a very capable learner. He was mastering all the lessons his parents were teaching him about violent problem solving. He was good at yelling, threatening, and intimidating. He knew how to hit and inflict injury, and he was becoming very skillful at blaming others when he got caught.

Steven understood his parents' words clearly when they told him not to hit, but their spoken rules were not the ones they practiced. What did they practice? Hitting —lots of it. That was the way they solved problems, and that was the real rule Steven was learning. By their example, Steven's parents were teaching a different lesson than they intended.

Permissive Rules

Permissive training methods also lead to breakdowns in the teaching and learning process. Parents who use this

39

approach tend to confuse their words for actions and become frustrated when their message doesn't get across. Natalie's mom, a single parent, was a good example. She arrived at my office very frustrated by all the resistance she was encountering.

"Natalie is a self-centered and disrespectful twelve-year-old," complained her mother. "She knows my rules, but she doesn't care to follow them. When I try to explain why I have those rules, she just tunes me out and does exactly what she wants." Natalie's mom shared an incident that happens just about every morning before school.

"Natalie knows she's not supposed to play her stereo too loudly in the morning, but every morning it's the same thing. She blasts her music so loudly that you can hear it across the street. It drives me crazy."

"What do you do when this happens?" I asked.

"Well, first I go in and tell her to turn it down," said her mother, "but that doesn't do any good. I've told her over and over again. She never listens."

"What do you do next?" I inquired.

"I get really angry. I walk in her room and tell her to turn it down or turn it off. Sometimes I threaten to take her stereo away," said her mother.

"Does she cooperate then?" I asked.

"She usually turns it down a little," said her mother, "but you can still hear it throughout the house, and after awhile she just turns it up again anyway."

"Do you take it away then?" I asked, wondering if eventually she did get around to using consequences.

"I haven't yet," she said, "but that day isn't far off. I just shut her door. She can ruin her own ears."

Natalie's mom doesn't realize that she is actually communicating two rules to her daughter about playing the stereo — one with her words, another with her actions. Her words (rule in theory) say "turn it down," but her actions (rule in practice) say "you really don't have to if you don't want to." Natalie's choice is clear. She wants to play it loudly, and that's what she does.

The examples of Steven and Natalie illustrate how easily the teaching and learning process can break down when our words are inconsistent with our actions. The parents in each of these examples were unaware of their ineffective action messages. They sincerely believed their rules were getting across with their words.

Teaching Effectively

What type of action messages are you using? Do you find yourself teaching the same old lessons over and over again without success like Steven and Natalie's parents? If so, you'll be relieved to know that teaching effectively requires less time and energy than you're using now and gives you better results. Teaching rules is easy when we're using the right tools — clear words and clear action messages. Let's look at two examples.

Kenny, age eight, received the birthday present he really wanted: a new ten-speed mountain bike. Before he tried it out, however, his father went over some ground rules. "That bike is a real nice one," said his father. "A lot of people would like to have it. When you take it to school, I expect you to lock it up, and when you're done with it each night, I expect you to put it away in the garage."

"I will," said Kenny, but only two days later his father arrived home from work and noticed Kenny's bike was still out in the front yard. It was dark.

"Maybe he'll remember to put it away after dinner," his father thought to himself, but dinner came and went and the bike stayed where it was. So after Kenny went to bed, his father tied the bike to the rafters in the garage.

The next morning, as he was leaving for school,

41

Kenny discovered his bike hanging from the rafters. "What happened to my bike?" he said, very excited.

"You can have it back on Saturday," said his father matter-of-factly. "It was left out in the front yard last night."

"I'm really sorry," said Kenny remorsefully. "I won't do it again. I promise. Can't I take it to school just this once?"

Kenny's pleading was very convincing, but his father remained firm. "You can have it back on Saturday," he said. Kenny left to catch the bus.

Like many of us, Kenny's father was probably tempted to give in, but he realized that giving in would send the wrong message about his rules. Instead, he held firm and gave a consistent message. His words said "Put the bike away," and his actions supported his rule. Kenny received a clear message, and he learned to be more responsible about putting his bike away.

Shelly's mom also was clear about her rules when her daughter showed up two hours late after school one night. Shelly, sixteen years old, knew she was supposed to be in by 6 P.M. on weeknights, but since she got her own car she had been getting home late with increasing frequency.

Her excuses were always good ones, and nobody thought much of it at first. Then, one night she didn't arrive home until after 8 P.M. She didn't call, either.

"Where were you?" asked her mother, looking relieved and worried at the same time as Shelly walked in the house. "I was concerned that something might have happened to you."

"I was at Carolyn's house. I just lost track of the time, I guess," said Shelly. "What's the big deal anyway? I've got my own car. I know how to get home."

"I know you do," replied her mother, "but you're expected home by 6:00 on weeknights, and if something comes up we expect the courtesy of a call. We'll try it

without the car keys for the rest of the week. If e
goes well, you can have them back on Monday. N
them, please?''

Reluctantly, Shelly handed over her keys, but her
mother's message had gotten through. Shelly made it
home on time every night that week and also in the weeks
that followed. When it looked like she might be late, she
always called to let her parents know.

Shelly's mom was teaching her rules very effectively.
Her actions spoke as clearly as her words.

Summary

Children learn concretely. Their beliefs and perceptions
about our rules are based primarily on what they experience, not necessarily on what they are told. This fact has
important implications for how we go about teaching our
rules. We do this in two basic ways — with our words and
with our actions. Both teach a lesson, but only our actions
are concrete. Our actions define our rules.

When our words match our actions consistently, children learn to trust our words and to recognize our rules
behind them. When our words do not match our actions,
however, children learn to ignore our words and base
their beliefs on what they experience. In reality, they are
learning two sets of rules — our spoken rules and the rules
we practice.

This fundamental miscommunication about rules
and expectations is the reason why most of our well-
intended lessons break down. Most of us are unaware it's
even happening. Like Steven and Natalie's parents, we
continue to teach with our words while our children learn
from our actions. The solution is clear words and clear
action messages. These tools are the key to teaching our
rules the way children learn best.

Questions About Rules

1. *When I ask my six-year-old to do something, she frequently asks me why she has to do it. I thought that providing an explanation would help her to better understand my rules. Is this practice making matters worse?*

Answer: It's challenging enough for most young children (three to seven years) to understand and master our basic rules without understanding the rationale behind them. When they ask us why they have to cooperate, frequently it's not because they are interested in a convincing rationale as much as it is to determine if our rules are firm or soft. Why? translates into: Do I really have to do it?

If they can successfully engage us in long explanations, arguments, or debates, or possibly get us to give in, then they'll know that our limits are negotiable and subject to change. If you provide an explanation but remain firm with your limits, you'll probably find your child asking why less often. What I'm suggesting is that why is often a form of limit testing to determine if we really mean what we say.

If you choose to provide explanations for your younger child, the best time to do so is before your rules have been violated or after your consequences have been carried out. If you do so during an incident of misbehavior, you may be inviting limit testing and sending the message that your limits are negotiable.

2. *If consistency between our words and actions is important, then wouldn't the word no followed by a spanking convey a clear message about my rules?*

Answer: The answer depends upon the rules you intend to teach. If you're trying to convey a rule about stopping a specific misbehavior (such as throwing rocks), then your child would probably get the message.

44

If you used spankings on a regular basis
your action message would also convey an
—hitting is the way we solve problems.
lesson you want to teach?

3. *How important is consistency between parents when teaching family rules?*

Answer: Consistency between parents is very important if we intend to teach our family rules in the clearest and most understandable way. For example, if both mom and dad say, "Do your chores before playing," and they both enforce their rule with their actions consistently, then their children receive a clear message about their parents' rules and expectations.

If, on the other hand, both parents say, "Do your chores before playing," but only mom enforces that rule consistently with her actions, what do the children learn about their parents' rule? Of course, that only mom really expects you to do it. In effect, there are two rules operating, mom's rule and dad's rule. Only mom's rule requires compliance. When dad is around, the parents can expect their rule to be tested.

PARENT STUDY GROUP QUESTIONS

1. Piaget's research has shown us children learn concretely. What does this mean? Why is it important for setting limits?

2. Four-year-old Nicholas was asked three times to pick up his building blocks before he could watch his cartoon show. He picked up a few, but as soon as his show started he planted himself in front of the set and his mom picked up the rest. What message did she convey with her words? What message did her actions convey? What is the real rule about picking up toys before TV? What do you think Nicholas will do next time he is asked to pick up?

3. If you have been using permissive methods, what have your children been learning from your actions? Is this the lesson you intended?

4. If you have been using punitive methods, what have your children been learning from your actions? Is this the lesson you intended?

5. When our words and our actions are in conflict, which do children follow to learn our rules?

6. What does hitting (slapping, spanking) teach children about our rules for solving problems?

7. What do children learn when we try to enlist their cooperation by wearing them down with words?

8. What is the key to teaching your rules in the clearest and most understandable manner?

▼
Chapter

3

The Family Dance

Nearly every family that operates with unclear or ineffective limits develops its own special dance of miscommunication that it performs over and over again in conflict situations. This learned pattern of ineffective problem solving invariably leads to escalating conflicts and power struggles. Over time, the dance becomes such a familiar and deeply ingrained habit that family members experience it as their normal way of doing things. They are not even aware they are dancing.

Families, such as the ones we'll follow in this chapter, can easily become stuck in these destructive patterns of communication. Without awareness and new skills, they have little choice but to keep on dancing the only dance they know. Awareness is the first step toward breaking free.

If you suspect that you've become stuck in a family dance, this chapter should help you begin to break free. In the pages that follow, you'll learn how these dances begin, how they end, and what keeps them going. Most importantly, you'll learn how to step off the dance floor so you can move on to more effective methods of problem solving. Let's take a look at how one couple discovered their dance.

A Permissive Dance

Paul and Julie work full-time jobs and are parents of three children ages four, six, and eight. Their home is a busy place. They came for counseling because Julie was feeling tense and anxious about all the yelling and conflict that was taking place in their home.

"No matter what we say, they just do what they want," said Julie. "Everything is a battle. We seem to be yelling at them all the time. When we're not yelling at them, they're yelling at each other. It's more than I can stand!"

Paul was also feeling discouraged. "We really do love our children," he said, "but I can honestly say I don't enjoy them very much anymore. We try to treat them with fairness, but they walk all over us."

They didn't realize it, but Paul and Julie were dancing with their children. They were stuck in an escalating pattern of conflicts and power struggles. My first objective was to help them recognize their dance.

"Pick a typical misbehavior in your house and describe in a very step-by-step manner exactly what you say and do when your children behave this way."

Before the words left my mouth, both parents said, almost in chorus, "breakfast times."

"OK," I said, "describe to me what happens during breakfast." Julie went first. As she described what usually happens, I diagrammed out each step in the interactional sequence. Visual diagrams are a great way to help parents get acquainted with their dance. When she finished, we both paused for a moment to look at her diagram (Figure 3A).

Figure 3A. Julie's diagram

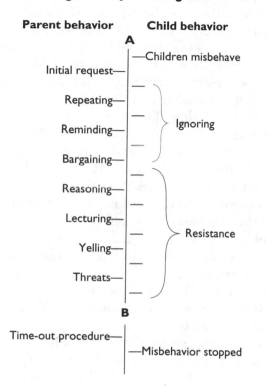

"I never realized I did so much talking," she said. "No wonder I feel so wiped out! I must go through this half a dozen times a day with chores, homework, dinner, baths, and bedtimes."

"Yes. That's quite a dance," I replied, giving it the label it deserved.

For many parents, family dances are like saving "stress coupons." When we collect enough of them in the course of a day or a week, we get a prize—headaches, stomachaches, or a variety of other upsets. All of this doesn't make us feel very much like being around our kids.

49

Julie's diagram was revealing. From the time she first intervened to the time she finished, she tried many different forms of persuasion, but none of them were very effective for stopping the children's misbehavior.

Like most permissive parents, Julie started off with a lot of repeating and reminding, but her requests were usually ignored. She then moved on to bargaining, reasoning, and lecturing. The resistance continued.

The more she talked, the madder she got until lecturing turned to yelling and bargaining gave way to threats. When she finally reached her breaking point, she sent them to their rooms (time-out procedure), which stopped the misbehavior but made her feel guilty.

As the two parents looked on, I returned to Julie's diagram and drew a circle around all the steps that used words. This took up nearly all of her diagram. I labeled these as verbal steps. Then I drew a box around the words time-out at the end of her diagram and labeled this as an action step. The box took up only a small portion of her diagram (Figure 3B).

"Which step stopped the misbehavior?" I asked. From the look on her face, I could see she already understood my point. Julie was spending all her time and energy doing the things that didn't work. No wonder she felt frustrated and drained! Her efforts were getting her nowhere.

"At what point in the dance do you begin to get angry?" I asked next.

"In all honesty," said Julie, "I'm angry from the beginning. I know they're not going to cooperate with me, but I don't start acting angry until further along when I can't stand it anymore." She pointed to her diagram, "That's the spot. Somewhere between my bargaining and my lecturing, I start to wear down, and I begin to lose it."

At the beginning of Julie's diagram, I wrote the

Figure 3B. Julie's diagram, divided into verbal and action steps

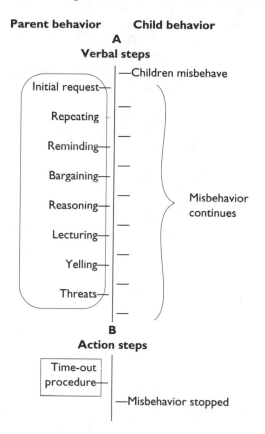

words "getting mad," and at the end of her diagram, I wrote the words "very mad."

The pattern was clear (Figure 3C). I summarized what Julie's diagram was telling us. "It seems that the more you talk, the more your kids resist you, and the angrier you become. Your dance continues to heat up until you finally stop it with your action step." Julie nodded in agreement.

Figure 3C. Julie's diagram, showing her anger

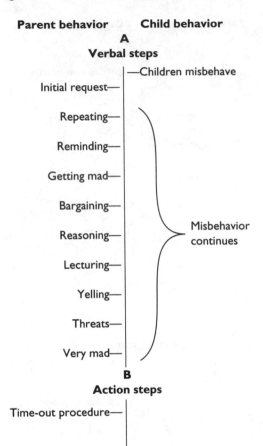

Parent behavior   Child behavior

A

Verbal steps

—Children misbehave

Initial request—

Repeating—

Reminding—

Getting mad—

Bargaining—

Reasoning—   Misbehavior continues

Lecturing—

Yelling—

Threats—

Very mad—

B

Action steps

Time-out procedure—

"Let's hold on to that thought for awhile and get back to it after we look at the methods your parents used with you. What did they do when you misbehaved?" I asked. As she gave her description, I drew a second diagram.

"My mom handled most of the discipline when I was growing up," Julie reported. "She did a lot of repeating and reminding, some bargaining, and a lot of lecturing and yelling. When things went too far, she threatened to tell my father when he got home. He usually spanked, so we rarely pushed things after she'd threaten us."

"At what point did your mom begin getting angry?" I asked.

"She became very angry if we didn't pay attention to her lectures," Julie recalled, noticing a familiar pattern.

I circled all the verbal steps and put a box around the action step. When the diagram was complete, I placed it next to Julie's diagram. Except for the ending, the two diagrams looked very similar (Figure 3D).

Figure 3D. Julie's parents' diagram

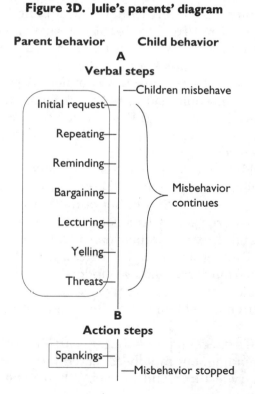

Parent behavior   Child behavior

A
Verbal steps

—Children misbehave

Initial request

Repeating

Reminding

Bargaining   Misbehavior
                  continues

Lecturing

Yelling

Threats

B
Action steps

Spankings

—Misbehavior stopped

"I'm surprised," Julie confessed. "I thought I was doing things differently than my parents."

Julie's reaction was not unusual. Many parents are surprised when they realize how much they still rely on their parents as their models for child training. We may make modifications on the basic theme to correct what we believe to be our parents' mistakes. If we felt our parents were too strict, we may compensate by becoming more lenient. If we believe they were too lenient, we may compensate by becoming more strict. Most often, we end up like Julie, doing the same dance with a different ending and passing our basic script on to our children.

It was time to look at Paul's diagram. "Paul, I'm curious to know what you do when the kids misbehave in the morning. Let's start from the beginning like we did with Julie." I returned to the blackboard and drew out Paul's diagram (Figure 3E) as he described how he handled the morning breakfast wars.

When Paul's diagram was complete, I paused once again so we all could take it in. "Look familiar?" I asked.

"Very familiar," said Paul. "I've done that dance so many times I could almost tell you every word I'm going to say before I say them."

"I'll bet your kids could too," I added. (Sometimes, when children are present in these situations, I ask them, "Do you know what your father or mother is going to say next?" It never ceases to amaze me how well children understand the steps to their dance.)

Paul's diagram also was revealing. Like Julie, he operated from the permissive model, but, unlike Julie, he never quite got around to his consequences. As a result, the children tested him more often, and his dances lasted longer.

Paul's dances typically began with a lot of repeating and reminding, but rapidly escalated into blaming, ridicule, angry lectures, and threats. When things got loud

Figure 3E. Paul's diagram

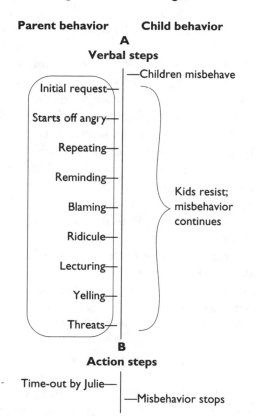

Parent behavior   **Child behavior**

A
Verbal steps

—Children misbehave

Initial request

Starts off angry

Repeating

Reminding

Blaming

Ridicule

Lecturing

Yelling

Threats

Kids resist;
misbehavior
continues

B
Action steps

Time-out by Julie—

—Misbehavior stops

and hot, Julie usually arrived on the scene and attempted to put out the fire with time-outs.

I drew a circle around all the steps in Paul's diagram that involved words and labeled them verbal steps. The circle covered his entire diagram. The action step that eventually ended his dances belonged to Julie.

"Paul, when do you find yourself getting angry?" I asked.

"Lately, I've been starting off angry and staying that

hole time," he said. "It hasn't always been this
w months ago, I started off calmly like Julie, but
nobody listened to me. So I got angry and started yelling."

At the beginning of Paul's diagram, I wrote the
words, "starts off angry." His dances were angry ones.

Paul's diagram was now complete, but I didn't need
to summarize it for him. The pattern was clear. The more
he talked, the more the kids tested and resisted, and the
angrier he became. He also could see why Julie was becoming so upset. She was involved in all of his dances. It
was her job to stop them.

"What did your parents do when you misbehaved as
a child?" I asked, hoping Paul might connect his present
methods with those of his parents.

"My parents did a lot of yelling, criticizing, blaming,
and spanking," Paul recalled. "When my father arrived
home from work each day, the first report he'd hear from
my mother was about our behavior. If the report was
negative, he headed for the belt. We lived in constant
fear."

Paul described his father as someone who always
seemed to be in a state of angry agitation. The children
went to great lengths to avoid his wrath. His thick leather
belt, which hung visibly from a peg in the kitchen, served
as an ever-present reminder of his authority. Paul's mem-
ories of that belt and the spankings it delivered were so
painful that he promised himself he would never hit or
mistreat his own children.

Like many parents, Paul carries emotional scars from
a painful family dance, one he was determined not to
repeat. He associated the pain, however, with the spankings at the end of the dance and not with all the steps that
led up to them. He was trying to change his family dance
by eliminating its painful ending.

I showed him his parents' diagram (Figure 3F). "You

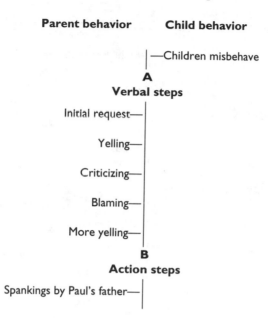

Figure 3F. Paul's parents' diagram

Parent behavior   **Child behavior**

—Children misbehave
A
Verbal steps

Initial request—

Yelling—

Criticizing—

Blaming—

More yelling—
B
Action steps

Spankings by Paul's father—

look surprised," I said, noticing the look on Paul's face as he continued to examine his two diagrams.

"I am," he said. "I never thought I would end up doing many of the same things my parents did."

The diagrams were persuasive evidence that Paul and Julie were repeating scripts they learned in their families of origin. They were doing the only dance they knew, and, in the process, they were teaching that dance to their children.

Getting off the Dance Floor

"So how do we get off this treadmill?" asked Paul.

"You've already taken the most important step by learning to recognize your dance," I said. "Next, you will

Figure 3G. Julie and Paul's new diagram

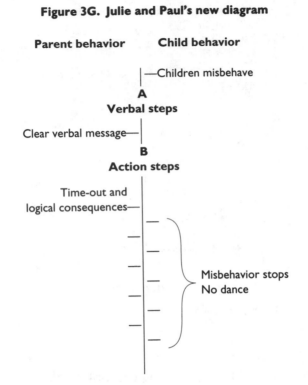

Parent behavior   Child behavior

—Children misbehave

A

Verbal steps

Clear verbal message—

B

Action steps

Time-out and
logical consequences—

Misbehavior stops
No dance

need to begin putting your verbal and action steps closer together. Let me summarize the process briefly by referring back to Julie's diagram.

"Remember how Julie spent most of her time and energy getting bogged down with a lot of ineffective verbal steps? She used too many words and not enough action. Her dance continued until she arrived at her action step. You can stop your dances by eliminating all the ineffective verbal steps between points A and B. When we begin with a clear message at point A and move on directly to our action step at point B, our communication is clear. There aren't many opportunities to dance." Julie and

Paul's new diagram soon looked like Figure 3G. So can yours.

A Punitive Dance

Rick and Linda, parents of two children ages seven and thirteen, had a dance I won't soon forget. I caught my first glimpse of it in the reception room before they even made it back to my office.

"Come on, Lisa," Linda said to her thirteen-year-old when they were called. But Lisa just sat there, her arms folded tightly.

"You go in," Lisa said to her parents. "You're the ones that need the counseling."

"If you would just do what you're told once in awhile, we wouldn't be here at all," her mother shot back angrily.

"No, you'd find something else to complain about," Lisa retorted. "That's what you're best at."

"I'm not going to stand here and listen to any more of your disrespectful back talk," said Linda.

"Oh yeah! What are you going to do? Ground me? It doesn't seem to bother you when you treat me disrespectfully," Lisa shot back.

"I'm the parent," Linda countered.

"No, you're the dictator," said Lisa, still in her chair.

"That's enough, Lisa," Rick intervened. "Come on. It's time to go back to his office." Reluctantly, Lisa accompanied her parents back to my office, but before we were even seated the dance started up again.

"See what she's like," Linda complained, trying to get me to take sides.

Before I could establish a neutral position, Lisa got in one last barb. "Yeah, you're a real pleasure to be around too," she sneered.

"I can see you're all pretty angry and frustrated," I said, trying to take the focus off Lisa. "I'm not very good at solving problems when I'm feeling that way. Let's take a few minutes and give ourselves a chance to calm down." I handed each parent some forms to look over while we waited.

The session had barely begun, but they were already getting acquainted with a technique they would need fairly often to interrupt their dances: the cool down. When calm was restored, I asked Rick, "Is the argument that happened earlier similar to what happens at home?"

"It's been happening all the time since Lisa got grounded six weeks ago," he replied. Rick described the events that led up to their appointment.

The problem began when Lisa arrived home with her midsemester progress report. She was getting Ds in science and math, her hardest subjects. When Linda saw the progress report, she got angry. "Ds are not acceptable grades in this house!" she declared.

"I've got six weeks until the end of the semester. That's plenty of time to get them up," said Lisa.

"You have more time than you think," said Linda, "because you're not going anywhere after school until those grades come up." Lisa was grounded to the house.

When she tried to protest her mother's decision, her mother threatened to take away even more privileges and informed Lisa that the matter was final. Lisa exploded. "You're mean and unfair!" she shouted. So her mother took away Lisa's phone privileges too for the same period.

"Keep it up if you want to lose even more privileges," Linda taunted. Lisa ran to her room and slammed the door.

That evening, Rick tried to mediate the dispute, but things just got worse. First, Linda blamed Lisa for being lazy and disrespectful. Then, Lisa accused Linda of being mean and unfair. Linda started shouting, and Lisa shouted back. In the heat of the exchange, Lisa called

Linda a bitch. Lisa regretted it the moment she said it, but it was already too late. Linda was just about to slap Lisa in the face when Rick stepped in. He took away one of the things Lisa loved most — her Saturday skating privileges, gone until further notice.

"I didn't know what else to do," said Rick, clearly frustrated. Lisa was already grounded to the house on weeknights, and she'd lost her phone privileges too. "She's too big to spank, but I couldn't let her get away with it either." Like Linda, Rick had dug them all in a little deeper with his consequences.

"What do you usually do when Lisa or Cody misbehave?" I asked. As Rick described his methods, I diagrammed them out on the blackboard.

"First, I tell them to stop," he said.

"In the same tone of voice you're using now?" I asked. He nodded. "Do they stop?"

"No, I usually have to tell them a couple of times or raise my voice to get their attention," he said.

"What do you do next?" I asked.

"I usually try to reason with them so they can understand what they did wrong," Rick replied.

"Do they cooperate then?"

"Not often," he said. "Most of the time we end up arguing about why they should do what I asked."

"How do you begin to feel?" I inquired.

"I get angry," said Rick. "I usually end up saying something like: Can't you just do what I ask?"

"Don't leave out the threats and angry lectures," Lisa added, getting interested in the discussion.

"Yeah, I guess I do a little of that too," Rick confessed.

"A little?" said Lisa, rolling her eyes.

"OK, I probably do a lot of it, but it wouldn't happen if you guys would just cooperate the first time you were asked," he said.

"Then what happens?" I asked, wondering if his consequences were getting close.

"If Cody pushes me too far, he usually gets spanked, or I may take away some of his privileges for a week or so. When he's done something really bad, I do both. I stopped spanking Lisa when she turned twelve. Now I usually take away her phone, TV, stereo, time with friends, skating privileges, or ground her to the house for a few weeks when she gets mouthy or misbehaves."

"Does that stop their misbehavior?" I asked.

"It does at the time," Rick replied, "but then we have to live with a couple of angry and resentful kids for awhile until their punishment is over. Sometimes, I think it's harder on us than on them," he said. I could see Linda nodding her head in agreement.

Rick's diagram was complete (Figure 3H). I stood back and gave everybody a chance to look it over. "Look familiar?" I asked.

"You've captured something," said Rick. "I'm not sure what it is, but whatever it is, I'm doing a lot of it."

"I call them dances, and you're not alone. There are a lot of parents out there doing dances to get their children to cooperate. Let's take a look at the steps in your dance," I said.

I returned to Rick's diagram and drew a circle around all of the steps that relied on words and labeled them verbal steps. They took up most of his diagram. Next, I put a box around the steps that involved actions and labeled these action steps. These took up only a small section at the end of his diagram (Figure 3I).

"You're using two types of steps to get your kids to cooperate: verbal steps and action steps," I said. "Which one stopped the misbehavior?" I asked.

"My action step at the end," he replied.

"Exactly," I said. "Your action steps stop the dance for awhile. Now, let's look at how you're feeling when

Figure 3H. Rick's diagram

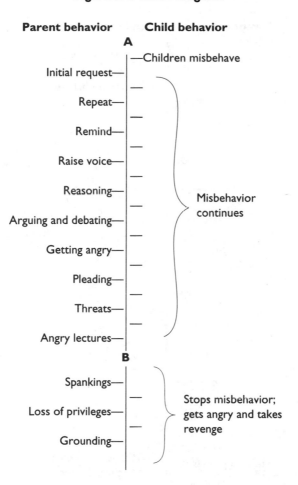

you're doing these steps. Earlier, you said you get angry when your kids argue with you while you're trying to reason with them. The arguments usually lead to lectures and threats. It sounds like things just get hotter until the dance ends with your action step."

Rick nodded. He could see that the more he talked

Figure 31. Rick's diagram, divided into verbal and action steps

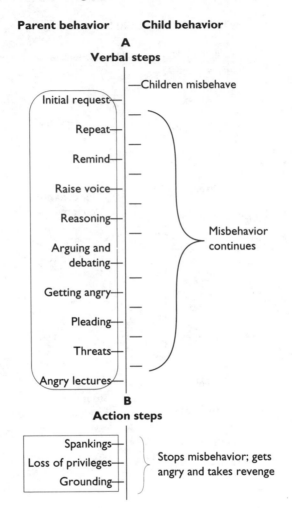

the more resistance he encountered and the angrier he became. He was spending most of his time doing the things that weren't working for him.

"Let's take a look at your action steps," I suggested. "Your action steps stop the kids' misbehavior at the moment, but what happens later on? They get angry and resentful and take it out on you. Then you end up doing many shorter versions of the same dance without action steps."

"That's where I get stuck," he admitted. "I don't know what else to do at that point. Usually, there isn't much left to take away, but I can't just let them get away with it either. They need to know that they can't misbehave and that they have to cooperate when we ask them to." I agreed.

"If there was a way to get that message across without hooking their anger and resentment, would you be willing to use that method?" I asked.

"Of course," said Rick. "I'm tired of all the hassles."

"Good," I said, "because that's exactly what you will be learning to do. Now, let's see if we can find out how your dance got started. What did your parents do when you misbehaved as a child?" As Rick described his parents' methods, I diagrammed them out on the board (Figure 3J).

"My parents did things very differently than Linda and I," Rick began. "My dad handled all the punishment in our house, and my mom just threatened to hand things over to my dad if we misbehaved. My dad was a very harsh disciplinarian. By today's standards, he'd probably be considered abusive."

"Did he spank a lot?" I asked.

"Spankings were the easy part," said Rick. "When we misbehaved, he'd get this cold angry look on his face with his eyes kind of glazed over; then he'd yell and threaten us to let us know what was coming. We would

Figure 3J. Rick's parents' diagram

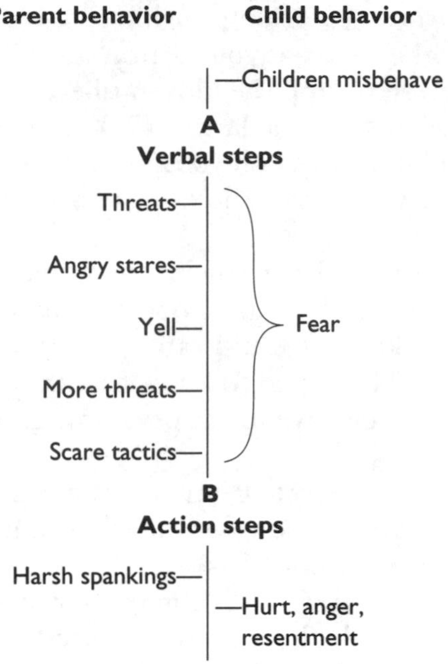

Parent behavior   **Child behavior**

—Children misbehave

A
Verbal steps

Threats—

Angry stares—

Yell—   } Fear

More threats—

Scare tactics—

B
Action steps

Harsh spankings—

—Hurt, anger,
resentment

shriek in fear and run to our rooms to get away from him. Then, to add to our terror, he'd take his belt off and smack it against a chair or table. And then he would come after us. . . . ''

From the tears in Rick's eyes, it was clear he still carried a lot of hurt and anger from that painful family dance. I could also see why he believed he and Linda were doing things differently. In comparison, their methods must seem quite mild, but as we inspected the two diagrams that stood in front of us, Rick couldn't help but notice the similarities. Lisa's resentment was beginning to look more familiar.

I placed Rick's parents' diagram under his own and

turned my attention to Linda. "Linda, what do you do when the kids misbehave?" I asked.

"I do almost everything Rick does," she said, "but I don't have nearly the patience he does. I start off angry and yelling from the beginning, and I usually stay that way the whole time."

I drew a diagram for Linda identical to Rick's except that I wrote in the words "starts off angry" at the beginning of her diagram. "Is that it?" I asked when the diagram was complete.

"I think you left out a few things," Lisa noted. "What about the taunting and challenging? You're always saying to us, 'Go ahead, do it again. I dare you.' Dad doesn't do that."

"Yes, I guess I get a little carried away sometimes," Linda admitted, "especially when they keep arguing with me after I threaten to take their privileges away."

I went back and made the correction on Linda's diagram. Then, as before, I drew a circle around all of the verbal steps and a box around her action steps. The diagram was complete (Figure 3K). "Is that the dance?" I asked. Linda nodded. We all took a minute to look it over.

Linda's dance was more emotional and dramatic than Rick's, but in many ways it was very similar. Like Rick, she spent most of her time in a verbal sparring match with the kids. The more she talked the more they resisted and the angrier she became. When she decided things had gone far enough, she would end the dance with hurtful consequences — spankings, grounding, or long-term loss of privileges.

As Linda inspected her diagram, I posed a hypothetical question. "What would happen if you went directly from point A to your action step at point B and eliminated all these other steps in between?"

"Well, there would be a lot less arguing," she acknowledged.

Figure 3K. Linda's diagram

"And you would be a lot less angry too," I said. "Eliminating all those steps would stop their misbehavior more quickly with less time and energy. But the kids would still be angry and resentful about your action step. Now, let's suppose you had some action steps that stopped their misbehavior and didn't make them angry or resentful. Would there be any need for the dance?" Linda shook her head.

"You make it sound so simple," she said.

"I think you'll find that the methods I'm going to show you are simple once you learn to use them," I replied. "The hardest part will be stopping yourself from doing your old dance. You've already taken the most important step by becoming aware of it. Now, let's take a look at how you learned your dance. What did your parents do when you misbehaved as a child?"

"Well, I think I know where I got my flair for dramatics," said Linda. "My mom was always yelling and screaming at us about one thing or another. She did a lot of nagging and reminding. We usually cooperated with her eventually, but if we didn't she took our privileges away or grounded us. I remember being grounded to the house for weeks at a time over little things."

"How did you feel when that happened?" I asked.

"Angry and resentful," she said.

"Like Lisa?" I asked.

Linda understood what I was trying to say. "I was a lot like Lisa," Linda reported, "and I also did a lot of rebelling when I thought my mom was unfair. I loved her, but our relationship was stormy."

"Was it anything like your relationship with Lisa?" I inquired.

Linda smiled again. She could see that the dance she did with her mother (Figure 3L) was a lot like the dance she was doing with Lisa. The relationships that developed around those dances were also very similar.

"What methods did your father use?" I asked.

"My father punished us, but he never yelled or threatened us or acted angry in any way," Linda reported. "He just told us to stop and if we didn't he spanked us, not very hard, but hard enough to make us stop misbehaving. When we got older, he also took away

Figure 3L. Linda's mother's diagram

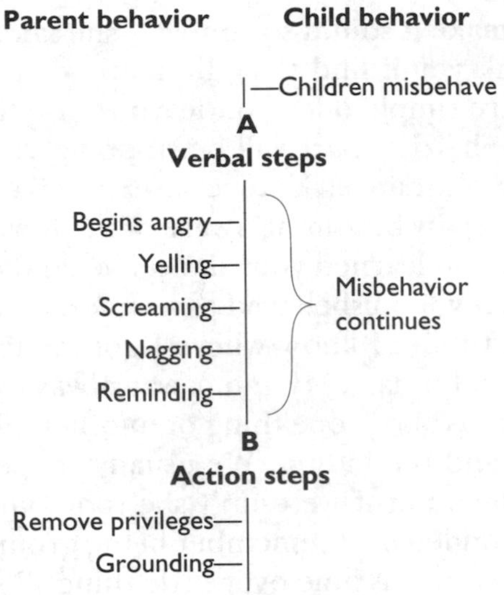

Parent behavior   **Child behavior**

```
                        |—Children misbehave
                     A
              Verbal steps

  Begins angry—|  ⎫
      Yelling—|   ⎬  Misbehavior
    Screaming—|   ⎬  continues
      Nagging—|   ⎪
    Reminding—|   ⎭
                     B
              Action steps

Remove privileges—|
        Grounding—|
```

our privileges and grounded us, but not as long as my mom. He tried very hard to be fair." (See Figure 3M.)

Linda could see from the diagrams that she was using a combination of her parents' methods. Her verbal steps resembled those used by her mother, while her action steps incorporated both of her parents' methods.

Rick and Linda left that session with an awareness of the things that weren't working for them. They recognized their dances and the scripts that went along with them. They were ready to try something new.

In the sessions that followed, they learned how to start off with clear messages and use the cool down and cut off techniques (see Chapter Five) when things got too hot. Threats and angry lectures were replaced by firm messages and encouragement. Spankings and groundings were exchanged for time-outs and logical consequences. It wasn't long before their new diagrams looked like Figure 3N. So can yours.

Figure 3M. Linda's father's diagram

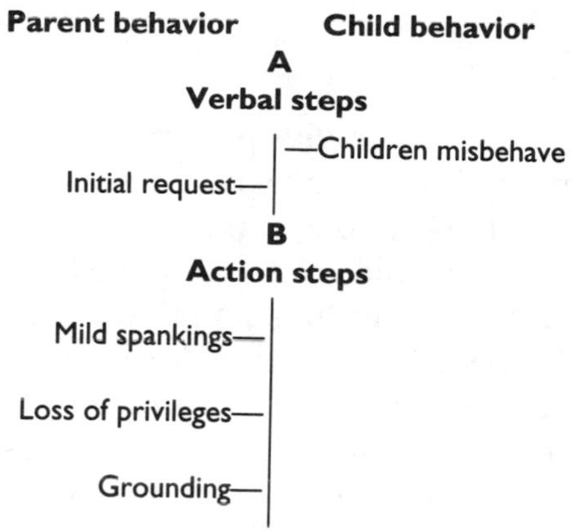

Parent behavior   Child behavior

A
Verbal steps

—Children misbehave

Initial request—|

B
Action steps

Mild spankings—|

Loss of privileges—|

Grounding—|

Figure 3N. Rick and Linda's new diagram

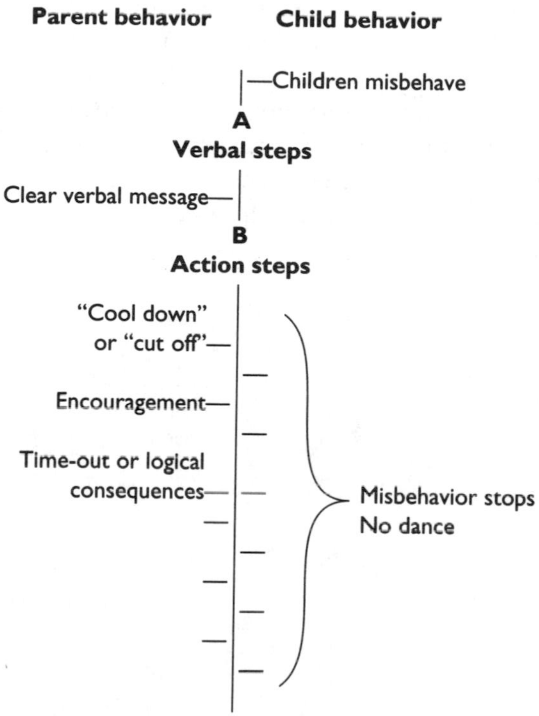

Parent behavior   Child behavior

|—Children misbehave

A
Verbal steps

Clear verbal message—|

B
Action steps

"Cool down"
or "cut off"—|

Encouragement—|

Time-out or logical
consequences—|

Misbehavior stops
No dance

ᴍary

dances are destructive patterns of communication and problem solving that are passed on from generation to generation. They all begin with unclear or ineffective messages about our rules. They're fueled by anger, resistance, and misunderstanding, and they all lead to escalating conflicts and power struggles. Most are just your basic household variety of power struggle.

Over time, these dances become such a familiar and deeply ingrained habit that family members experience them as their normal way of doing things. Like the families we followed in this chapter, they are not even aware they are dancing. Awareness is the first step toward breaking free.

The best way to stop a dance is not to start one in the beginning. Parents can avoid dances altogether by giving clear verbal messages about their rules and expectations and by supporting those messages with effective action. Sound simple? The process is easier than you might think once you discover the messages that aren't working for you. The next chapter will help you do that.

Parent Study Group Questions

1. Are you dancing with your children? If so, is it a permissive dance? A punitive dance? Some of each? How long has it been going on?

2. Can you identify the steps in your dance? Pick a typical misbehavior that you handle frequently with your children. How do you typically begin? How do you end your discipline? What do you and your children do to keep it going? Fill in the steps to your dance in the diagram below (Figure 3O). (This activity can be done

Figure 3O. Your diagram

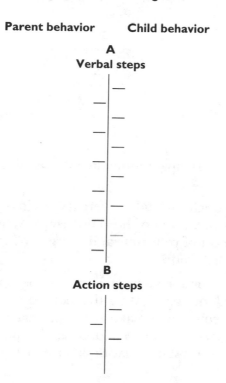

73

Figure 3P. Diagram of your mother's methods

Parent behavior   Child behavior

A
Verbal steps

B
Action steps

by each participant individually, then shared with the group.)

3. Draw a circle around the verbal steps in your diagram. Draw a box around the action steps. Which steps require most of your time and energy? Which steps stop the misbehavior?

4. At what point in your dance do you become annoyed, irritated, or angry? Mark that point on your diagram. Do you sometimes make angry, critical, or discouraging remarks to your children at this point? (such as "Can't you just do what I ask once in awhile?")

Figure 3Q. Diagram of your father's methods

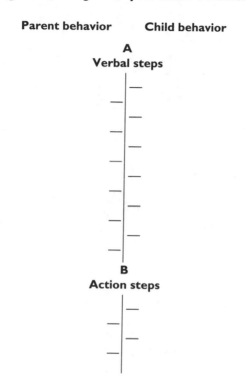

Parent behavior   Child behavior

A
Verbal steps

B
Action steps

5. Do the consequences you use to stop your dance change when you become angry or upset?

6. What methods did your parents use with you (Figures 3P, 3Q)? How did they begin their discipline? How did they end? How did you respond?

7. Do you notice similarities between your parents' methods and your own? In what way?

8. Are the conflicts you have with your children similar to the conflicts you had with your parents? How much do you think this has to do with your methods?

Chapter

4

Are Your Limits Firm or Soft?

When you drive down a city street and approach a traffic light, and the light begins to turn yellow, do you always stop at the yellow light even though you have plenty of time to make it safely through the intersection? Most adults don't, and neither do children when their parents hold up these signals to stop their misbehavior. Children don't stop at yellow lights for the same reasons adults don't. Stopping is optional, not required.

Many parents today are holding up the wrong signals to stop their children's misbehavior. They don't realize that their stop signs don't really require stopping or that their attempts to say no sound more like yes, sometimes, or maybe to their children. The problem, in most cases, is unclear communication about limits.

Limits come in two basic varieties, firm and soft. Each differs considerably in its effectiveness in communicating our intended message. In this chapter, you will discover which type of limits you've been using and why your chil-

77

dren respond to your limits the way they do. You'll learn how to reduce your children's need for testing by starting off with a clear message about your rules and expectations.

Why Limits Are Important

As we discussed in Chapter Two, limits are the messages we use to communicate our rules and expectations for acceptable behavior. They answer some very basic questions. On the surface, they operate like traffic signals and provide information in the form of green lights (do that again) and red lights (stop that) for acceptable and unacceptable behavior. These signals answer the questions: What's OK? and What's not OK?

Beneath the surface, however, limits answer a very different set of questions about the power and authority of the person setting the limits: Who's boss? Who's in control? How far can I go? What happens when I go too far? The answers define the balance of power and authority in parent-child relationships and help children determine whether compliance with their parents' rules is optional or required.

Limit-Testing Behavior

How do children clarify our rules and expectations? Rarely do they come up and ask: Do you really mean what you say? How much power and authority do you have anyway? And what are you going to do if I don't do what you ask? My guess is that you probably haven't had this experience very often, if at all.

Children don't normally ask these questions with words, but they do think about them, and they do ask them with their behavior. They just go ahead and do whatever it was we said we didn't want them to do, and they wait to see what happens. This is limit-testing behavior, and it answers their questions just as effectively as words.

Much of what we consider to be children's misbehavior is actually limit-testing behavior or their attempts to find answers to their basic questions. Testing is the best way to get their questions answered with any certainty. Consider the following example.

Six-year-old Heather is typical of many of the children I see in my family counseling work. She is bright and capable, but she resists doing what she is asked both at home and at school.

In her parents' words, "Heather pushes everything to the limit and doesn't seem to be satisfied until she gets everybody upset." I had a good suspicion that I was about to meet a child with a lot of unanswered questions.

When Heather arrived at my office with her parents, she plunked herself down in one of my comfortable upholstered swivel chairs and began sizing me up. Within a very few minutes, she went right to work on me.

What do Heather and many other children do when they first sit in my chairs? That's right. They spin them, and sometimes they put their feet in them too. They know their parents don't approve of this behavior, but they do it anyway. They look at me, then at their parents, and go ahead and see what happens. This is limit-testing behavior. When it happens, I wait to see how the parents respond because I know I am about to learn a great deal about how the family communicates about limits.

Heather's parents responded to her chair spinning the way most parents do. They gave a look of disapproval —the one where one eyebrow is raised, the head is cocked, and the eyes are fixed in a stern disapproving stare.

79

Heather did what most children do when this happens. She acknowledged the look, stopped her behavior briefly, and resumed her spinning as soon as her parents looked the other way. Heather and her parents were re-enacting their family dance, the same dance they go through dozens of times each week.

With her behavior, Heather was asking the same questions she asks at home and in the classroom: Who's boss? Who's in control? How far can I go? And what happens when I go too far? She was conducting her own personal research study to determine my actual power and authority and the rules that operated in my office. Between the disapproving looks, she continued to spin the chair. I watched to see what her parents would do next.

After a few minutes, Heather's father did what many parents do. He reached over and stopped the chair with his hand. Her mother continued with the disapproving looks. Both messages elicited the same response. Heather acknowledged her mother's look and her father's new attempt, stopped briefly, and resumed her spinning as soon as the look was gone and the hand was pulled away.

Heather's parents were doing their best to say stop, but Heather knew that stopping was not really expected or required. All the gestures and words were meaningless steps in a drama. The spinning continued. I could see why she wasn't stopping at her teacher's signals in the classroom.

Five minutes had gone by, and Heather still had not received a clear or firm message from her parents. Exasperated, her mother finally turned to me and said, "This is the same thing she does at home!"

At this point, I intervened and attempted to answer some of Heather's questions. In a matter-of-fact voice, I said, "Heather, my chairs are comfortable, and I would like you to be able to use them, but you'll have to follow two rules if you do — don't spin them and don't put your feet in them. I'm confident you can follow my rules, but if you decide not to you'll be sitting in my orange chair for the rest of the session." I keep an old orange plastic chair in my office for these situations.

What do you think Heather did? Sure, she did the same thing most children do. She tested. Not right away, but within a few minutes, she continued her research on me by giving the chair another spin and looking for my reaction. With her behavior, she was asking: Do you really mean what you say? Is that really the way it is?

I pulled out the orange chair, and said calmly, "This will be your seat for the rest of the session. You may try my blue chairs again next session."

What did Heather and I just work out? I answered her questions and provided her with the information she was looking for. She understood my rules and my expectations for her behavior. Now she had the information she needed to make more acceptable choices. With this encounter behind us, it was time for her parents and me to talk about soft and firm limits.

Soft Limits: When No Means Yes, Sometimes, or Maybe

Five-year-old Kevin knows that he's not supposed to have any soft drinks without his mother's permission, but when she is busy on the phone he sneaks into the refrigerator and helps himself to a can of Pepsi. When his mother discovers it, she says, "Kevin! You know you're not supposed to get into the Pepsi without my permission." Kevin looks guilty and apologetic, but he continues to drink the soda.

His mother adds, "If I let you drink sodas any time you wanted, your teeth would rot. I really wish you would ask first. OK?" Kevin nods contritely, but he also continues to drink. As he slurps down the last few swallows, his mother says, "All right, honey, next time you'll ask, won't you?" Kevin nods.

Kevin's mother is using soft limits. By the time she's finished talking, she seems to believe that her message has gotten across, but has it really? What has Kevin really learned about drinking soda without permission?

Kevin certainly understood the words and gave many of the appropriate responses, but he polished off the entire can of Pepsi while his mother lectured! What Kevin really learned from this episode is something he already knew — that drinking sodas without permission is really OK if he is willing to endure his mother's lectures. The limits Kevin's mother used in this instance communicated a much different message than she intended.

Soft limits are rules in theory, not in practice. They invite testing because they carry a mixed message. The verbal message seems to say stop, but the action message says that stopping is neither expected nor required. Kevin understood this clearly and responded the way most adults do at intersections when the light turns yellow. He acknowledged the signal but continued on his way. Kevin and his mother will likely go through many more of these dances over her rules about drinking Pepsi.

From a training perspective, soft limits are ineffective because they don't accomplish any of our basic training goals. They don't stop misbehavior; they don't encourage acceptable behavior; and they don't promote positive learning about our rules or expectations. They simply don't work.

Worse yet, they frequently achieve the opposite of their intended effect. They invite testing and predictably lead to escalating misbehavior and power struggles. Soft limits are the cause of most family dances.

Children trained with soft limits often learn to communicate with mixed messages more skillfully than their parents. When asked to do their chores or homework, they respond with "I will" or "In a minute" when they really mean "I won't" and "Probably never." If their intent is to go to the mall, which is off limits, they're more likely to tell their parents that they're going for a bike ride. They know that providing an acceptable verbal message is an effective way to mask their real intentions, avoid responsibility, and get their own way.

Soft limits come in a variety of forms. They can be ineffective verbal messages or ineffective action messages. Sometimes, they are both at the same time. All share the common feature of being ineffective at communicating our intended message. Compliance is neither expected nor required. Let's look at some typical examples.

Wishes, Hopes, and Shoulds

Four-year-old Jessica knows she is not supposed to play with her father's computer, but all the dials and buttons are more than she can resist. She turns the power on and plays with the keyboard as her mother arrives on the scene.

"Jessica, I really wish you wouldn't play with Daddy's computer." Jessica just ignores her.

So her mother tries again, "Jessica, you know Daddy doesn't like you playing with his computer," but Jessica continues to bang away on the keys.

"Jessica! I'm getting mad, and I really hope you stop before I get any madder!" but Jessica still has her hands on the keyboard.

Did you hear a clear message that Jessica was expected or required to stop playing with the computer? Jessica didn't. Wishes, hopes, and shoulds are another way of saying: Stopping would be nice, but you really don't have to. Compliance is optional, not required. When children confront these messages, they usually test for clarification. This is exactly what Jessica did when she continued to play with the computer.

Repeating and Reminding

Terry sits in the living room watching his favorite television show with the volume turned up high. Annoyed, his father yells from the other room, "Terry, turn the TV down!" but Terry ignores the request. Several minutes go by, and his father yells again, "Terry, how many times do I have to tell you? Turn the TV down! Are you deaf?"

Terry continues to ignore him. Angry now, Terry's father walks into the room, stands between Terry and the TV, and, with one hand on the on/off button, says, "You can turn it down or I'll turn it off." Terry turns the volume down.

When Terry ignored his father's first request, nothing happened. Terry got what he wanted. The second request followed the same pattern. If Terry's father did not mean what he said the first time, why should Terry take his words any more seriously the second or third time? He doesn't.

The verbal message says: Turn it down, but the action message says: I am not going to do anything about it, at least not for awhile. If you wanted to watch your program with the volume on high, which message would you follow?

Parents who repeat and remind are unintentionally training their children to ignore and tune them out. Like many children, Terry doesn't comply with his father's request until he is required to.

Speeches, Lectures, and Sermons

Nine-year-old Sandra knows she's supposed to be in for dinner by 6 P.M., but she's having a great time playing with her friends. She arrives home forty-five minutes late.

"Where have you been, young lady?" says her annoyed mother. "You know what time you're supposed to be here. Your dad and brother are hungry, and I've had to keep everything warm in the oven while we waited for you. What kind of a house would this be if everybody just showed up for dinner whenever they pleased? Now clean up and come to the table, so we can all get started."

Was there any clear message that showing up late for dinner would not be tolerated? Sandra didn't hear one. Will this lecture help Sandra to arrive on time in the future? Not likely. What then did Sandra learn from all of this?

She learned that showing up late is really not such a bad deal, except for an annoying lecture, if she wants to play an extra forty-five minutes. She can even count on her mom to keep everything warm and ready for her when she returns. Her mom's action message was a yellow light.

Ignoring the Misbehavior

Three-year-old Tina discovered the pleasures of blowing bubbles in her cup during mealtimes. Her parents find this behavior quite annoying but do their best to ignore it in the hopes that it will go away. Tina's two older brothers, however, find her behavior quite amusing. Her parents tell the boys not to encourage her, but Tina hasn't stopped. Mealtimes haven't been much fun for Tina's parents.

Is the absence of a green light the same as a red light? If it was, Tina probably would have stopped blowing bubbles a long time ago. What makes us believe that children will give up a behavior they enjoy simply because we ignore it? When we ignore misbehavior, we are really saying: It's OK to do that. Go ahead. You don't have to stop.

If Tina's parents really want her to stop blowing bub-

85

bles, they need to provide the right signals. They need to say stop with their words, and, if needed, they need to follow through effectively with their actions and take the cup away.

Unclear Directions

Sixteen-year-old Janet leaves the house to go on a date with her boyfriend. As she walks out the door, her father calls out, "Don't stay out too late."

What does "too late" mean? Eleven P.M.? Twelve P.M.? One A.M.? Or later? And who decides? Isn't Janet's father making the assumption that he and his daughter share the same beliefs about his rule for getting home on time?

Unclear or open-ended directions invite testing and set both parents and children up for conflict. If Janet is having a good time and wants to stay out longer, do you think she is likely to call home and see what her father really meant? Not likely.

Consider what four-year-old Tyler learns when he pretends he's a ninja warrior and tries out a flying karate kick on his friend, Harold. It works! Harold gets one right in the stomach and doubles over in tears. Tyler's mother sees what is happening from the kitchen window and intervenes.

"Tyler, you're playing much too rough!" she says. "You should be gentler." She consoles Harold as he regains his breath. When she returns to the kitchen, she sees Tyler starting the same karate game all over again.

Did Tyler hear a message that said he must stop kicking? No. He was told he was "playing too rough" and that he should be "gentler." What do these words mean to a four-year-old? Who decides what's too rough?

Without a clear verbal message to stop kicking, Tyler returned to the game he was enjoying. If we really want

86

misbehavior to stop, we need to state our di| direct and specific messages.

Ineffective Role-Modeling

Paul and Chris, two brothers, hassle over a remote control car. Their arguing disturbs their dad who is reading the paper in the next room. Annoyed, he enters the room and sees both boys squared off.

In a loud voice, Dad says, "I've had it with all the racket, and I'm sick and tired of playing referee to all your squabbles!" He gives each boy a swat on the seat and leaves the room saying, "Now keep it quiet for awhile."

What did the boys learn from this? They were attempting to resolve a conflict with yelling and hitting, but their efforts disturbed their dad. So what did he do? He resolved the conflict with more yelling and hitting.

His tactics stopped their quarrel, but what did he teach them in the process? His actions conveyed a message he didn't intend: Yelling and hitting are how we resolve conflicts. In effect, he was training them to do the very thing he was punishing them for.

Bargaining

Nathan knows he's supposed to mow the lawns on Saturdays, but he decides to take off with his friends and tell his parents he forgot. As he walks out the door, his mom reminds, "Nathan, don't forget to mow the lawns before you go anywhere."

"But Mom, do I have to?" Nathan asks. "The grass is not that long."

"It's been two weeks since it was last mowed," says his mom, "and it looks long to me."

"Can't I do it after lunch? I promise I will," says Nathan.

"If you get the job done when you're supposed to, I might even consider letting you stay up an hour later tonight," offers his mom.

"But Mom," pleads Nathan, "what if I do the front lawn now and the back lawn later? Can I still stay up an hour later?"

Frustrated by her weakening position, his mom responds, "I'm getting a little tired of talking about this!"

"Please Mom, just this once. I promise," says Nathan convincingly.

"Well, maybe just this once, but next week you'll have to do both lawns before playing," she insists.

"I will," says Nathan.

Did you hear a clear verbal message that mowing the lawns before playing was required? Nathan didn't. Instead, his mom used persuasion and bargaining to enlist his cooperation. In doing so, she was really saying that her rules were negotiable.

To children, negotiable feels a lot like optional, and Nathan tests to see how much he can get away with. By the time everything was said and done, he understood that the real rule is: Mow the lawns sometime on Saturdays unless you can talk your way out of it. Parents who are willing to bargain over their limits are, in effect, inviting children to test and to redefine their rules.

Arguing and Debating

Nine-year-old Karen is asked to clean up her room before she goes out to play. "I don't see why I have to clean my room before I go out if you don't have to clean yours," complains Karen.

"Our room is clean, Karen. Now, do what you were told," her father replies.

"Your bed isn't made. It doesn't look very clean to me," Karen shoots back.

"That's because your mother is changing the linen today—now do what you were told," insists her father.

"That's not fair! You guys get to choose when you want to make the bed, but we don't," Karen complains.

"I've had about enough of your sass, and I'm sick of listening to your complaints!" responds her dad. "You know the rules. Now do it."

"Yeah, they're lousy rules!" Karen snaps back as she heads off reluctantly to clean her room.

What is the message Karen's father sends by arguing and debating over his rules? And what is not happening while the arguing and debating is going on? Karen is not cleaning up her room. That won't happen until the argument is over, and some arguments can go on for quite awhile.

By participating in a verbal sparring match with his daughter, Karen's father is really saying that his rules are subject to further discussion and debate. He is unintentionally inviting a power struggle by encouraging Karen to test his limits and prolong her misbehavior.

Bribes and Special Rewards

Justin's mother is frustrated because her ten-year-old son won't do anything he's asked. A well-intentioned neighbor suggests, "Kids his age love money. Why don't you try paying him for doing what you want?"

Maybe she's right, Justin's mother thinks to herself. *Justin is always asking me for money.* She decides to give it a try.

The next day, Justin leaves a mess on the living room floor, and his mother asks him to clean it up. "No way!" says Justin, "I'm going to Charley's house to play commandos."

"I'll pay you seventy-five cents if you do it before you go," his mother says.

"Make it a dollar and I'll do it," says Justin.

"OK, a dollar," his mother says reluctantly, "but you have to do it now." He did, and she paid him.

Not bad, Justin thinks to himself as he scampers out the door.

Justin's mother used this approach many times that first week with good success — at least she thought. After all, she was getting him to do more chores than he was willing to do before. By the end of the week, she realized that she had paid out nearly $20. The second week, the payout was $25, and the third week it was nearly $30. The neighbor was right. Justin did love money, but what was his mother really teaching him?

One month after she started this plan, Justin's mother had paid out nearly $90 to get her son to do things he was supposed to do anyway. She began to question the wisdom of her approach.

"Nobody had to pay me to cooperate when I was a child." The more she thought about it, the madder she got.

That evening, she asked Justin to put away some toys he had left out on the front lawn. "How much do I get?" he said.

"I shouldn't have to pay you anything for doing what you're supposed to do," his mother said.

"Then I won't do it!" said Justin indignantly. "Not unless you pay me."

Justin's mother realized she had been sending the wrong message. When we offer children bribes and special rewards in return for cooperation, aren't we really saying, with our actions, that we don't expect them to cooperate unless we pay them off? Bribes and special rewards are just another way of saying that cooperation is optional and contingent upon receiving rewards.

Like Justin's mother, many parents who offer bribes and special rewards do so in the belief that they are teaching cooperation, responsibility, and compliance with their rules. What they are really teaching, however, is that the only tasks worth doing are those they get paid for. Justin understood this clearly. His cooperation stopped as soon as the reward was withheld.

Inconsistency Between Parents

When mom says, "Jimmy, pick up your toys before you go out to play," and dad says, "Let him go dear. His friends are waiting," and holds the door open for Jimmy to scamper out, what message is Jimmy getting about the rules he has to follow?

In effect, there are two sets of rules operating here: mom's rules that say do it and dad's rules that say don't do it. Since Jimmy got to leave without picking up, the action message says that dad's rules prevail.

The next time Jimmy is asked to pick up his toys before going out, he will likely play one parent against the other and test to see which set of rules is really operating. If mom asks him, he will say, "Dad says I don't have to." If dad asks him, he will say, "You didn't make me do it last time." In either event, inconsistent messages set all three up for conflicts.

Ineffective Follow-Through

Jake knows he's not supposed to have any cookies or sweets before dinner, but three or four times a week he sneaks into the cookie jar and grabs himself a handful. Sometimes he gets caught. When he does, he quickly gulps down whatever is in his hand as his mother reminds him that he's supposed to stay out of the cookie jar before dinner.

Jake's mother's words say stop, but her actions are a clear green light that says eating cookies before dinner is really OK until you get caught. That's not such a bad deal for someone who likes cookies. If Jake's mother really wants her son to stop eating cookies before dinner, she needs to follow through with an action message that communicates her rule more clearly (such as keeping the cookie jar empty for a week each time he violates her rule).

More Examples of Ineffective Verbal Messages (Soft Limits)

"It's time to take a bath, OK?"

"Would you just try to be nice once in awhile?"

"Come on, get your act together."

"Would you do me a favor and cooperate for once?"

"Can't you see I'm on the phone?"

"Would you yell a little softer? You're waking the baby!"

"You better shape up."

"I don't like your attitude."

"It would be nice to see your homework done early."

"Would you like it if I interrupted you?"

"Stop acting like a jerk!"

"Would it be asking too much to have a little cooperation?"

"That's enough from you!"

More Examples of Ineffective Action Messages (Soft Limits)

Allowing children to walk away from a mess.

Cleaning up children's messes for them.

Dressing children when they can dress themselves.

Ignoring misbehavior in the hope it will go away.

Overlooking unacceptable behavior when you're in a good mood.

Slapping a child who hits to show them how it feels.

Firm Limits: When No Really Means No

Eight-year-old Patrick sits at the breakfast table playing with a whistle he got out of his cereal package. Like most children, he's anxious to try it out. He blows it a couple of times to make sure it works. It works too well. His two brothers are covering their ears and yelling for him to stop. Patrick enjoys the commotion. He continues to blast away.

Aroused by the commotion, Patrick's father walks into the room. He says, matter-of-factly, "Patrick, stop blowing the whistle. That's an outdoor toy." Patrick gives his father a defiant look but complies with the request and puts the whistle down.

As soon as his father leaves the room, however, Patrick picks the whistle up and lets out several defiant blasts. His father returns to the room, and, without any further comments, takes the whistle away.

Patrick's father is using firm limits to communicate his rule about blowing whistles in the house. His words say stop and so do his actions when he takes the whistle away. Patrick receives a very clear message. He understands that compliance with the rule is both expected and required, and he has all the information he needs to make more acceptable choices in the future.

Firm limits send clear signals about our rules and expectations. Children trained with these signals understand what we mean because they experience what we say.

93

Words are consistent with actions. They learn to take our words seriously and cooperate when asked. The result — better communication, less testing, and no family dances. Firm limits are highly effective training tools.

Guidelines for Stating Firm Limits

Effective guidance begins with a clear message about our rules and expectations. We begin this step with our words, and most often that's where communication breaks down. The following tips will help you improve the quality of your verbal messages.

1. Keep the focus of your message on behavior.

Our goal is to reject unacceptable behavior, not the child performing the behavior. Therefore, we need to keep the focus of our message on behavior and corrective action, not on attitude, or feelings, or the worth of the child.

For example, if you want Kenny, age six, to stop teasing his younger brother, your message should be, "Kenny, stop teasing your brother now," not "Kenny, don't be such a pest!" or "Nobody likes your snotty attitude" or "Kenny, how do you think that makes your brother feel?"

If you want eight-year-old Melinda to stop interrupting you while you're on the phone, your message should be, "Melinda, stop interrupting please," or "Melinda, you need to wait until I'm off the phone," not "Can't you see I'm busy!" or "Do you have to be such a pest!" or "You're so inconsiderate!"

2. Be direct and specific.

A firm limit-setting message is one that informs children, directly and specifically, what it is you want them to do. If necessary, you should be prepared to tell them when and how you want them to do it. The fewer the words, the better.

For example, if you want your twelve-year-old home for dinner by 6:30, your message should be, "Be home for dinner by 6:30," not "Don't stay out too late" or "Try to be back on time." If you use the latter two messages, who decides what "too late" or "on time" means, you or your twelve-year-old? And who defines "try?" Both of these messages open the door for testing.

If your ten-year-old is doing a careless job of cleaning her bathroom, your message should be, "Jill, your bathroom needs to be cleaned thoroughly. That means picking the towels off the floor, putting your dirty clothes in the hamper, and wiping the hair and toothpaste off the counter."

If instead your message was, "Jill, I hope you do a better job cleaning the bathroom" or "The bathroom could be a little cleaner," who decides what "a better job" or "a little cleaner" means, you or Jill? Without a direct and specific message, Jill's performance will probably still fall short of your expectations.

3. Use your normal voice.

The tone of your voice is very important. A raised voice sends the wrong action message — loss of control. You want your tone to convey that you are in control and that you are firm and resolute in your expectation that your child must do what you've asked. The best way to communicate this expectation is simply to state your message matter-of-factly in your normal voice.

Firm limits are not stated harshly. There is no need to yell, scream, or raise your voice to convince your child that you really mean what you say. If needed, your actions (consequences) will convey that message more powerfully than your words. Just say what you want them to do in your normal voice and be prepared to move on to your action step if needed.

4. Specify your consequences if necessary.

If you expect to be tested or if your children have not been following your rules consistently, you may need to specify the consequences for noncompliance at the same time you make your request. This is not a threat. You are simply establishing your credibility and providing them with the information they may need to make an acceptable choice.

For example, if you ask your child to stop riding his scooter in the street, but you expect him to try it anyway, your message should be, "Please don't ride your scooter in the street. If you do, I'll have to put it away for the rest of the day."

Now your child has all the information he needs to cooperate. He may still decide to test, but if he does, follow through with your action step and put the scooter away. After a few encounters like this, he will begin to take your words seriously and do what you request. You will no longer need to specify the consequence to establish your credibility.

5. Support your words with action.

Remember, your words are only the first part of your overall message. In many cases, your words may be all you will need, but even the clearest verbal message will be ineffective if you fail to support your message with action.

For example, if I tell my sons, "No playing until your chores are done," but fail to act when they sneak out to play without finishing, are they likely to take my words seriously the next time I make this request? Of course not. They know that my words are only as credible as the actions that support them.

Examples of Effective Verbal Messages (Firm Limits)

"Stop hitting now."

"Don't eat popsicles in the living room."

"Take your feet off the sofa, please."

"Pick up your building toys and put them back in their box before you go outside to play."

"Be home by 5:30."

"You can play by the rules or find another game to play. What would you like to do?"

"Turn the TV down, please, or it will be turned off."

"You can play with the toy the right way or we'll have to take it away."

Examples of Effective Action Messages (Firm Limits)

Using a time-out consequence for a child who hits.

Removing the popsicle from a child who ignores your request not to eat it in the living room.

Removing building toys for a few days if your child refuses to pick them up.

Temporarily revising afterschool play time for a child who fails to be in on time (such as, "We'll try 5:00 for the rest of the week. If you handle that, then we can try 5:30 again next week.").

Not allowing your child to play a game for awhile (perhaps an hour or so) when he refuses to play by the rules.

97

Turning the TV off when your child refuses to turn it down.

Removing the toy when your child refuses to play with it in an acceptable way.

Refusing to wash clothes that aren't placed in the hamper.

Not replacing a toy that was damaged due to carelessness.

Summary

In this chapter, we learned why limits are such an important part of the child-training process. They are the messages that convey our rules and define the balance of power and authority in our relationships. We saw how children use limit testing to clarify our rules that are unclear.

Limits come in two basic varieties, firm and soft (see Figure 4A). Firm limits (when no means no) are highly effective. They send clear messages about our rules and expectations. Children trained with firm limits do less testing because they understand that compliance is both expected and required.

Soft limits (when no means yes, sometimes, or maybe) are rules in theory, not in practice. These ineffective messages encourage limit testing and resistance as children attempt to clarify what we really mean. Soft limits come in a wide variety of forms, but all invite limit testing and noncompliance. They are a major source of conflicts, power struggles, and destructive family dances.

You probably have a better idea now of the type of limits you've been using and why your children respond to your limits the way they do. Following on page 100 are the questions parents most frequently ask about firm and soft limits.

Figure 4A. Comparison of firm and soft limits

	Firm limits	Soft limits
Characteristics	Stated in clear, direct, concrete behavioral terms	Stated in unclear terms or as "mixed messages"
	Words supported by actions	Actions do not support intended rule
	Compliance expected and required	Compliance optional; not required
	Provides information needed to make acceptable choices and cooperate	Does not provide information needed to make acceptable choices
	Provides accountability	Lacks accountability
Predictable outcomes	Cooperation	Resistance
	Decreased limit testing	Increased limit testing
	Clear understanding of rules and expectations	Escalating misbehavior, power struggles
	Regard parents' words seriously	Ignore and tune out parents' words
Children learn	"No" means "no."	"No" means "yes," "sometimes," or "maybe."
	"I'm expected and required to follow the rules."	"I'm not expected to follow rules."
	"Rules apply to me like everyone else."	"Rules are for others, not me."
	"I am responsible for my own behavior."	"I make my own rules and do what I want."
	Adults mean what they say.	"Adults don't mean what they say."
		"Adults are responsible for my behavior."

Questions about Firm and Soft Limits

1. *My husband is willing to overlook some things my children do that I consider to be misbehavior. This is often a source of conflict between us. How do we know what things should and should not be overlooked? What are some guidelines for setting limits?*

Answer: The home is the training ground for the world. If your child is behaving in ways that would be unacceptable outside the home (in the school, neighborhood, or community), limits should be set on those behaviors. In short, the rules for acceptable behavior in the home should parallel the rules for acceptable behavior at school and out in the community.

When we overlook misbehavior, we are really saying, by our lack of action, that the behavior is OK. To children, the absence of a red light is usually a green light, or a yellow light at best. We know that yellow lights do not stop misbehavior. Failure to act is setting limits by omission. Our lack of action also conveys a message about our rules.

2. *What can I do to further clarify the type of limits I'm using with my children?*

Answer: Perhaps the best indicator of your limits is your children's reaction to them. If your children are responding to your requests with testing and resistance, the likelihood is good that you're using soft limits. Beyond this, there are several other methods for getting direct feedback about your messages:

    a. Ask your spouse or friend to listen to you when you set limits and tell you exactly what you said and did.

    b. Some parents have even used tape recorders to record messages at times of the day when conflicts are most likely to occur (such as getting off in the morning, arriving home, homework and chore times, mealtimes, going to bed).

c. Use the check-in procedure you will learn in the next chapter. This is a simple and effective way to get direct feedback from your child.

3. *How do I avoid the old repeating and reminding routine when I'm not sure my children heard or understood my limits?*

Answer: Repeating and reminding is exactly what children want us to do when they ignore or tune us out, and it is very hard to resist not doing what they want. You'll need some specific techniques. In the next chapter, you will learn three effective strategies for interrupting your family dance and avoiding the repeating and reminding routine.

4. *If I begin using firm limits consistently, how long will it take before my children show a significant decrease in their limit-testing behavior?*

Answer: This will vary depending on the child, the child's age, and the length of time you've been using soft limits. Younger children (three to seven years old) generally respond more quickly than older children because they have less history to overcome.

You will likely encounter the heaviest testing during the first four to eight weeks, then you should find a gradual but steady reduction in limit testing from that point on. Compared to the amount of time your child will be at home, the investment of consistent effort on your part will pay big dividends in cooperation. The change process will be covered more thoroughly in Chapter Twelve.

5. *I've read in a number of parenting books that parents' rules should be flexible and negotiable. Do you agree? Firm limits do not sound very flexible.*

Answer: Yes, I agree. Parents' rules should be flexible in the sense that they can be negotiated and revised as children outgrow them or as changing circumstances require. But the time to be flexible and negotiate your rules is not when they are being tested or violated.

Firm limits do not bend or collapse when tested or violated. In this sense, they are not flexible, but they are certainly subject to discussion, negotiation, and revision at other, more appropriate, times.

Parent Study Group Questions

1. How do children clarify our rules when our messages are unclear or ineffective? Why is this a normal part of learning? Share examples of how your children do this to clarify your rules and expectations.

2. How do children usually respond to soft limits? What do they learn? Do your children show this kind of behavior? In what situations? Why are soft limits such ineffective training tools?

3. How do children usually respond to firm limits? What makes these messages effective training tools?

4. Can you identify the type of limits you've been using? Share some examples of your messages with other group members and describe how your children respond to them. Do they respond like the children in the examples?

5. What is your plan for improving the quality of your verbal messages? Discuss guidelines for using firm limits. Discuss your plan with other group members.

   Practice Exercise. Practice giving clear messages (firm limits) with your children. Note their responses and how often this step alone achieves their cooperation. Be prepared to share your experiences next session.

Getting off the Dance Floor

Sherman is only five, but when it comes to family dances he's a young Fred Astaire. He knows how to execute a perfect stall when he's asked to get dressed in the morning, and he knows just the right moment to cry or get upset when his parents are close to giving in. Sherman can turn a no into a yes faster than any child on his block.

What Sherman doesn't know, however, is that his parents are catching on to his tricks. They are beginning to see his behavior for what it is — part of a dance — and they're ready to put an end to it.

One morning, as Sherman begins his usual stall, his mother announces, "Sherman, you have fifteen minutes to finish dressing, then you're out the door ready or not. I'll set the timer."

She doesn't mean it, Sherman thinks to himself. *She'll remind me a few more times, then come over and help me finish up.* He continues to dawdle. Fifteen minutes go by and he only has his socks, underwear, and T-shirt on. The buzzer goes off.

"Time to go," says his mother matter-of-factly. She puts his remaining clothes in a shopping bag and escorts him to the door. No reminders. No lectures. No pleading or cajoling. What's going on? Sherman can't believe his eyes. He's in a state of shock.

"You can't do this!" he screams, but by this time they're already out the door, and the commotion catches the attention of other children heading off to school. *Oh no!* thinks Sherman, embarrassed. His drama is not intended for them. They know he's capable of getting dressed and out the door. He sprints for the car.

"Here's the bag, Sherman," his mother says as the two of them get into the car. With tears streaming down his face, Sherman scrambles to finish dressing. His pants, shirt, and shoes are on before they even back out of the driveway. Nothing further is said. The next morning, Sherman is dressed on time.

Let's look at a diagram of what took place (Figure 5A). As the diagram illustrates, the best way to stop a dance is not to start one. We need to begin with a clear verbal message about our expectations and move on quickly to our action step. Sherman's mother does this very effectively. You can, too, but you shouldn't expect your children to give up their testing quickly.

In the beginning, they will likely challenge even your clearest verbal messages and do everything they can to get you back out on the floor. You'll probably be very tempted to go along with it. The three techniques you'll learn in this chapter will help you resist that temptation and to interrupt your dance before it gets started. Let's see how they work.

Figure 5A. Sherman's diagram

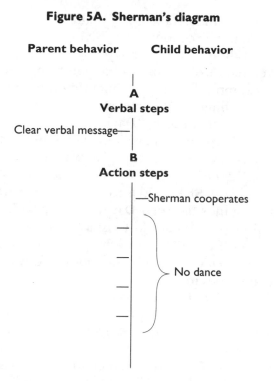

The Check-in Procedure

When we state a firm limit, but our children don't respond as expected or tune us out, sometimes we're not
sure whether our message was really heard or understood. We're left wondering: Did my message get across?
Am I being ignored? Is it time to move on to my action
step?

The *check-in procedure* is a simple technique that
helps parents answer these questions without getting
hooked into the old repeating and reminding routine.
When in doubt, simply check-in with your child by saying
one of the following:

107

"Did you understand what I said?"

"Were my directions clear?"

"What did you hear me say?"

"Tell me in your words what you heard me say."

For example, it's nearly dinner time, and six-year-old David is watching his favorite cartoon show. His mother calls from the other room, "David, it's time to turn off the TV and wash up for dinner," but David just looks at her with a blank stare and continues to watch his program.

Did he hear what I said? she wonders. *If he did, he sure doesn't act like it.* She decides to check-in. She walks into the room, stands between David and the TV, and says matter-of-factly, "What did I just ask you to do?"

"Turn off the TV and wash up," replies David.

"Then do it please," says his mother. David turns off the TV and goes to wash up.

What got into her? he wonders. *That's not how she's supposed to act. What happened to all the reminders, warnings, and threats? I should have gotten at least another five minutes from her.*

In this case, David received his mother's message but chose to ignore it. He was limit testing. He fully expected her to repeat and remind and do a great deal of talking before he would actually have to stop watching his show. But it didn't happen. By using the check-in procedure, David's mother eliminated the dance and the payoffs for ignoring (Figure 5B).

Let's add a new wrinkle to the example above. Let's say, for the sake of argument, that when David's mother checks-in he responds with a blank stare because he really was tuned out, completely. What should his mother do?

She should give him the information he missed the first time and support it with her action step by turning off the TV. Now she knows that her message got across. So does David.

The check-in procedure also is useful in situations

Figure 5B. The check-in procedure

Parent behavior   Child behavior

A
Verbal steps

Clear verbal message—

—David ignores request

Check-in procedure—

—David cooperates

No dance

where children give us the right verbal response but continue to do as they wish. Hilary, age ten, is a pro at this.

It's Saturday night and Hilary has been invited to join some friends for a slumber party. Her ride is arriving in twenty minutes. As she waits in front of the TV, her father notices a mess she left in the living room. "Hilary, this mess needs to be picked up before you leave," he says.

"I will," says Hilary, but fifteen minutes go by, and she hasn't made a move. She's hoping to make it out the door. Hilary's father suspects this also, so he decides to check-in.

"Hilary, what did I ask you to do?" he inquires.

"I'll pick it up," she says as convincingly as the first time, but she continues to watch the TV.

109

Her father clarifies the message, "Your words say, 'I will,' but your actions say, 'I won't.' Let me be more clear—you won't be leaving until it's picked up." Now, his message is very clear.

Rats! He didn't go for it, Hilary says to herself. Realizing that the game is over, she runs into the living room to pick up the mess so she can leave when her ride arrives. No dances this time.

The Cut-off Technique

The *cut-off technique* is another method of interrupting a dance when children try to hook us into arguing, debating, bargaining, or compromising our limits. As the term implies, the cut off ends the interaction by stating a consequence if it continues. If your child still decides to test, then follow through with your consequence. Either way, the dance stops.

When your child tries to engage you in arguments, debates, bargaining, or other forms of verbal sparring, you should say the following:

"We're done talking about it. If you bring it up again, then . . ." (follow through with your action step).

"Discussion time is over. You can do what you were asked, or you can spend the next ten minutes in your room getting ready to do it [time-out consequence]. What would you like to do?"

Thirteen-year-old Erin knows she's not supposed to take her mother's costume jewelry without asking, but she notices a new pair of earrings that would look great with her new outfit. She puts them on and tries to get out the door unnoticed.

"Erin, are those my new earrings?" her mother asks as Erin is getting ready to head off. "Aren't you supposed to ask before you take my jewelry?"

"I forgot," Erin says in her most remorseful voice. "Can I wear them? Please Mom? They go perfectly with my new outfit."

She's right, Erin's mom thinks to herself. *They do look great with that outfit, but we also have a rule that she's supposed to follow here. She didn't even consider if I wanted to wear them today. If I give in, she's just going to do it again.*

Erin's mom remains firm. "Not today," she says. "Maybe another time if you ask me first."

"But Mom!" pleads Erin, "I'm asking you now. Can't I wear them? Please? I'll ask next time. I promise." Erin is giving it her best shot to try to break down the rule by opening the topic up for debate. All she needs is a little wiggle room to begin to wear her mom down.

The bait was presented skillfully, and Erin's mom was really tempted to bite, but then she remembers what she learned in the workshop. *No,* she says to herself, *we're not going through this again. I'm going to sit this dance out.*

"Put them back, Erin," says her mom firmly. "We're done discussing it." Erin's mom walks back into the kitchen, and Erin puts the earrings away. Erin's mom has taken an important step toward interrupting her permissive dance (Figure 5C).

Zack's dad also used the cut-off technique effectively when his sixteen-year-old tried to wiggle out of doing a chore. "I want you to clean the garage before you go anywhere on Saturday," his father said earlier in the week.

"No problem," said Zack, but when Saturday came he spent most of the day lounging around watching basketball games on TV. By late afternoon, the garage still hadn't been touched.

"Dad, may I take the car to the basketball game tonight?" Zack asked.

"Not until the garage is done," said his father.

"But Dad . . ." pleaded Zack. "It's almost five

Figure 5C. The cut-off technique

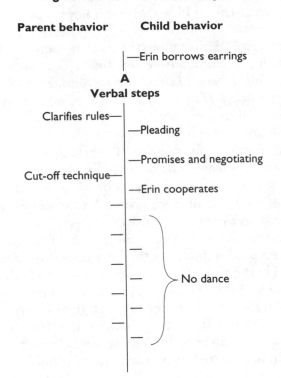

Parent behavior   **Child behavior**

—Erin borrows earrings

A
Verbal steps

Clarifies rules—

—Pleading

—Promises and negotiating

Cut-off technique—

—Erin cooperates

No dance

o'clock, and it will take at least two hours to do the garage. Can't I do it tomorrow, please?" Zack maneuvered for a little opening. He fully expected to bargain his way out of it, but Zack's father was prepared. He held firm.

"You better get started on the garage if you want to go," said his father.

"But Dad! You're not being fair," Zack protested, dangling a delicious piece of bait his father could hardly resist. "I'll finish my chores just as soon as I get home. I promise!"

Zack's father was just about to debate the issue of fairness when he remembered the technique he read about in the book. "We're done talking about it, Zack," said his father. "If you bring it up again, you may not go even after the garage is done."

Zack knew that if he decided to test this limit, he might not like the answer. Besides, he really wanted to go. He gave it his best shot, and it didn't work. Reluctantly, he headed off to clean the garage.

The Cool Down

Effective problem solving is difficult for anyone to do, parents or children, in an atmosphere of anger and frustration. The *cool down* is an excellent technique for restoring self-control and stopping angry family dances before they begin. This method keeps both sides off the dance floor until the time is right for problem solving. You may want to think of it as a time-out for both parents and children.

The technique is easy to carry out. In situations of anger or upset, you should separate yourself from your child by saying something like the following:

(When both sides are upset) "I think we both need a little time to cool down. Wait for me in your room [living room, den, etc.], and we'll talk in five minutes [or however much time you need to restore control]." Set the timer.

(When the child is upset) "You look pretty angry to me. Let's take a few minutes to cool down. I'll set the timer for five minutes. You can cool off in your room or the living room. What would you like to do?"

(When the parent is upset) "I"m feeling very angry, and I need some time to cool off. I'll be in my room for awhile, and when I'm calmed down we can talk."

To ensure the success of this technique, both parties should be in separate rooms or areas (away from each

113

other) during the cool-down period and sufficient time should be provided for both of you to restore control before resuming problem solving. Don't assume that your child has calmed down because you have. You may want to preface your problem solving with a question such as "Are you ready to talk?" If things break down a second time, use the technique again. Use it as often as you need it. Consider the following example.

When I first met nine-year-old Sam and his dad, they were stuck in an angry dance. Whenever Sam misbehaved, his dad began yelling, and, before he knew it, he was saying hurtful things he later regretted.

Sam felt angry and hurt and was becoming skillful at hurting back. They both needed some way to interrupt their painful dance. I suggested the cool-down technique and showed them how it worked. They agreed to give it a try.

Shortly after our first appointment, Sam was in the garage building something with nails. When he finished his project, he left a number of nails scattered on the garage floor. When his dad noticed the nails, his first response was to explode.

"Sam! Get in here!" he shouted, but as the words left his mouth he remembered what we discussed.

Sam arrived expecting the worst, but to his astonishment, his father said, "Sam, I need a few minutes to cool off. Wait for me in your room, please."

It took about five minutes for Sam's dad to calm down. Then, he went to Sam's room and calmly asked him to pick up the nails. No yelling, no insults, and no injured feelings! It felt strange to be treated respectfully, but Sam was more than happy to comply. Both had taken a big step toward ending their angry dance and improving their communication (Figure 5D).

My counseling work sometimes involves assisting parents who are trying to break the cycle of violence and

Figure 5D. The cool-down technique

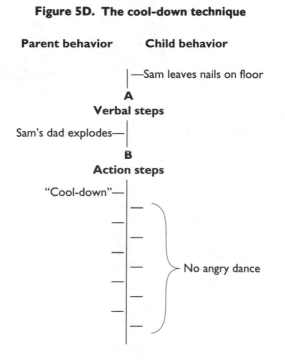

Parent behavior   **Child behavior**

—Sam leaves nails on floor

A
Verbal steps

Sam's dad explodes—

B
Action steps

"Cool-down"—

No angry dance

abuse in their families. Most of these parents were abused themselves. They grew up with angry and violent dances, and they are repeating those dances with their children.

My first goal is to help these parents find a way off the dance floor before their anger turns to violence. The cool down is often the solution. Let's see how one parent used this technique to break the cycle of violence in her family.

When I first met Sandra, she was being reunited with her children for the second time in as many years. She had been through a number of parenting classes and had learned some useful techniques. She knew how to use time-out and encouragement, but for some reason these techniques were not enough.

"I can't help it," said Sandra. "I can only stand so

115

Figure 5E. Sandra's dance

Parent behavior   Child behavior

—Children misbehave

A
Verbal steps

Clear verbal message—
Blaming—
—Denial
Accusations—
Getting angry—
—Arguing
Arguing—
Very angry—
—More arguing
Yelling—

B
Action steps

Time-outs (75%
of time)—
Hitting (25%
of time)—

much arguing and hassling before I lose my temper and lash out.''

I asked Sandra to describe her methods from beginning to end. As she did, I diagrammed them out for her on the board (Figure 5E).

Sandra was doing a very punitive dance, the same dance she grew up with. Typically she started off with a lot of blaming and accusations. When her kids denied their guilt and argued back, she got angry. The more they argued, the angrier she became. Talking turned to yell-

116

ing, and, before she knew it, she was losing her control. She tried to end her dances with a time-out instead of hitting, but sometimes things went too far.

From Sandra's description, I could see it was the dance that was putting her over the edge. She needed a way to stop it before she reached her boiling point. Time-out was the right approach, but she was using it much too late.

We practiced how to give the kids a clear message at the beginning without blaming and accusations. It felt strange, but she was willing. Then, I introduced the cut-off technique and showed her how to follow it up with the cool down. We practiced these methods until she felt comfortable.

"Use the methods as often as you need them," I said, "particularly when the arguments begin." I gave her a week to practice and asked her to call if problems came up.

When Sandra returned the following week, she wore a smile of accomplishment. "It worked!" she said. "When they started arguing, I told them we were done talking about it. When they kept it up, I sent them to their rooms for a ten-minute cool down, and I took one myself." No yelling. No threats. And no hitting. Sandra found a useful tool for interrupting an angry dance.

PARENT STUDY GROUP QUESTIONS

1. Describe your experiences giving clear verbal messages (firm limits) that you practiced since last session. How did your children respond? Did you notice improved cooperation?

2. What is the best way to stop a dance? How do each of the strategies in this chapter always begin?

3. Karen, age fifteen, is a skillful debater. When her parents ask her to do something, Karen has a persuasive argument and a ready set of reasons for why she can't. Their dances often involve exhaustive debates about what she's supposed to do. What strategy should Karen's parents use to stop this destructive pattern?

   Practice Exercise. Select another group member and practice using the technique Karen's parents should use to stop the dance. Take turns being Karen and her parents.

4. Kevin, age eight, is a master at ignoring his parents' requests, or maybe he really is tuned out, completely. His parents aren't really sure, but they end up repeating and reminding many times throughout the day. How can they stop this dance?

   Practice Exercise. Select another group member and practice using the technique Kevin's parents should use when Kevin gives a blank stare to a request to come in for dinner. Take turns being Kevin and his parents.

5. Christy's mom has a very short fuse and tends to explode in a torrent of angry words and punitive consequences whenever Christy challenges or defies her mom's requests. How can Christy's mom put an end to her angry dance?

118

Practice Exercise. Select another group member and practice using the technique Christy's mom should use to end the dance. Take turns being Christy and her mother.

Practice Exercise. At home, practice using the strategies you need to interrupt your dance. Note what it feels like not to go through the dance. Does it feel strange? Do you feel a strong desire to do what you did before? Be prepared to share your observations next session.

Chapter

6

Encouragement: The Language of Cooperation

How do you feel when you ask someone to cooperate with you in the best way you know how only to encounter their resistance? Angry? Frustrated? Discouraged? All of the above?

This is how many parents feel who use soft limits. They get angry and frustrated when they don't get the response they expect, and they end up saying discouraging things to their children. They assume that the problem is their children's lack of cooperation, not the way that cooperation is being requested. Discouraging messages and soft limits go hand-in-hand.

Parents who use firm limits, on the other hand, expect cooperation, but they also recognize that children are most likely to cooperate when they are asked in a respectful manner. Encouraging messages inspire cooperation. Firm limits and encouraging messages also go hand-in-hand.

Encouraging and discouraging messages have very different effects on children's behavior. One leads to co-operation, while the other leads predictably to resistance. In this chapter, you will learn how to use encouraging messages as an effective motivational tool. You will see that the type of message you use has a lot to do with the type of limits you set.

Discouraging Messages Inspire Resistance

Randy, nine years old, teases his younger sister and gets the intended response. She screams for mom, who is reading in another room. Randy's mother has a good idea what's going on from the sound of things.

"Randy, I hope you're not teasing your sister again. You know how I feel about that," she says, but Randy continues with his teasing and his sister screams again.

Angered by the lack of cooperation, Randy's mother enters the room and unleashes a barrage of discouraging messages. "Can't you see that you're making your sister upset?" she shouts. "Would it be asking too much from you to have you cooperate just once in awhile? I would expect your behavior from a three-year-old, but certainly not from you. Would you just grow up and stop making life miserable for everyone?"

Randy retaliates. "Do you enjoy being such a witch all the time?" he says. The hurtful dance moves into high gear.

"That's enough from you, young man!" his mother shoots back. "I'm sick and tired of all your crap!" She hands him a pencil and a sheet of stationery. "Now you sit down and write 100 times — I won't sass my mother."

"You can't make me if I don't want to," Randy counters.

"There will be no playing or TV the rest of the week if you don't!" she threatens.

"So what! See what I care," Randy snaps defiantly, as his mother leaves the room.

Like most parents, Randy's mother did not start off with the intention of discouraging her son or provoking a power struggle. Her goal was to stop his misbehavior and enlist his cooperation. But she was using one of the surest methods to not achieve that goal.

Discouraging messages usually achieve the opposite of their intended effect. They inspire resistance, not cooperation, and they lead predictably to escalating misbehavior and power struggles. They are the fuel for hurtful family dances. Let's take a closer look at the steps in this dance (Figure 6A).

Randy's mother begins her dance with a soft limit and becomes angered at the predictable response — Randy's noncompliance. She then tries to shame him into cooperating with a series of discouraging messages. The focus is on Randy's worth and capabilities, not his behavior. Her messages convey no confidence in his ability to behave acceptably. In effect, she is saying: "You're not capable; I have no confidence in you; and I don't expect you to cooperate." He doesn't.

Would you feel like cooperating if someone said these things to you? Or would you feel hurt and more inclined to retaliate? Randy responds the way many of us would — with resistance and retaliation. He perceives his mother's message as a personal attack.

Let's not overlook the action message that accompanies her discouraging statements. By role modeling this method of problem solving, isn't his mother teaching him that hurtful and discouraging statements are an acceptable way to get others to cooperate? Without realizing

123

Figure 6A. Randy's dance

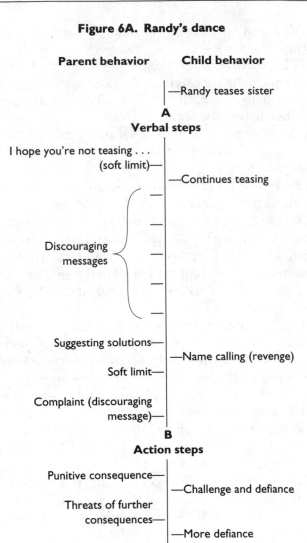

Parent behavior   **Child behavior**

—Randy teases sister

A
Verbal steps

I hope you're not teasing . . .
(soft limit)—

—Continues teasing

Discouraging
messages

Suggesting solutions—

—Name calling (revenge)

Soft limit—

Complaint (discouraging
message)—

B
Action steps

Punitive consequence—

—Challenge and defiance

Threats of further
consequences—

—More defiance

it, she is teaching the very behavior she's trying to stop.

Discouraging Verbal Messages

Discouraging messages come in a variety of forms. Some can be subtle as in the case of the parent who is overinvolved or helps too much. Others are explicit and direct as in the example of Randy and his mother. All discouraging messages convey little confidence in the child's ability to make good choices and behave acceptably. Many personalize misbehavior and carry an underlying message of shame or blame. Let's look at the underlying message in each of the following examples:

"Do you think you can cooperate just once in awhile?" The underlying message is "I don't believe you can cooperate." The effect is to blame, diminish, single out, and humiliate.

"Show me you have a brain and make a good choice for a change." The underlying message is "You're stupid, and I don't believe you can make good choices." The effect is to diminish, shame, and humiliate.

"Would it be asking too much for you to treat me respectfully?" The underlying message is "You're disrespectful." The effect is to blame and diminish.

"Is that the best you can do?" The underlying message is "You're not very competent and you don't live up to my expectations." The effect is to shame, diminish, and embarrass.

"I don't believe it! You actually did your chores for a change." The underlying message is "I don't expect your cooperation. The effect is to embarrass, shame, diminish, and single out.

"Try that again. I dare you." The underlying message is "Continue misbehaving because I don't expect your cooperation, and I want to show you I'm the boss." The

effect is to challenge, provoke, blame, diminish, and threaten.

"There's one jerk in every family." The underlying message is "You're not worthwhile or acceptable." The effect is to reject, humiliate, shame, single out, and diminish.

"Now that's real bright." The underlying message is "You make poor decisions. You're stupid." The effect is to humiliate, shame, embarrass, and diminish.

"I knew I couldn't leave you alone without trouble." The underlying message is "You're not capable of behaving acceptably on your own." The effect is to blame, shame, humiliate, and diminish.

Discouraging Action Messages

Verbal discouraging messages, like the ones in the previous examples, are overt and not difficult to recognize, but there is another type of discouraging message that is much more subtle and insidious. These are action messages, and their discouraging effects are often obscured by our good intentions.

Two-year-olds are usually the first to try to point this out to us. What do they say when we offer our well-intended but unsolicited help? They usually say, "I can do it myself!"

When we do things for children that they are capable of doing for themselves, the effect can be very discouraging. The underlying message comes across something like this: "You need me because you're not capable of doing this on your own." Let's look at the underlying message in each of the following examples.

A four-year-old begins to pour from a carton of milk into his cereal bowl. His father is afraid it might spill. He reaches over, takes the carton, and pours it for him. The underlying message is "You're not capable of handling this task on your own. You need me to do it for you."

An eight-year-old is doing her homework at the kitchen table while her mother prepares dinner. Her mother offers frequent help and suggestions. The underlying message is "You're not capable of doing your homework on your own. You need me to help you."

Two brothers, seven and nine, begin to argue about sharing a toy. Their father hurries over and helps them work it out. The underlying message is "You're not capable of solving problems on your own. You need my help."

A five-year-old goes to McDonald's with his parents. His parents order for him without asking what he would like. The underlying message is "You're not capable of making decisions on your own about what you would like to eat."

An eager four-year-old wants to help out in the kitchen. His parent refuses, saying he'll only make a mess. The underlying message is "You're not capable. Only I can do this job."

A six-year-old wants to pick out her own school clothes in the morning, but her mother insists on laying them out for her. The underlying message is "You're not capable of making good decisions without my help."

Encouraging Messages Inspire Cooperation

Jamie and Leah, two sisters ages nine and eleven, are playing a spirited game of Monopoly on the floor when someone lets the dog in the house. Eager for some attention, he heads into the living room and stands right in the middle of the Monopoly board.

"Get out of here, Buck!" the two girls shout, but it's too late. The damage is already done. Paper money and properties are scattered everywhere. As the two sisters attempt to sort out the confusion, a dispute breaks out.

"That's my stack of money!" says Leah as her sister places it on the pillow she was sitting on. "And those are my utilities too!" Leah protests.

"No, they are not!" insists Jamie. "I had them." She clutches them tightly to her chest.

"You're cheating," says Leah as she grabs for the disputed items, but Jamie holds on tightly.

The noisy quarrel catches the attention of their father in the other room. He's tempted to investigate, then reconsiders. *No, I'll give them a chance to work it out on their own,* he says to himself. But things only get louder, and eventually one of them lets out a scream.

When he comes to investigate, he sees the girls wrestling on the floor. Leah is pulling Jamie's hair with one hand and grabbing for the money and properties with the other. Jamie is kicking back and holding on tightly to the disputed items. Both girls are very upset.

"Get off your sister, Leah," her father says in a firm voice. When Leah tries to explain, her father adds, "We can talk about it when you two get back. First, you both need a little time to cool off. I'll set the timer for fifteen minutes." Both girls head to their rooms for a cool down.

When the timer goes off, the girls return to the living room. "Do you want to talk about it?" asks their father.

"She tried to take a stack of my money and properties when Buck walked through our game," explains Leah.

"No, I didn't," says Jamie. "I had them first."

Realizing the futility of trying to sort out what happened, their father focuses on the more important task at hand. "What are some other ways you guys might have handled this?" he asks. He looks at Leah first.

"I could have stopped playing with her," says Leah.

"That's one choice," says her father. "Any others?" This time he looks at Jamie.

"We could have started the game over since Buck really did mess things up," says Jamie.

"Both of those are good choices," says her father. "I'm sure you guys will handle things fine if this comes up again." He gives each a smile and returns to what he was doing.

"Do you want to start the game over again?" asks Leah.

"OK," says Jamie, "but let's put Buck out first."

Leah and Jamie's father is using encouragement very effectively. Much of his success, however, is due to the way he starts off. He begins with a firm limit-setting message and a cool-down period that establishes the right atmosphere for problem solving. No one is blamed or singled out. Now, his encouraging words can have their greatest impact.

Where does he focus his encouragement? On choices and behavior. He gets right to work helping the girls explore other, more effective choices for handling the situation. Then, he expresses confidence in their abilities to resolve similar problems on their own. His messages are inspiring: "You're capable; I have confidence in you; I expect you to cooperate."

How would you feel if someone said that to you? Would you feel accepted and supported? Would you feel like cooperating? Most of us would, and so did Jamie and Leah.

Encouraging messages make us feel good and motivate us to cooperate. They meet our needs for belonging, reaffirm our feelings of competence and self-worth, and instill confidence in our ability to master challenging problems. They are a powerful motivating force for change. Encouragement can make the difference between cooperation and resistance.

Alfred Adler, a major figure in the development of psychiatry with Freud, considered encouragement to be a fundamental component in the process of human change. His writings and those of his leading proponents (Rudolf Dreikurs, Donald Dinkemeyer) continue to have a major impact on practices in education, applied psychology, and many other fields. Encouragement is gaining the recognition it deserves as a powerful tool for motivating cooperative behavior. Let's look at some guidelines for using this tool most effectively.

Guidelines for Using Encouraging Messages

Knowing what to encourage is the key to using encouragement effectively. The focus of our messages should address our basic training goals. Let's refer back to those goals for a moment.

What are we trying to teach with our guidance methods? Better choices, acceptable actions, cooperation, independence, and improvement. All lead to greater responsibility. These characteristics should be the focus of our encouraging messages. Let's look at some examples.

Encouraging Better Choices

Being responsible involves making choices about our behavior and experiencing the outcome of those choices, positive or negative. Often, when children misbehave, they are unaware of the poor choices they've made or that there are other, more effective, choices available to them. When we help children explore their choices and encourage them to make better ones, we teach responsibility. Consider the following example.

Toby, age ten, arrives home with a note from his

130

teacher. The note says that Toby will have to serve a two-hour detention after school the next day because he was disruptive in class.

"What happened, Toby?" his mother asks, in a matter-of-fact voice.

"This kid who sits behind me in class keeps teasing me about a girl he thinks I like," says Toby. "He drives me crazy! I told him to stop, but he wouldn't listen. So, I turned around and called him a jerk. I guess I was a little loud."

"Sounds like he really annoyed you," replies his mother. "What are you going to do if he does it again?"

"My teacher said I should let her know, and she would take care of it," says Toby.

"That's one choice. What else could you do?" she asks.

"I guess I could just ignore him," says Toby, "but that's really hard. He's such a pest!"

"That is hard," agrees his mother, "but I think it would work. If he saw that you weren't bothered by his teasing, he'd probably give it up. You've got two good choices to use next time. I'm sure you'll handle it fine."

Toby left feeling supported and encouraged. He was aware of his options, and he was prepared to make a different choice the next time he was teased.

Encouraging Acceptable Actions

Making an acceptable choice is an important first step, but acting on that choice is our larger training goal. Sometimes, our encouragement is most effective when we focus directly on actions.

Penny, seven years old, is invited to go swimming and runs home to ask her mom. As she blasts into the house, she sees her mom talking with a neighbor in the living room. She knows she's not supposed to interrupt, but she's very excited about swimming. She interrupts anyway.

"Mom," Penny says excitedly, "can I go swimming at Paula's house?" She can tell by the look on her mother's face that the interruption wasn't appreciated.

"Penny, what are you supposed to do when you want to talk to me, but I'm in the middle of a conversation?" her mother asks.

"Wait until you're done and say excuse me," Penny replies.

"Right," says her mom. "Now, go back outside, come in, and try it over again."

Penny enters the house a second time, approaches her mother, and waits patiently for a pause in the conversation. "Hi Penny," says her mother. "What's up?"

"May I go swimming at Paula's house? Her mother said she would watch us."

"Sure," says her mother, "and thank you for the way you asked." She gives Penny an appreciative smile, and Penny goes to get her swimsuit. Penny got the message in a very positive way. She'll probably think twice before interrupting her mother next time.

Three-year-old Ted also needed a little encouragement about acceptable actions when he was eating dinner with his family. "I'm thirsty," he announces. "Give me some juice." His words had a commanding tone.

"How are we supposed to ask?" his father asks, matter-of-factly. Ted remembers.

"May I have some juice, please?" he asks.

"Sure pal," says his father. "That's the way I like to be asked. Here you go." He refills Ted's cup.

Ted's object lesson was quick, simple, and effective. He got what he wanted, and he felt good about asking the right way.

Encouraging Cooperation

We certainly don't need misbehavior to cue us to the need for encouragement. Any time a child helps out, cooperates, or makes a contribution, we have an opportunity to use encouraging messages. Our encouragement increases the likelihood that cooperation will continue.

Six-year-old Mel helps out with his younger sister while his mom is on the phone. She appreciates his help, and when she gets off the phone she lets him know.

"Mel, thanks a lot for helping with Sarah. I really appreciate it." She gives him a little smile and a wink.

Mel swells with pride and accomplishment. It felt good to have his contribution recognized. Next time his mom is on the phone, he's likely to pitch in again.

A word or two of encouragement at the right moment can have a big impact. Children are much more likely to develop the spirit of cooperation when their efforts are acknowledged. The following are just a few examples of how to do it.

"I like the way you handled that."
"Your room looks great today."
"Your helping out makes a big difference."
"Good job."
"I knew I could count on you."
"Thanks, I appreciate what you did."

Encouraging Independence

One of our larger goals in training children is to assist them to handle challenging tasks and problems on their own. We do this by teaching effective skills and by limiting our involvement so they have opportunities to practice those skills. Encouragement plays an important role in this process. It gives children the courage to take risks and to act independently.

Lee just turned four. He's sitting at the breakfast

table and decides to pour some juice from a large pitcher into his cup. He looks at his dad first before trying.

"Go ahead, Lee," says his dad encouragingly.

Lee lifts the pitcher with both hands and carefully aims for his cup. He pours, but the pitcher is so big that it obscures his view of the cup. A little juice spills on the table. Lee sets the pitcher down dejectedly. His father encourages him to try again.

"You were very close," he says. "Let's try it again, but this time let's set the cup off to one side so you can see it better." He moves the cup and hands the pitcher back to Lee.

Lee looks a little uncertain, but he takes the pitcher, aims, and pours. Bingo! A perfect hit.

"Good job, Lee," says his father. "I knew you could do it." Lee beams with pride and accomplishment. He now has the courage to do it independently.

Encouragement also helped Allison learn a better way to handle a problem with her sister. When Allison, age seven, saw her younger sister playing with the plastic medical instruments Allison received for Christmas, she ran to mom to tattle.

"Mommy, Gwen is playing with my doctor's kit again," Allison complained. "She might break them."

"Did you ask her to stop and to give it back to you?" inquired her mother.

"No," Allison replied, expecting her mother to solve the problem.

"Then, that's what you need to do," said her mother. "I'm sure you'll handle it fine." And she did. She also learned a lesson in independent problem solving.

Encouraging Improvement

Some skills, like learning homework and chore routines, require repeated effort and practice before they are mastered. The process is gradual. Parental impatience or expectations of immediate mastery can be very discouraging. Our energy is better directed toward encouraging improvement. Our focus should be on effort, not outcome; process, not product.

Glenn and Dana are five and seven. Their parents are trying to get them into the habit of clearing their dishes and silverware from the table after meals. They've been working on this for three weeks, and they still have a ways to go.

"This is taking longer than I expected," their father commented to his wife one evening. "Maybe we should take fifteen minutes off their bedtimes for every time they forget."

"Let's try using a little more encouragement first and see what happens," suggested his wife. "Each time one of them remembers on their own, let's tell them how much we appreciate it, and when we have to prompt them, let's thank them after they do it."

The next morning when breakfast was finished, Dana remembered on her own. "Thank you for clearing your place, Dana," said her mother. "I really appreciate it." The words weren't lost on Glenn. He didn't miss his opportunity for a little positive attention.

"Thank you, Glenn," said his mother. "I really appreciate you remembering on your own." He probably wouldn't have had it not been for Dana's encouragement, but he was happy to take the credit all the same.

Not bad! thought their mother after the kids left for school. She used the same strategy the next few days with similar results. They didn't always remember on their own, but they were doing it much more frequently than before.

By the end of the week, the parents noticed a minor breakthrough. The kids remembered to clear their places entirely on their own for three consecutive days. They were well on their way to mastering a new routine. Encouragement, not consequences, was getting it done.

Summary

In this chapter, we examined two contrasting methods for motivating children's cooperation. We saw how discouraging messages, which often accompany soft limits, achieve the opposite of their intended effect. They inspire resistance, not cooperation, and often fuel angry power struggles.

Encouraging messages, on the other hand, are highly effective for motivating cooperation — particularly when used with firm limits. Encouraging messages meet children's needs for belonging, reaffirm feelings of competence and self-worth, and inspire children to tackle challenging tasks and problems on their own. Encouraging messages can make the difference between cooperation and resistance. (See Figure 6B for a comparison.)

Knowing what to encourage is the key to using encouragement effectively. Our messages have their greatest impact when they focus on better choices, acceptable actions, cooperation, independence, and improvement.

Figure 6B. Encouraging vs. discouraging messages

Encouraging messages	Discouraging messages
Inspire cooperation	Inspire resistance, retaliation
Motivate and empower	Discourage and humiliate
Convey respect, confidence, support	Diminish, blame, reject
Create cooperative relationships	Create adversarial relationships
Meet needs for belonging, competence, self-worth	Perceived as personal attack
Focus on choices and behavior	Focus on child's worth and capabilities

136

PARENT STUDY GROUP QUESTIONS

1. Share your experiences practicing the strategies for interrupting your dance. Describe how you felt and how your children responded. Did you feel a strong desire to do what you have always done?

2. What type of messages have you been using to inspire your children's cooperation? Have you been getting the responses you expect?

3. Cindy has been asked three times to pick up her dirty laundry but shows no sign that she's about to do it. Her dad is getting frustrated. "Would it be asking too much to get a little cooperation from you for a change?" he says. "Does everything have to be such a battle with you?"

   What really triggered Cindy's resistant response? What type of behavior is her father inspiring? Where is the focus of his message? On Cindy's behavior — or on Cindy as a person? Would you feel like cooperating if someone asked you in this way?

   Practice Exercise. What is another way Cindy's father might have made his request with a greater likelihood of getting cooperation? Use clear, firm messages and encouragement to state the request more effectively.

4. Chris, age eight, is helping his father repair a fence in the backyard. "Would you pound this nail in while I hold this board in place?" asks his father. Chris takes aim but misses and bends the nail in half. His father grabs the hammer out of his hand, gives him a disgusted look, and says impatiently, "You hold the board and I'll do the hammering."

137

What kind of action message is Chris's father using? What is the underlying message? How do you think Chris feels about this? What would be another way Chris's father might have handled this?

5. Emily, age four, is doing a pretty good job of getting herself ready for church. She has her underwear and socks on and is trying to get on her dress when her mother walks in and starts assisting with the dressing. What is the message to Emily? How might her mother handle this differently?

6. Ted, age eight, wants to help his mother make a cake. He pours the mix into the bowl, adds two eggs, and fishes out the pieces of eggshell. Then he wipes his hands on his shirt. "What are you doing?" shouts his mother. "Can't you do this without making a mess all over yourself?"

   What is another way Ted's mother might have gotten her message across more positively? Where should she focus her message? On the behavior she wants to stop or on the corrective behavior she wants to encourage?

7. What is your plan for inspiring your children's cooperation? Where do you need to focus your encouragement? Discuss your plan with other group members.

Practice Exercise. Practice using encouraging messages with your children at home. Note how often they decide to cooperate without the need for consequences. Be prepared to share your observations and experiences with the group at the beginning of the next session.

▼

Chapter

7

Teaching Problem-Solving Skills

If you didn't know how to swim and I lectured you for two hours about swimming, would that make you a better swimmer? Not likely. You would have to get into the pool and practice your skills many times before that would happen, and you would probably need more instruction.

Children learn much the same way. Our words help the learning process along, but providing information is not always enough. Sometimes, they need practice and additional instruction before they can fully master the lessons we're trying to teach.

In this chapter, you will learn four simple and highly effective techniques for teaching decision-making and problem-solving skills. Your consistent application of these techniques will provide your children with the practice they need to master your lessons and to make better choices about their behavior.

Information Is Sometimes Not Enough

Kaley, age six, and her mother arrived at my office with an interesting dilemma. Each day, Kaley left for school with a carefully prepared lunch, but the best items in her lunchbox always seemed to end up in some other child's hands. Kaley frequently arrived home in tears.

"I don't understand it," explained her frustrated mother. "She knows what to do. I've told her over and over again to say 'no' when the older kids ask for her lunch items, but she continues to give them away anyway! Her teacher said there's nothing she can do if Kaley chooses to give her lunch away."

I suspected her mother was right. Kaley probably did know what to do, but I wanted to check this out with Kaley to be sure.

"Kaley, what are you supposed to do when other kids ask for your lunch items?" I asked. She parroted back the words her mother told her.

"I'm supposed to say, 'no' and tell the teacher if they take them anyway," she said.

Her mother was right. On an intellectual level, Kaley understood what she was supposed to do. But knowing what to do and actually doing it are two different skills. I suspected her skill training was incomplete, so I explored the problem a little further.

"Saying 'no' to big kids is sometimes hard to do," I said. Kaley nodded her agreement.

"I get scared," she said.

"Let's practice saying 'no' to big kids for awhile," I suggested, "and see if we can help you feel more comfortable." I wanted Kaley to see, hear, and feel what it was like to do what she was being asked.

I asked her mother to pretend that she was the big kid, and I pretended to be Kaley. When her mother approached me and made a pitch for my chips, I said, "No, they're mine. Sorry, but you can't have them." We went through this procedure several times, and I role-modeled different ways to say "no."

"Now, it's your turn to practice, Kaley," I said. "This time, I'll be the big kid, and you can hold the lunchbox." I approached her and asked for her chips. She didn't make eye contact, but she did say, "no" very clearly.

"That was a very clear 'no,'" I said. "That would have worked just fine. Let's try it again."

We went through the situation again many times. Each time, I encouraged her to say "no" a different way to see which way felt most comfortable to her. She preferred the simple two-word approach, "No, sorry," and she discovered that she felt more comfortable when she didn't have to look at me while she said it. She was gaining confidence.

"Ready to try this out at school?" I asked.

"I guess so," said Kaley.

I asked her mother to practice the procedure with Kaley a few more times before Kaley left for school the next day and to offer some words of encouragement. We scheduled a follow-up appointment for later that week.

"How did it go?" I asked when they arrived for the follow-up visit. I could tell from the look on Kaley's face that she must have had some success.

"It went fine," said her mother. "The practice really helped. Her lunch stayed in her hands all week." Kaley had a proud look of accomplishment.

"Congratulations!" I said. She had mastered an important skill, one she could put to good use in other situations as well.

When Kaley first arrived at my office, her skill training was incomplete. Providing information was a helpful first step, but she needed practice and further instruction before she could actually do what she was asked. The simple training technique of role-modeling and a little encouragement helped Kaley complete the lesson her mother had begun.

Role-Modeling Corrective Behavior

Role-modeling corrective behavior is a simple and effective training technique with varied applications. It can be used for teaching independent problem-solving skills as in the case above or for teaching acceptable corrective behavior after children misbehave.

This instructional method is very concrete and therefore particularly effective with younger children ages two to seven years. Children have opportunities to see, hear, feel, and practice the corrective behavior we want them to carry out. The action step conveys a clear message about our expectations.

When your focus is on teaching skills when no misbehavior is involved, use the following steps:

1. Role-model the corrective behavior you want your child to use.
2. Encourage your child to "try it again" using the corrective behavior (practice several times, if necessary).
3. Encourage effort and improvement.

Let's look at several examples of how this technique can be used.

Three-year-old Tyler loves to help his father feed their dog in the mornings. When his father pours in the kibble and moistens it, Tyler does the stirring. Then his dad carries the bowl to the back patio.

"Can I carry it today?" Tyler asks. The bowl is pretty

heavy, and Tyler is only three, but his father gives him a try.

"Go ahead," says his father, "but be careful."

Tyler is careful. He places both hands firmly on the sides of the bowl, takes two steps, and plop! The bowl slips from his hands and spills on the kitchen floor. Tyler's eyes fill with tears of disappointment.

"You almost made it," says his father, as the two of them wipe up the floor and put the kibble back in the bowl. "You'll do fine next time, but first, watch how I hold it." Tyler's father role-models the proper way to hold the bowl. "See how both my hands are on the bottom of the bowl. Now it can't slip when I carry it." He hands the bowl back to Tyler.

"Now, try it again," says his father with a nod of encouragement. With both hands gripped firmly around the bottom of the bowl, Tyler heads out to the patio. Success.

"Good work!" says his father. "I can see you're ready to do that job on your own now."

Now, let's take a look at the second application of this technique. When your focus is on teaching corrective behavior following an incident of misbehavior, use the following steps:

1. Provide a firm limit-setting message.
2. Role-model the acceptable corrective behavior.
3. Encourage your child to "try it again" using the corrective behavior.
4. Encourage effort and improvement.

Trent, a four-year-old, gives his friend a push because the friend is in Trent's way. Trent's father inter-venes.

"Trent, we don't push when other people are in our way," his father says. "We say, 'excuse me,' or we ask them to 'move, please' like this [father role-models the corrective behavior]. Now, let's try it again."

Trent walks up to his friend and says, "Move, please." His friend moves over to let Trent by.

"Thanks, Trent," says his father.

Seven-year-old Brian craves his dad's affectionate hugs and head rubs but doesn't know how to ask for them. Lately, Brian has been sneaking up on his dad and swatting him on the backside or tickling him to get attention in the mornings. His dad is getting annoyed. On one of these occasions, Brian swats his dad while he is shaving. His father nicks himself.

"Brian, it's not OK to sneak up and hit or tickle me," his father says. "If you want a hug, just ask for one like this: 'Dad, I want a hug.' [He role-models corrective behavior.] Now, you give it a try, and I'll show you it works."

"I want a hug. Can I have one?" asks Brian, a little embarrassed.

"You bet," says his dad. He gives Brian a big one. "That approach will work every time."

Try It Again

Try it again is a simple, concrete, and highly effective teaching technique that is used almost intuitively by pre-school teachers when addressing minor misbehaviors. The applications of this technique, however, extend well beyond the preschool level. It can be used with older children and adolescents as well.

The procedure is easy to carry out. After an incident of minor misbehavior, state a firm limit and encourage your child to carry out the corrective behavior with "try it again." The child is simply given another opportunity to demonstrate that he or she can make a better choice and cooperate. If your child chooses to resist instead, then this technique leads smoothly to limited choices or logical consequences (discussed later in this chapter and in Chapter Eight). Consider the following examples.

Six-year-old Claire arrives home from school. As she enters the house, she drops her lunchbox on the floor and flings her sweater and mittens onto the couch.

"Claire, that's not where your things belong," her mother says. "Your sweater goes in the closet. Your lunchbox goes on the counter, and your mittens go in the top drawer of your dresser." She hands the items to Claire and walks her back to the front door. "Let's try it again." Claire does it the right way the second time.

Jim, sixteen years old, is impatient with his father for insisting that he finish unloading the dishwasher before heading off to a friend's house. "Can your little slave use the car to go to Dave's house?" Jim asks, in a sarcastic and disrespectful tone.

"Not when you talk to me like that," says his father. "Let's try asking that question again."

"May I use the car to go to Dave's house?" Jim says in a much more respectful tone.

"Sure," says his dad. "Thanks for asking the right way."

Three girls are playing jump rope in the front yard, but the two that are swinging the rope are doing so in a dangerous manner. A parent intervenes.

"That's not how we use the jump rope, girls," says the parent. "Does everyone know how to use it the right way?" The girls nod. "Good, then let's try it again the right way."

Nate, age nine, is in the kitchen helping his mom get things ready for dinner. "Nate, would you call your brother and sister to the table?" his mom asks. "They're playing upstairs."

So Nate yells out, "Kirk and Beth, come to the table!"

"Nate, that wasn't what I had in mind. I meant go upstairs and ask them. Let's try that again," she says. He does.

Exploring Choices

Sometimes children are simply unaware of other, more effective choices for solving problems or behaving acceptably. *Exploring choices* is a guidance technique that teaches children alternate choices for behavior and encourages them to exercise those choices responsibly. This technique can be used as a training step after consequences have been applied or to teach problem-solving skills when no misbehavior has occurred.

From a developmental perspective, exploring choices is most appropriate for teens and older children because it requires abstract thinking skills — the ability to think ahead into the future. The method can also be adapted for use with younger children, but you will probably need to suggest the choices yourself and combine the technique with role-modeling and "try it again" to make the learning experience more concrete.

Use the following steps:

1. Explore with your child, in a question format, other available choices for solving the problem or handling the situation more effectively.

2. Encourage your child to carry out one of the better choices.

146

Let's look at some examples.

Eight-year-old Pete just completed a ten-minute time-out for hitting his sister. His dad takes a few minutes to explore Pete's choices for handling the problem next time it comes up.

"Hitting Meg to get your radio back did not turn out to be a good choice. Hitting will always get you time-outs. What could you do differently next time Meg refuses to give back your radio?"

"I don't know," says Pete.

"You could ask her again politely," says his dad. "If that doesn't work, you can ask your mom or me to help. Both of those are good choices. What are you going to do next time?"

"I'll ask you or mom if she won't give it to me," says Pete.

"Good choice," says his father. "That'll work, and I know you can handle it well."

Mark, a fifteen-year-old, has an 11 P.M. curfew on weekends, but doesn't return home from a party Saturday evening until 1 A.M. As a consequence, Mark's parents revoked his party privileges for the next three weeks and revised his curfew time to 10:30.

"It wasn't my fault," Mark insisted. "There was nothing I could do. My ride didn't want to leave, so I was stuck."

His parents helped him explore other choices. "Doing nothing turned out not to be a good choice. Let's look at some other things you might have done. You could have tried to talk him out of staying because he knew you needed to be home by 11. Or you could have called us so we could have given you a ride. What are you going to do next time?"

"I'll call," said Mark.

"Good choice," said his dad.

Six-year-old Tim arrived home in tears because one of his friends called him names. His mother provided some comfort, then explored other choices for handling name calling in the future.

"I bet Jason knows that calling names is not OK," said Tim's mom, "but he chose to do it anyway. What are some other things you can do if he does it again?"

"I could tell on him and get him in trouble," said Tim.

"That's one choice," his mom said, "but that will probably make Jason mad, and he'll find some other way to get back at you. What else could you do?"

"I don't know," said Tim, looking puzzled.

"Well, you could try ignoring him and see if that works. Or you could tell him that if he doesn't stop you won't play with him and leave if he continues. What are you going to do next time?" she asked.

"I'll try ignoring him first," said Tim, "and if that doesn't work, I'll leave."

"Good choices," replied his mom. "Let's practice it for a minute. I'll pretend to be Jason, and let's imagine I just called you some names. What are you going to do?"

Tim pretended to ignore her, then said, "If you don't stop, I'm not going to play with you."

"I think Jason will get the message," said his mom.

Limited Choices

Alex, age eight, received a remote-controlled four-wheel-drive truck for Christmas. He can't wait to play with it, but first his dad goes over some ground rules.

"Alex, you can run your truck anywhere in the front

148

or back yards except for the flower beds," he says. "Keep it out of the flower beds, please."

"I will, Dad," says Alex, and he did, too, for awhile. But Alex soon discovered that the bedding areas had the best terrain for his four-wheeler. There were mounds and redwood bark and all kinds of flowers and shrubs to navigate around. He couldn't resist. When his dad walked out in the front yard, there was Alex running his truck through the bedding areas.

"Alex, you can run your truck where you were asked, or I will have to put it away for the rest of the day," said his dad. "Those are your choices. What would you like to do?"

"I'll keep it out of the flower beds," Alex replied.

"Thanks for cooperating," said his dad.

Alex's dad is using *limited choices*, a highly effective method for teaching children decision making and responsibility. The way he sets this situation up, Alex could not avoid being responsible for his behavior. The rules were clear, and so were the consequences for not following them. Alex had all the information he needed to make an acceptable decision.

In this case, he decided to follow his dad's rules and cooperate. But what if Alex had decided to test? Then his dad would have followed through with a logical consequence and taken the truck away. Either way, Alex would have learned the lesson his dad was trying to teach.

Guidelines for Using Limited Choices

1. Restrict the number of choices you present to two or three and be sure the desired corrective step is one of them. For example, if you don't want your kids to throw the Frisbee in the house, you might say, "You can throw the Frisbee in the front yard or backyard, but not in the house. What would you like to do?"

149

2. Remember, the choices are your limits. State them firmly with no wiggle room, or you may invite limit testing. For example, if you don't want your children eating drippy popsicles anywhere in the house except for the kitchen table, you should say, "You can eat the popsicles at the table or outdoors." Choices presented with soft limits will reduce the effectiveness of this technique (such as "I'd really prefer that you eat the popsicle at the table or outside.").

3. After presenting your limited choices, ask your child, "What would you like to do?" This question places the responsibility for decision making and corrective action where it belongs — on your child's shoulders.

4. When your children state their intention to comply with an acceptable choice but fail to do so, follow through with a logical consequence (action message) that supports your rules. For example, if you say, "You can ride your scooter on the sidewalk or driveway, but not in the street," and your child continues to ride in the street, then it's time to take the scooter away for a while. Don't be seduced into repeating the choices or trying to persuade your child to follow them. It's time for action.

Questions about Limited Choices

1. *What should I do if my child attempts to introduce other choices that are unacceptable to me or attempts to engage me in bargaining?*

Answer: Some children are very skillful at changing limited choices into "let's make a deal." This is limit testing. If your child attempts to introduce another choice that is not acceptable to you, you should respond firmly: "That's not one of your choices."

If your child attempts to bargain with you over the

choices, you should say firmly: "Those are your *only* choices. What would you like to do?" Use the cut-off technique if the child persists.

2. *Should I use limited choices even though my child frequently tests or violates my rules?*

Answer: Yes. Limited choices are also effective with persistent limit testers, but you will need to specify a logical consequence at the same time you present your choices. In effect, the logical consequence becomes the choice for noncompliance.

For example, if your child is making a mess by filling up his squirt gun in the house, you might say, "You can fill up your squirt gun with the garden hoses or at the sink in the garage, but if you do it again in the house, I'll take the squirt gun away."

Now, your child has all the information needed to cooperate. If the choice is to test or violate your rule, you simply follow through with your logical consequence.

3. *What should I do if I give my child limited choices, and the result is a refusal to respond or a blank stare?*

Answer: If you suspect your child is tuned out, use the check-in procedure you learned in Chapter Five. If your child is intentionally ignoring you, then wait to see what the child does. Actions will convey the response as clearly as words. If the actions reveal that the child has chosen not to cooperate, then follow through with a logical consequence. Your child will soon discover that a decision not to choose is also a choice.

The following examples illustrate some of the many ways limited choices can be used. Often, this technique will lead to a cooperative choice, but I've also tried to include examples where the child decides to test or defy so you can see how to follow up with a logical consequence.

151

Jill, age five, is making burping noises at the dinner table to the amusement of her two brothers. Her mother asks her to stop, and she does briefly, then starts up again.

Her mother says, "Jill, you can stop making noises or you can spend the next five minutes in your room getting yourself ready to cooperate [time-out procedure]. What would you like to do?" Jill decides to cooperate.

Phillip, age eight, is cheating at a table game. When his sisters ask him to play fairly, he ignores them. They complain to their dad who intervenes with limited choices.

"Phillip, you can play by the rules or find a different game to play," says his dad. "What would you like to do?"

"I'll play fair," says Phillip, but five minutes later he's back at it again. His sisters complain, but this time their father follows through with a consequence.

"Phillip, you're going to have to find something else to do," his father says. "Shelly and Stephanie are playing by themselves now." Phillip heads off to find something new to do.

It's lunch time, and the kids seem to think mom is a short-order cook. One asks for soup; another asks for spaghetti. "We're having sandwiches today," says their mom. "What would you like, ham or bologna?"

"How about pizza?" asks one of the kids.

"That's not one of your choices today," says their mom.

Aaron, age ten, refuses to go to his room for a time-out after treating his mother disrespectfully. His mother uses limited choices.

"Aaron, you can go to your room on your own for ten minutes, or I can take you back there for twenty minutes," she says matter-of-factly. "What would you like to do?"

Ten is better than twenty, Aaron thinks to himself. *There's no point in testing this issue further.* Reluctantly, he heads back on his own.

Two brothers are quarrelling loudly over some baseball cards. A few shoves are exchanged, then they start to yell. Their dad intervenes.

"Guys, can you work this out quietly, or do you need some time in your rooms to cool off?" The boys decide to work it out quietly.

Ben and Karen's dad is setting the ground rules for eating Halloween candy. He anticipates limit testing. "You can have three pieces a day after dinner," he says. "If you take more than that or eat it before dinner, the candy will be thrown away. It's up to you."

"What about two pieces at lunch and two after dinner?" asks Ben, hoping for some bargaining room.

"That's not one of your choices," said their dad.

Maria, age thirteen, is playing her stereo in her room with the volume cranked up high. It is so loud that the rest of the family can't hear their television program downstairs. Her mother heads upstairs.

"Maria, please turn the volume down. We can't hear our program downstairs." But Maria just stares at her defiantly and makes no move to cooperate. Her mother decides to use limited choices.

"Maria, you can turn your stereo down, or I'll turn it off and keep it in my room for the rest of the week. What would you like to do?"

Maria's options are clear. There's no payoff for defiance, and she really wants to keep the stereo in her room. She decides to cooperate. She turns the volume down to an acceptable level.

"Thanks," says her mother, as she heads back to enjoy her program.

Summary

Providing information for children about how to make choices or solve problems is often helpful, but knowing what to do and actually doing it are two different skills. Sometimes, children need practice and additional instruction before they can actually do what we request. They need further training.

In this chapter, we learned four simple and effective techniques for giving children the practice and instruction they need to master challenging decision-making and problem-solving skills. The focus of each of these techniques is on making acceptable choices and performing corrective behavior. When combined with firm limits and encouraging messages, these techniques are powerful tools for teaching children to solve problems on their own and to make more acceptable choices about their behavior.

PARENT STUDY GROUP QUESTIONS

1. Share your observations and experiences using encouraging messages. Did you get greater cooperation without the need for consequences?

2. Why is providing information sometimes not enough for teaching children the skills we intend? What more do they need? How do we provide it?

3. Alyssa, age seven, is sitting in the living room with her father, who asks her to bring him the newspaper. She picks it up and flings it across the room. Several sections of the paper are scattered about the room. What technique could he use to show Alyssa how she is supposed to bring him the paper? Why is this technique particularly effective with younger children?

4. Ben, age five, is eager to get the frozen yogurt bar his mother is passing out to him and his friends. While the other kids wait their turn, Ben reaches in and grabs one. What technique or techniques can Ben's mother use to show him a more acceptable way to wait for his turn?

5. Amber, age thirteen, lost her skating privileges for two weeks because she wasn't at the rink when her father arrived to pick her up. She was at a nearby mall with her friends.

   "There was nothing I could do," Amber complained. "My friends all decided to go to the mall even though they knew you were coming to pick us up. I just went along." What strategy could Amber's father use to help her make a better choice the next time her friends decide to take off?

Practice Exercise. Select a partner and practice the technique Amber's father should use. Take turns being Amber and her father.

6. Greg, age ten, was asked not to ride his skateboard at the shopping center near his house. Greg's friends like to hang out there, and Greg's parents suspect he will try to do it again. What technique can they use to convey their rules and expectations and place the responsibility on Greg? What would you say if you were Greg's parent?

7. Practice giving limited choices for the following misbehaviors:

   a. Eleven-year-old refuses to turn down his radio.

   b. Five-year-old refuses to stop teasing his sister.

   c. Sixteen-year-old argues about his midnight curfew.

   d. Eight-year-old ignores his mother's request to stop leaning back in his chair.

   e. Your children all request different items for lunch.

Practice Exercise. Select two or three methods to practice at home between sessions. Be prepared to share your experiences with the group next session.

Supporting Your Rules with Consequences

So far, you've learned how to give clear messages about your rules, how to inspire cooperation with encouragement, and how to teach effective problem-solving skills. These steps provide children with all the verbal information they need to behave acceptably, but, as you know, your words are only the first part of your total message.

Your children may still decide to test your rules, and when they do, the time for talking is over. It's time to act and to answer their questions with concrete action messages they really understand. Consequences are the second part of your limit-setting message. They speak louder than your words.

In this chapter, you will learn how to support your rules with consequences that communicate your intended message in the clearest and most understandable way. If you've relied on permissiveness in the past, the consequences will help you regain your credibility and authority and teach your children to tune back in to your words.

If you've relied on punishment in the past, the consequences will help you rebuild a cooperative relationship with your children based on mutual respect rather than fear. For anyone recovering from a bad case of soft limits, the consequences in this chapter will be a big step in the direction of effective communication and problem solving.

Why Consequences Are Important

Consequences are like walls. They stop misbehavior. They provide clear and definitive answers to children's questions about what's acceptable and who's in charge, and they teach responsibility by holding children accountable for their choices and behavior. When used consistently, consequences will teach your children to tune back in and take your words seriously.

You will probably need to use consequences often during the first four to eight weeks of this program. Why? Because your children will probably test you frequently. This is the only way they will know that your rules have changed and that your walls are really solid. You will probably hear comments like "You're not fair!" or "You're mean!" as they attempt to break down your walls and get you to revert back to your old behavior.

This is what Monica's parents encountered after they attended one of my workshops looking for more effective ways to deal with their twelve-year-old daughter's resistant, defiant, and argumentative behavior. They soon recognized that their approach was permissive, their limits were soft, and their consequences were late and ineffective. On the evening of the final workshop, they sat down with Monica and told her that things were going to be different.

"We're not going to repeat and remind anymore

when we ask you to do the things you're supposed to do," said her father. "We'll ask you once. No arguments or debates. No lectures or raised voices. If you choose not to cooperate, then we will be using some new consequences." They explained logical consequences and time-out.

I'll believe it when I see it, Monica thought to herself very skeptically. Based on all of her previous experiences, she had no reason to regard their words very seriously.

But Monica's parents kept their word. When they asked her to do something, they stated their request once, firmly. When Monica tuned them out, which she did most of the time, they used the check-in procedure. No more repeating and reminding. When she attempted to argue or debate, her parents used the cut-off technique. If she chose to push them to the limit and not cooperate, they used logical consequences or time-out.

The methods worked. For the first time, Monica was accountable for her poor choices and unacceptable behavior. She began to understand that she was responsible for her misbehavior, not her parents. But her testing didn't stop right away.

In fact, she intensified her resistance during the first three weeks and tested nearly everything to the point of consequences. When her parents held firm, Monica frequently added comments like "You're not fair" or "I hate you" in an attempt to make her parents feel guilty and give in. Monica tried everything she knew to get her parents to revert back to their old ways, but none of it worked.

Four weeks after they started, Monica's parents noticed a change in her behavior. The change was subtle at first. She did less testing and more cooperating. She was beginning to change her beliefs about her parents' rules and to take their words seriously.

Monica's initial increase in testing during the first

four weeks is a normal part of the learning process. After all, her parents told her that the rules had changed. How could she know they really meant what they said? Testing was the only way she could be sure, and when she tested her parents answered her questions clearly and consistently with consequences.

Your consequences will accomplish your immediate goal of stopping your children's misbehavior when it occurs, but teaching your children to tune back in to your words will take some time. How much time? This will depend on your consistency, the length of time you've been using soft limits, and the amount of training your child needs to learn that your rules have changed.

As you accumulate hours of consistency between your words and your actions, you will notice that you'll be tested less often and that you will have a decreasing need for consequences. This will be your signal that your children are starting to change their beliefs about your rules.

What Makes a Consequence Effective?

Effective consequences accomplish our basic training goals. They stop misbehavior. They send clear messages about our rules, and they teach responsibility by holding children accountable for their behavior.

The effectiveness of your consequences will depend largely upon how you apply them. If you apply them in a punitive or permissive manner, your consequences will have limited training value because you will be most responsible for solving the problems. If you apply them in a democratic manner and incorporate the following characteristics, your consequences will have their greatest instructional value. Let's look at some of the characteristics effective consequences have in common.

160

Immediacy

Five-year-old Danny decides to use his soup spoon to cata-
pult peas at his sister. His father promptly requests that he
stop. He does initially, but after a few minutes he decides
to test and shoots another one. Without any further
words, his father applies a logical consequence and removes his spoon from the table.

Consequences are most effective when they are applied immediately after the unacceptable behavior. The
immediacy of the consequence helped Danny to make the
cause-and-effect connection between his misbehavior and
the consequence. If Danny's father had chosen instead to
remove the spoon at the next meal, the consequence
would have had far less impact.

Consistency

Thirteen-year-old Sherry knows she's not supposed to use
the phone after 9 P.M. on school nights but wants very
much to talk to one of her friends. She asks her mother if
this time can be an exception to the rule, but her mother
remains firm. When Sherry does not get the response she
wants, she decides to plead her case to her father, but he
also remains firm.

Sherry remembers what happened the last time she
violated her parents' rule. She lost her phone privileges
for a week. But she decides to sneak upstairs and try it
anyway. She gets caught. Once again, she loses her phone
privileges for a week.

Consistent consequences are vital to effective child
training, but as this example illustrates, consistency has
many dimensions. There's consistency between the verbal message and the action message. There's consistency
by parents individually and collectively, and there's consistency in the way consequences are applied from one

occasion to the next. The training process can break down when we are inconsistent in any of these important areas.

Sherry's parents were consistent individually, collectively, and from one time to the next. Their words were supported by their actions, and their daughter received the clearest possible signal about her parents' rules. Compliance was both expected and required.

Sherry may still decide to test the rules from time to time, but when she does she will experience the same answers. If she wants to maximize her phone privileges, she will learn to live within her parents' rules.

For the sake of argument, let's say that Sherry's parents were only 60 percent consistent in enforcing their rule about using the phone after 9 P.M. on school nights. What can they expect from their daughter? More testing? Sure. In reality, the rule is only in effect 60 percent of the time. How will Sherry know when it is and when it is not in effect? She will have to test. Inconsistency is an invitation for limit testing.

Relatedness

When we fail to pay our phone bills for several months at a time, the phone company does not respond by suspending our cable TV privileges. That would not stop us from using the phone without paying. Instead, the phone company does something that really works. It shuts off the phone service. This teaches us to live within its ground rules.

It makes little sense to take away a child's bicycle privileges or withhold a favorite dessert because that child refuses to share a video game with his brother or sister. Bicycle privileges or desserts have nothing to do with sharing and taking turns.

A more instructive consequence would be to temporarily suspend the child's video game privileges ("If you don't share the video game, then you won't be able to play with it anymore this evening. We'll try it again tomorrow."). Consequences are most effective when they are logically related to the unacceptable behavior they're trying to stop.

Acceptable Role-Modeling

Five-year-old Devin stabs his baked potato with his steak knife at the dinner table and makes a squealing sound each time he does. His younger sister giggles, but his parents aren't amused.

"Devin, that's not how we use knives at the dinner table," says his father. "You can use it the right way or I'll have to take it away until next meal. What would you like to do?"

"OK," says Devin. "I'll use it the right way," and he does for a few minutes, but when his father gets up to refill his water glass Devin stabs his potato again. Without any further words, his father takes the knife away.

Devin gets a clear message about his father's rules, but he also receives an important object lesson in respectful problem solving. No one is blamed or criticized, and no one gets their feelings hurt.

Now, let's start this example over, but this time let's assume Devin's father responds punitively. When he sees his son stabbing his potato, he explodes.

"Damn it!" his father shouts, as he smacks Devin on the side of the head. "I knew you weren't ready to use a knife like a big boy. If that's the way you're going to act, you can just forget about using one again for quite awhile." He takes the knife away. His consequence stops Devin's misbehavior, but what does Devin learn about problem solving?

The method we use is the method we are teaching.

163

The method itself communicates a message about accept-able behavior. When we use spankings or hurtful conse-quences to stop children's misbehavior, we are really teaching that hitting or inflicting pain on others is an acceptable way to solve conflicts and get others to cooper-ate.

Time Limits

Seven-year-old Kelsey makes loud robot noises while her family watches their favorite television show. Her father asks her to stop, and she does briefly, then resumes the disruptive noises. Annoyed, her father sends her to her room for the rest of the evening (nearly two hours).

When it comes to applying consequences, more is not necessarily better. Consequences of brief duration often achieve our training goals more effectively than long-term consequences.

Our goals are to stop the misbehavior and to encour-age the corrective behavior. If we can accomplish these goals with a brief consequence, then more time is avail-able for children to demonstrate that they can cooperate and behave acceptably.

By sending Kelsey to her room for the entire eve-ning, her father removed an opportunity for Kelsey to demonstrate that she could cooperate and behave accept-ably in that situation. Ten minutes would probably have accomplished his purpose adequately.

Consequences of unclear duration also create prob-lems. For example, four-year-old Tim was asked "to go to his room until further notice" because he wouldn't stop playing with his father's camera. Tim went to his room, but every few minutes he stuck his head out the door and called, "Is it time yet?" After five or six times, Tim's mom was considering adding more time.

Most effective consequences have a beginning and an

end that are clear and well-defined. Unclear or open-ended consequences invite the type of testing Tim did. If Tim's mom had specified five minutes as the amount of time Tim needed to spend in his room, her consequence would have been clearer. Tim probably wouldn't have kept popping in and out of his room.

Clean Slates

Three weeks ago, Jill, nine years old, informed her mother that she was going to the park to play and that she would be back by 6 P.M. in time for dinner. At 6:45, Jill had not shown up, so her worried mother went to the park to look for her.

Jill was not at the park. Instead, she was found playing in an off-limit drainage area. Jill's mom took away Jill's afterschool play privileges for the following day. In addition, because she did not show up in time for dinner, her meal was not reheated.

For the next three weeks, Jill arrived home by 6 P.M. When her mother spot-checked, Jill was playing where she said she would. Despite Jill's compliance, her mother continued to remind her almost every day about the time she got home late and what happened.

Jill's mother can't seem to let go. Her focus is stuck on stopping the unacceptable behavior when it should be directed to encouraging Jill's present cooperation. Jill needs a clean slate and a fresh opportunity to show that she can make acceptable choices and be responsible for herself.

Now that we have a better idea about what makes consequences effective, let's look at different types of consequences we can use for handling typical misbehaviors. We'll begin with the one that requires the least amount of our involvement — natural consequences.

Natural Consequences

Five-year-old Darren and his family are eating ice cream cones at the ice cream shop. Darren has a junior cone with two scoops. To amuse his brother and sister, Darren decides to wave his cone in the air like an airplane coming in for a landing. His father gives him a disapproving look and shakes his head, but Darren keeps on going.

As he tilts the cone in the air, the two scoops fall to the floor. Darren's eyes fill with tears. "May I have another one?" he pleads.

His father remains firm. "One is all we get tonight," he says.

Darren's parents are letting the natural consequence of spilling the ice cream teach their son the lesson he needs to learn. Like many of us, they were probably tempted to say "I told you so" or to provide a lecture on the poor choice of playing airplanes with an ice cream cone. They also realized, however, that any further words on their part would take responsibility away from Darren and sabotage the effectiveness of the real-life consequence he was experiencing. Darren will probably think carefully before he chooses to play airplanes with his cone again.

Natural consequences, as the name implies, follow naturally from an event or situation. They send the right action messages to children because they place responsibility where it belongs—on the child. Natural consequences require little or no involvement from parents other than not trying to make it right. A lecture or an "I told you so" comment can easily sabotage the training value of the natural lesson.

Some parents find natural consequences easy to use and welcome opportunities to let their children learn from their own mistakes. For other parents, natural consequences are not easy to use. When something happens, these parents find themselves fighting their desire to take charge. Doing nothing when you want to do something is frustrating. If this happens to you, practice limiting your involvement to restating the obvious facts of the situation (such as "When the toy is broken, we can't play with it." "When the Pepsi is spilled, it's gone.").

Now, let's look at some of the many situations where you can use natural consequences.

Situations for Using Natural Consequences

1. *When toys, play items, or favorite items of clothing are lost, damaged, or stolen due to carelessness, misuse, or lack of responsibility.*

Natural consequence: Don't repair or replace the lost or damaged item, at least not until enough time has passed for the child to experience its loss.

I recall one parent who told me her daughter, a second-grader, had received an expensive designer jacket as a gift from her grandparents. Within two days of receiving the gift, the girl left the jacket at a neighborhood park and it disappeared. Her daughter pleaded and begged for another, and her mother gave in and bought one. The second jacket lasted about three weeks before it too was lost.

The parent had learned her lesson, but the child had not. When the child begged for another, her mother announced a different plan. "We're going to buy an inexpensive sweatshirt," she said. "When you show me you can take care of it and get it home consistently without losing it, we'll be ready to talk about jackets once again."

2. *When children make a habit out of forgetting.*

Natural consequence: Don't remind them or take away their responsibility by doing for them what they should be doing for themselves.

Nine-year-old Kendra had a habit of forgetting her homework and lunch money in the mornings. Each time this occurred, one of her parents would drop the forgotten item off at school. Noticing that this had become a pattern, Kendra's teacher suggested that the parents not make any extra trips to school for a two-week period. Kendra was a good student. If she missed one or two lunches or assignments, it wasn't going to hurt her. The parents agreed.

On Tuesday of the first week, Kendra forgot her lunch money. When lunchtime arrived, she asked her teacher if her parents had dropped off her lunch money. "Not yet," said her teacher.

That night, Kendra complained to her parents, "You forgot my lunch money! I couldn't eat lunch today."

"I'm sure you'll remember it tomorrow," her father said matter-of-factly. Nothing further was said.

Kendra did remember her lunch money, but on Thursday she left without her homework. Like before, she asked her teacher if her parents had dropped it off. "Not yet," said her teacher. Kendra got a zero on the assignment.

Kendra complained once again to her parents, "You forgot to bring my homework. I got a zero on that assignment!"

"You're a very good student," said her mother. "I'm sure you'll remember it tomorrow." She did.

3. *When children fail to do their part.*

Natural consequence: Let them experience the result.

Allen, age twelve, knows that it's his job to put all his dirty clothes in the hamper downstairs so his mother can wash them, but he chooses instead to leave them all over his bedroom. In the past, his parents picked his clothes up

168

for him, but they decided it was time he started handling it himself. Both agreed they wouldn't pick up any more of Allen's dirty clothes. If he wanted them washed, he must take the responsibility to get them into the hamper.

Nearly two weeks passed before Allen discovered that he was out of clean socks and nearly out of underwear. "Mom, I'm out of clean socks," Allen stated, somewhat annoyed, on the morning of his discovery.

"I didn't see any in the hamper," said his mother. "If it's not in the hamper, it can't be washed. I guess you'll have to wear a dirty pair today."

Reluctantly, Allen wore the dirty socks that day and the next, but the fragrance in his room soon forced him to pick up his clothes and put them in the hamper. He hasn't complained since.

Logical Consequences

Ten-year-old Chuck takes pride in the fact that his friends refer to him as a master at video games. Unfortunately, Chuck is not a master at sharing, and when his friends come over they frequently complain that he won't take turns.

Initially, Chuck's parents decided not to intervene and to let the kids work it out for themselves, but nothing improved. The parents agreed a different approach was needed.

The next day, Chuck and his friends were once again playing video games, and the familiar chorus of complaints began.

"You just had a turn!" protested one of Chuck's friends. "It's my turn now."

"No, it's not," said Chuck. "It's my house, and I decide whose turn it is."

Chuck's dad entered the room and said calmly,

"Chuck, you can share the game and take one turn at a time or the game will be put away. What would you like to do?"

"OK, I'll share," said Chuck.

"Good choice," said his dad. But less than fifteen minutes later, the complaints began again. As Chuck's dad entered the room the second time, he could see his son clutching the controls and trying to persuade his friends that he had won a bonus game by making it to the highest level.

"Looks like we're going to have to put the game away for now, guys," said Chuck's father. "We can try it again tomorrow."

Chuck's father is using *logical consequences*, a highly effective guidance approach popularized by Rudolf Dreikurs and proponents of Adlerian psychology. Unlike natural consequences, logical consequences are arranged by the parent and are logically related to the situation or misbehavior. Chuck temporarily lost the privilege of playing his video game because he chose not to abide by his parent's rules for sharing. The logical consequence removed some of Chuck's power and control but not his responsibility. In effect, he chose the consequence he experienced.

Logical consequences send clear action messages that children really understand. They stop misbehavior. They teach our rules, and they answer questions that were not answered with our words. When children experience logical consequences, they know where they stand and what we expect of them.

Guidelines for Using Logical Consequences

Your logical consequences will achieve their best results when they are immediate, consistent, temporary (time-limited), and followed by a clean slate.

1. *Use your normal voice.*

Logical consequences are most effective when carried out in a matter-of-fact manner with your normal voice. Language that sounds angry, punitive, or emotionally loaded conveys overinvolvement on your part and takes responsibility away from your child. When this occurs, your object lesson in responsibility may backfire into a power struggle or clash of wills. Remember, your consequence is intended to stop your child's misbehavior, not to discourage your child.

2. *Think in simple terms.*

Many parents have difficulty using logical consequences because they think too hard and get lost in all the details. The appropriate logical consequence is usually apparent when we think in simple terms.

For example, most incidents of misbehavior involve at least one of the following circumstances: children with other children, children with objects, children with activities, or children with privileges. In most cases, you can apply a logical consequence by temporarily separating one child from another, a child from an object (such as a toy), a child from an activity (such as a game), or a child from a privilege (such as TV privileges or afterschool play privileges).

3. *Before the misbehavior, set them up with limited choices.*

Sometimes, particularly in cases of limit testing or before your rules have been violated, you will have opportunities to arrange logical consequences for your child before you'll actually need to apply them. This can be done very effectively with limited choices.

Eight-year-old Brad likes skateboarding with his friends, but he lives on a steep hilly street. Several of his friends have experienced serious injuries. For this reason,

Brad is not permitted to ride his skateboard unless he's wearing his safety helmet. Brad's friends, however, don't have to, and Brad doesn't like being the only child wearing a helmet.

On one occasion, Brad and his friends are leaving the house to go skateboarding. Brad had his board under his arm, but he did not have a helmet.

"Don't forget your helmet, Brad," reminds his father.

"Come on, Dad! Do I have to?" says Brad.

"You can ride with a helmet or not at all," says his dad (limited choices). "What would you like to do?"

"OK," says Brad. Reluctantly, he returns to the house for his helmet.

Brad was testing, and his father was able to intervene before his rule was violated. In situations like this, limited choices is an ideal method for setting up logical consequences. If Brad had chosen to persist with his testing by riding without his helmet, his father would have followed through with the consequence of removing Brad's skateboarding privileges for the rest of the day. Brad would have been held accountable for his poor choice, and he would have experienced that his father's rule was mandatory, not optional.

4. *After the misbehavior, apply logical consequences directly.*

We cannot always set up our consequences with limited choices. In some cases, we don't arrive on the scene until after the misbehavior has occurred and our rules have already been violated. In these situations, we need to apply our logical consequences directly.

Judy, age seven, and her younger sister, Lynn, age five, are sitting on the couch watching Saturday morning cartoons while their parents are upstairs sleeping in. Both girls want to lay down, but there's only enough room for one. A quarrel breaks out. Judy orders Lynn to sit up.

When Lynn doesn't, Judy gives her a kick in the stomach. Lynn wails, and mom comes downstairs to investigate.

"She kicked me in the stomach," Lynn wails as she holds her stomach.

"Is that what happened, Judy?" her mom inquires.

"I asked her nicely, but she wouldn't move," explains Judy.

"We don't kick others to get them to move," states her mom. "I'll set the timer for ten minutes. You need to spend some time in your room."

When Judy's mother arrived on the scene, her daughter had already violated the family's rule about kicking. The time for limited choices had passed. Judy needed a clear action message to reinforce the rule. By separating her temporarily from the room and the company of others (time-out consequence), Judy experienced a logical consequence that supported her mother's rule: Kicking others is not acceptable behavior.

5. *Use your kitchen timer for dawdling and procrastinating.*

Timers can be useful in situations when children test and resist limits by dawdling or procrastinating. Consider the case of Logan, a five-year-old who is fully capable of completing his few morning chores before school but chooses instead to delay and procrastinate until the last possible minute. This usually brings his parents on the scene, who coerce him into picking up his room and making his bed. For Logan's parents, getting out the door in the morning is a real battle. For Logan, it is one of the best games in the house.

Frustrated, Logan's parents decided to use a different approach. They would use a timer and apply a logical consequence. At 7:10 the next morning, Logan's father announced, "You have twenty minutes to finish your chores. I'll set the timer. If they are not done when the timer goes off, I'll be leaving for work, and I won't be

available to give you a ride to school. You'll have to walk.''
The school was only eight blocks away, but Logan really
enjoyed his morning ride with his father.

As expected, Logan tested. When the timer went off
at 7:30, Logan's father followed through with the logical
consequence. He left for work.

Logan couldn't believe his eyes! No repeating or reminding? No last-minute assistance? What was going on?
He burst into tears and followed his father out to the car,
but his father held firm. "We'll try it again tomorrow,"
was all he said. The next day, Logan completed his chores
and made it out the door on time.

6. *Use logical consequences as often as you need them.*

Your logical consequences are training tools. Use
them as often as needed to stop misbehavior and to support your rules. If you need to use the same consequence
three or more times a day for the same misbehavior, don't
be too quick to assume that your consequence is ineffective. More likely, your child has more learning to do and
needs to bump up against your walls a few times to realize
that your rules have really changed. Well-established beliefs don't change overnight.

When to Use Logical Consequences

Logical consequences can be used in a wide variety of
situations. The following are just a few of the many possibilities.

1. *Misuse of toys, play items, or possessions.* The logical consequence is temporary loss of the item.

When Danny's mom walks into the backyard, she sees
Danny hitting a sprinkler head with a baseball bat.
"Danny, that's not how we use bats," she says, as she takes

174

the bat away. "You can have it back tomorrow if you use it the right way."

2. *Making a mess.* The logical consequence is cleaning it up.

Tina, age eight, leaves a mess in the living room and tries to get out the door without cleaning it up. Her mother notices. "Tina, you need to clean up your mess before you play."

"I'll do it later," says Tina. "I promise."

"There won't be any playing until it's done," says her mother. Tina really wants to play. Reluctantly, she heads back and cleans up the mess.

3. *Destructive behavior.* The logical consequence is to repair, replace, or pay for the item.

Ted, age ten, is annoyed with his younger sister for hanging around when his friends visit. He asks her to leave. She doesn't, so he threatens to break one of her favorite miniature horses.

"I'll tell mom if you do," says his sister. She still doesn't leave. Ted snaps the plastic horse in half. His sister wails, and mom arrives to see what all the commotion is about.

"She was bugging us!" says Ted, trying to justify his actions. "She's always hanging around when my friends are over, and she won't leave when I ask her either."

"I can understand how you would be annoyed, but it's not OK to break her toys," says his mom. "What's another way you can handle this next time?"

"I could ask you for help if she doesn't leave," Ted replies.

"Good, that will work much better," says his mom. "I'm happy to help if you ask her first and she doesn't cooperate. This time you'll have to buy your sister a new horse with your allowance money."

4. *Misuse or abuse of privileges.* The logical consequence is temporary loss or modification of the privilege.

Sandra, age sixteen, borrowed her mom's car but arrived home nearly two hours after the agreed-upon time, causing her mother to miss an appointment.

"What happened?" asked her mother, as Sandra walked into the house. "I missed my appointment, and I was getting worried."

"I just forgot," said Sandra. "I'm sorry."

"When we agree that you'll be home at a certain time, I expect that to happen unless there's an emergency," said her mother. "The car is off limits for the rest of the week. We can try it again next week."

What to Do When Your Consequences Don't Work

Sometimes children don't respond to our logical consequences the way we expect them to, and we're left wondering what went wrong. In many cases, we can determine what went wrong and correct the problem in the future by referring back to our characteristics of effective consequences. Check yourself out on the following questions:

1. Was your consequence immediate? That is, did your child experience the consequence soon after the misbehavior?

2. Was your consequence applied in a consistent manner? That is, did you do what you said you would? Did you do the same thing the last time your child misbehaved in this way and the time before? Was your consequence consistent with that of your partner?

3. Was your consequence related to the misbehavior?

4. Did you use acceptable role-modeling when you applied your consequence? If you carried it out in a punitive or permissive manner, you may have sent a different message than the one you intended.

5. Was your consequence temporary in duration? Did it have a clear beginning and an end? When you said it was over, was it really over? Or did you add an "I told you so" at the end?

6. Was your consequence followed by a clean slate?

Questions about Logical Consequences

1. *When I take away toys that my son refuses to pick up, he often responds, "I don't care." This really annoys me. How should I handle this?*

Answer: Two things are likely going on. First, there is the possibility that your son really doesn't care about the toys you take away, and this is why he refuses to be responsible for them. If this is the case, both of you may be better off without these items. Removing the toys is the appropriate step.

You will be glad to learn about "Saturday baskets" in Chapter Ten. When items end up in the Saturday basket on a regular basis, you have a good indication that your child really doesn't care about the toy. Removing those toys for longer periods of time (such as several weeks or permanently) is the appropriate step.

The second and more likely possibility is that your son is trying to annoy you with his comment ("I don't care") and hook you into a dance — lectures, sermons, reminders, or some other form of verbal sparring. Don't take the bait. If you act unconcerned, then the "hot potato" of responsibility sits in his lap, not yours.

Removing the item will hold him accountable for his unacceptable behavior.

2. *When I remove a toy or privilege temporarily, my daughter becomes argumentative and disrespectful. What should I do when this happens?*

Answer: Most likely, your daughter is trying to get you to dance with the goal of wearing you down so you'll give in. Don't take the bait. Remain firm with your limits. Use the cut-off or cool-down techniques you learned in Chapter Five. If she persists, follow through with a time-out. If your daughter is really interested in discussing your rules, the best time to do so is when both of you are calmed down, not when your rules are being violated.

3. *I'm beginning to think logical consequences are ineffective. When I remove a toy or privilege, my child will do the same misbehavior all over again a few days later. What's going on?*

Answer: Applying consequences is part of a teaching and learning process. The fact that you need to repeat your instructive consequences many times does not mean those consequences are ineffective. Rather, it means that your child has more learning to do before he or she realizes that your rules are firm and that compliance is both expected and required. Changing their beliefs about your rules takes time.

The Time-Out Procedure

At breakfast one morning, nine-year-old Shawna decides to give her younger brother a sharp kick under the table and pretend that it was an accident when he complains. Shawna is unaware, however, that her father is watching from the kitchen.

"Kicking your brother was not a good choice," says her father. "I'll set the timer for ten minutes. You need some time in your room."

"Oh come on, Dad," Shawna pleads in her most convincing voice. "It was an accident."

Her father remains firm. "We'll see you in ten minutes," he says as she heads off to her room.

In another situation, six-year-old Riley arrives home from school. As he enters the house, he drops his backpack and lunchbox on the floor and flings his jacket and some papers onto the nearest chair. "I'm home," he shouts as he heads out the door to play.

But before he makes it, his mom calls him back. "Riley, you need to put away your things before you do anything else," she says.

"But Mom!" says Riley in a very annoyed tone, "I'll do it when I get back from playing."

"It must be done before playing," says his mom matter-of-factly.

"Well! I won't do it!" says Riley defiantly.

"That's up to you," says his mom. "But if you don't, you'll be spending some time in your room getting ready to do it." Riley digs in his heels. His message is clear.

"OK," says his mom, "I'll set the timer. You'll have another chance in five minutes."

Both parents in these examples are using the *time-out procedure*. Time-out is a highly effective guidance method when used as it was intended — as a logical consequence. Time-out sends all the right messages to children. It stops their misbehavior. It removes them from the dance floor. And it teaches them our rules with clear action messages. Best of all, time-out achieves our training goals nonviolently without injuring anyone's feelings in the process.

Unfortunately, the time-out method has been widely misused and misunderstood. Punitive parents have used it as a jail sentence to force children into submission. The

179

punitive version of time-out sounds something like this: (parent shouting) "You get to your room! Sit on your bed quietly, and don't come out until I tell you to. I don't want to hear a peep out of you!" Punitive time-outs can be quite lengthy (several hours or an entire evening), and they are often carried out in an atmosphere of anger or upset.

On the other extreme, permissive parents view time-out as a tool for the child to use. The child decides when it starts, when it ends, or whether it even happens at all. The permissive version of time-out sounds something like this: (parent suggesting) "I think it would be a good idea if you went to your room for awhile. OK? You can come back out when you feel you're ready." (The child decides the time, which is usually quite brief.)

In actuality, neither of those methods is really time-out. Time-out is not jail, nor is it an optional consequence for your children to use when they feel the need for it. When it is used in either of these ways, responsibility shifts in the wrong direction, and most of the training value of the consequence is lost.

Time-out is really "time away from reinforcement." In most families, reinforcement is the many rewards of daily living — time spent doing pleasurable activities such as playing with friends, watching TV, enjoying privileges, playing games, being in the company of other family members, or just having the freedom to do what one wants.

Does time-out still sound like jail? The two are similar to the extent that they both provide a solid set of walls that stop misbehavior. There are also some major differences.

Time-outs are generally brief (five to twenty minutes), whereas jail sentences are quite lengthy. There are few, if any, opportunities for children to practice responsible corrective behavior in jail. Corrective training and learning do not happen there. Time-outs, on the other hand, are brief and can be used repeatedly. There are many opportunities for practicing corrective behavior. Unlike jail, time-out doesn't stop the person from learning the lessons we're trying to teach.

Guidelines for Using Time-Out

Time-out is a quick, simple, and easy to carry out procedure that can be used with children of nearly all ages (three years through teens) and in many different settings. You will find this method to be most effective when you present it firmly and matter-of-factly as a logical consequence.

1. *Introduce time-out to your children before using it.*

A sample introduction might be: "I have a new plan for helping you cooperate and learn my rules better. I think it will help us to get along better too. Here's how it works: When I notice that you are not cooperating, I will first ask you to stop. It may sound like: 'Jimmy, that's not OK. You need to stop that now.' If you choose not to stop after I talk to you, then you'll be asked to go to your room for five to ten minutes or as long as it takes to get yourself back under control.

"Each time, I'll set the timer in the kitchen, and I'll let you know when the time is up. If you come out before the timer goes off, then you'll go back and the time will start over. We will use this method as often as it's needed. Do you understand? Tell me in your words how you think it works."

2. *Select an appropriate time-out area.*

Selection of an appropriate place for the time-out is critical. When at home, your child's room is preferable as long as it has four walls and a door and is not loaded with entertainment items (such as a TV, videocassette recorder, video games, or stereo). Remember, time-out is "time away from reinforcement." You won't be accomplishing your purpose if your child's room is an entertainment center. If this is the case, use another room (perhaps the den or bathroom). The quietest room with the least amount of traffic is best.

3. *Use a timer.*

Kitchen timers work fine. If unavailable, use an inexpensive egg timer or a watch with an audible beeper alarm. The time should not begin until the child is actually in the room. If the child decides to leave the room before the timer goes off, send him or her back and start the full time over again. Once you set the alarm, you effectively take yourself out of the picture. The remaining part is between your child and the timer.

I do not recommend that you permit your children to set the timer themselves or to keep the timer in their rooms during the time-out. Parents who use this practice often discover that time-outs become very brief.

How much time should your child spend in time-out? One minute for each year of age is a good rule of thumb (for example, five minutes for a five-year-old). For more extreme misbehaviors (such as hitting, kicking, or destructive behavior), doubling or tripling the time is recommended, but not more. If you have used punishment in the past, you will probably find this appealing, but I encourage you to guard against making longer time-outs a routine practice. The times specified will get your message across.

4. *For limit testing, set up a time-out with limited choices.*

When Rick's mom investigated a loud thud, she found her eight-year-old practicing cartwheels in the living room. She asked him to stop, and he did briefly, but as soon as she left the room he was back at it again. She decided to give Rick some choices.

182

"Rick, you can stop doing cartwheels in the house or you can spend some time in your room. What would you like to do?" His choices were clear. He decided to practice outside.

Rick's mom set up her time-out consequence with limited choices very effectively. The options were clear. There was no advantage to continue testing. When Rick found the wall he was looking for, he made the acceptable choice. When you encounter limit testing, you can usually set up your time-out consequence with limited choices like Rick's mom.

5. *When rules have been violated, apply time-out directly.*

Five-year-old Alicia and her younger brother, Jerry, are pasting animal stickers into their sticker books. When Jerry reaches for a sticker Alicia wants, she hits him in the face with her book and wrestles the sticker away from him.

"She hit me," Jerry sobs as his father enters the room.

"Hitting is not OK, Alicia," her father says matter-of-factly. "You need to spend the next ten minutes in your room. I'll set the timer."

At the point that Alicia's father entered the room, the rule about hitting had already been violated. The time for limited choices and more verbal messages had passed. Alicia needed to experience the consequence associated with her behavior. Time-out achieved this purpose very effectively.

6. *After the time-out, provide a clean slate.*

When the timer goes off, the consequence should be over, provided your child has stopped misbehaving and is under control. If your child is not under control (for example, continues to throw a tantrum or rage), then the child is not ready to come out. You can say, "The timer went off. You can come out when you're calmed down but not before that time."

When your child is ready to come out, invite him or her back in a friendly voice. Try to resist the temptation to add an "I told you so" or a lecture that personalizes the object lesson and sabotages the effectiveness of the consequence. When you are friendly and encouraging, you communicate confidence in your child's ability to cooperate.

7. *Use time-out as often as you need it.*

Time-out is a training tool that will promote your child's learning when used appropriately. Don't assume that time-out is ineffective when your children persist with their testing or continue to violate your rules. Consistent repeated exposure to your consequences will lead to the learning you desire.

When to Use Time-Out

1. *Limit-testing behavior.*

Ten-year-old Sarah is told she cannot go skating, but tries her best to wear her mom down and turn a no into a yes. "Come on, Mom, please . . . ," Sarah pleads.

"We're done talking about it," says her mom, trying to stop the dance before it begins. "If you bring it up again, you'll be spending the next ten minutes in your room. It's up to you."

"But Mom!" Sarah protests. "You're not being fair! You let me go last weekend when we had people visiting." Her mom doesn't take the bait.

"I'll set the timer, Sarah," says her mother. "See you

in ten minutes." Reluctantly, Sarah marches off to her room. No dancing this time.

2. *Disrespectful behavior.*

Josh, nine years old, talks disrespectfully to his father because his father refuses to let Josh have dessert after barely picking at his dinner. "You're the meanest and cruelest dad anyone could have!" Josh shouts. "I hate you! I really hate you!"

"You may not talk to me like that," says his father matter-of-factly. "You can talk to me politely in your normal voice or you can spend the next ten minutes in your room. What would you like to do?"

Josh glares at his father and continues to shout. "I hate you!" he repeats again. "You are the meanest!"

"See you in ten minutes," says his dad. He sets the timer as Josh heads off to his room.

3. *Defiant behavior.*

Marla, eleven years old, made a peanut butter and jelly sandwich for lunch but refuses to clean up her mess on the counter. "The mess needs to be cleaned up before you go out," says her dad.

"Forget it!" she says. "I'm not cleaning it up."

"You can do what you were asked or you can spend some time in your room getting ready to do it," he replies calmly. "It's up to you. What would you like to do?"

"You heard me the first time. I'm not doing it," Marla shoots back defiantly.

"I'll see you in ten minutes. You'll have another opportunity to do it then." He sets the timer. When the timer goes off, he invites Marla back.

"I'm still not doing it!" she states firmly.

"That's up to you," replies her dad, still not taking the bait. He heads over to set the timer again, but before he does Marla has a sudden change of mind.

185

"OK, I'll clean it up," she says, realizing there's no advantage to resisting.

4. *Antagonistic or hurtful behavior.*

Mel, nine years old, wants to get his shower out of the way before watching his favorite TV program, but his teenage sister is using the bathroom. "Come on, hurry up!" he yells outside the door. "If you weren't such a zitface you wouldn't need to be in there so long."

Mel's dad overhears the comment. "Calling your sister hurtful names is not OK, Mel. See you in ten minutes. I'll set the timer." Mel heads off to his room.

5. *Violent or aggressive behavior.*

Richard, five years old, wants his dump truck back from his friend, Dale, but Dale doesn't want to share. When Richard grabs for it, Dale holds on tight. Both yell and struggle for control of the truck. When Richard's mother looks out the window to see what's going on, she sees Richard give Dale a punch in the face.

"We don't hit, Richard," his mother says firmly. "You need to spend the next ten minutes in your room. I'll set the timer." She doubled his usual time to emphasize her point.

When Richard comes back, his mother explores other choices for handling the situation. "Hitting your friend to get your toy back was not a good choice. What can you do next time?"

"I don't know," says Richard.

"Well, you can ask him nicely. If that doesn't work, you could ask me or your dad for help. Or we could use the timer and share the truck like you do with Kevin. Those are better choices. What are you going to do next time?"

"I'll ask you or dad," replies Richard. "The timer would be OK too."

"Good," says his mother.

6. *Tantrums.*

Robyn, age five, loves watching cartoons. If she had her own way, she would be watching them most of the day. For this reason, her parents limit her TV time to one hour a day. Robyn is not happy about this rule.

One afternoon, as Robyn is finishing her hour of cartoons, she sees the preview for the next show, "Looney Tunes" with Bugs Bunny, Daffy Duck, the Roadrunner, and all her favorites.

"Can't I watch a little more?" Robyn pleads. "'Looney Tunes' is my favorite show."

"The rule is one hour a day," says her dad. "It's time to turn the set off now."

"You're not fair!" protests Robyn, but the set is still on. "Looney Tunes" is beginning. Her dad gives Robyn some choices.

"You can turn the set off now or we'll leave the cartoons off tomorrow too. It's up to you. What would you like to do?" Robyn doesn't respond. She continues to watch the set.

Her dad turns the set off, but as soon as he does Robyn turns it back on. Her dad pulls the plug. Robyn throws a fit. She flings herself on the floor kicking and screaming, "You're not fair! You're not fair!"

I'm not giving in to this, her dad says to himself. He picks Robyn up and carries her to her room. "You can come out in five minutes if you're done crying," he says, but when the buzzer goes off Robyn is still wailing away.

When are they coming in to comfort me and give in? she wonders, but it doesn't happen. Twenty minutes after the

187

time-out began, she decides to come out. The tantrum didn't work, and the cartoons stayed off the next day too. Her parents' rule was firm.

Using Time-Out Outside the Home

Children know we're vulnerable when we're away from home, and often they want to see if our rules still apply. Fortunately, time-out can be used effectively outside the home, but certain modifications in the procedure are required. Let's look at how to handle some challenging situations.

1. *At the mall or shopping center.*

Dana's mom dreads trips to the mall because her four-year-old frequently bolts away from the shopping cart and runs down the aisles. Dana's mom decides to use time-out. She explains the plan as they arrive at the mall.

"Dana, you may not run down the aisles in the mall. You need to stay next to me the whole time. If you don't, you'll be doing a five-minute time-out to get yourself back under control."

A time-out in the mall? How's she going to do that? Dana thinks to herself, but she knows the quickest way to find out.

She is in the first store less than five minutes before she decides to test. When her mother is busy talking to a salesperson, Dana bolts.

"Excuse me," says Dana's mother to the salesperson. "Is there a quiet place where my daughter and I can sit down for about five minutes?" The salesperson points to a lounge area near the restrooms.

When Dana and her mother arrive at the lounge area, her mother says, "You need to sit down now." No angry lectures. No threats. No scoldings. Her mother doesn't respond to any of Dana's questions or comments.

Hey, this is no fun, Dana thinks. *I liked it better the old way when mom ran after me and got upset.*

"Are you ready to stay next to me now?" her mother asks when the five minutes is over.

"OK," says Dana, and she does.

Dana's mother may need to repeat this procedure a few more times before her daughter is convinced that time-outs will be used, but Dana will get the point. Her mother has a new tool for making shopping more bearable.

2. *At the supermarket.*

Bernie, age three, loves to go to the supermarket. When his mother pushes the cart near anything he likes, he grabs it and throws it in the cart. This is a great game for Bernie but very frustrating for his mother. She decides to try a new approach.

"Bernie, you may not grab things off the shelf unless I ask you to get them for me," she says. "If you grab things before I ask you to, you'll be spending some time in time-out."

Bernie hears the words, but he doesn't believe them. *How is she going to do that?* he wonders. After a few minutes in the shopping cart, he begins his old routine of grabbing things.

"Excuse me," Bernie's mother says to a clerk. "May I leave my cart here for a few minutes while I handle something with my child?"

"Of course," says the clerk, happy to help out.

Bernie's mother takes her son out of the cart and carries him to a bench outside the market. "You may not grab things off the shelves," she repeats. "We're going to sit here quietly for the next few minutes." She doesn't say

189

anything for the full three minutes. Bernie gets the answer he was looking for.

To Bernie, three minutes of sitting quietly is an eternity. He can't wait to get back to the supermarket, but this time he waits for his mother to point out items before he grabs.

Bernie and his mother may need to repeat this procedure several times before he learns to follow her rule. She may even need to use her car for the time-out area, but the training process will lead to the desired outcome.

3. *At the restaurant.*

Like most kids, Lynn, seven years old, likes going to restaurants with her parents, but sometimes she tries to get away with things she knows she can't do at home. On one occasion, she decides to get attention by talking loudly. People at other tables begin to look at her.

"Lynn, you're talking too loud," says her mother. "Use an indoor voice, please."

But Lynn keeps her volume up. *What are they going to do?* she thinks to herself. *We can't leave. We've already ordered our food.* Her father gives her some choices.

"Lynn, you can either lower your voice as you were asked or you can take a time-out. What would you like to do?" he asks.

"OK, I'll be quieter," says Lynn, but within a few minutes she's doing it again. Her father looks around for an empty booth or table.

"Come on, Lynn," he says. "You're going with me." He walks Lynn over to an empty booth and asks her to sit down. "You can come back in seven minutes," he says. He notifies the waiter before returning to his seat. When the seven minutes are up, he invites Lynn back. This time, she uses an indoor voice.

If the restaurant had been full and no booths were

available, Lynn's father would have used the family car as an alternate time-out area. He and Lynn would have spent seven quiet minutes together before returning to the restaurant. In either case, Lynn would have experienced a consequence that stopped her misbehavior.

4. *In the car.*

David and Sharon, ages six and nine, are grabbing and tickling each other while their father is driving the car. One of them lets out a scream. Their father tells them to stop.

"You may not grab or tickle each other while I'm driving," he says. "You can stop now or we can take a few minutes for you to get yourselves under control."

The kids do stop briefly, but a few minutes later they start up again. Their father looks for a safe place to pull over. "We're not going any further until you cooperate," he says.

When the car comes to a stop, the kids look at him in disbelief. They didn't think he'd actually do it, but he sits there quietly for what seems like a long time. They stop their grabbing and tickling. When ten minutes pass without any misbehavior, he starts the car and off they go. This time, the kids cooperate.

Questions about Time-Out

1. *What should I do if my children refuse to go to the time-out area?*

Answer: This is probably further limit testing. Give them a choice. (For example, "You can either go to your room on your own, or I will take you there and double the time. It's up to you. What would you like to do?") Give them twenty to thirty seconds to think it over.

Then, follow through based on the child's decision. In some cases, you may need to carry your children back to their rooms to show them that you really mean what you say and that there is no way out.

2. *What should I do if they leave the time-out area before the timer goes off?*

Answer: This is more limit testing. State to your children firmly that they must stay in their rooms until the time elapses. If they choose to leave the time-out area before the time elapses, tell them they will have to return to their rooms and the time will start over.

3. *What should I do if they leave the time-out area a second time?*

Answer: Your children are trying to determine if your walls are real. If they refuse to stay in their rooms and attempt to leave, make your walls real by holding the door shut while they are in there. No, this isn't cruel or unusual, and it won't injure their feelings or bodies. No one is being hit or humiliated. You are simply supporting your words with your actions. You may need to go through this sequence several times before they realize that you mean what you say.

4. *What should I do if my child yells and screams while in time-out?*

Answer: This is more drama for the parents' benefit. Children may also be discharging pent-up anger and frustration at not getting their own way. Do not reward the tantrum by giving in to it or by going back into the room with more convincing threats or lectures. Do not let your children leave the time-out area until the time-out is over or until they have been under control for several minutes.

192

5. *What should I do if my children throw their toys around or make a mess out of their rooms?*

Answer: When the time-out is over, remove any damaged or abused toys and inform your children that they can have them back in a few days. If they trash their rooms during the time-out, inform them that they will need to clean up the mess before they come out.

6. *What does it mean if my child comes out of time-out and does the same misbehavior all over again?*

Answer: Most likely, this means that your children have more learning to do before they will realize that your rules are really rules. Just repeat the time-out procedure all over again and use it as often as needed.

7. *I read a magazine article that said children whose bedrooms are used as the time-out area begin to regard their rooms as a place of punishment. How can I avoid this? I want my child to think of his room as a place of comfort and security.*

Answer: The child's reaction to time-out depends largely upon how time-out is applied. The method is not intended to be used punitively, but it can be misused that way. Children who receive punitive time-outs probably do begin to associate their rooms as a place of punishment because that is what they experience.

If time-outs are applied as they are intended, in an atmosphere of cooperation and mutual respect, your child shouldn't have any problem associating his bedroom, or any other room, as a negative or unpleasant place.

8. *When my child is asked to go to his room for time-out, sometimes he calls me names or talks disrespectfully on his* *way there. Should I add five more minutes each time he does this?*

Answer: No. That's probably what he wants you to do, and, if you played it out to the fullest extent, your time-outs would be "jail." He is probably trying to get you back out on the dance floor. As tempting as the bait must be, don't bite. If he's going to his room on his own and staying there the full time, then your time-outs are achieving their purpose.

Asserting Physical Control: A Last Resort

What is physical control and how do you do it? Physical control, as it's being presented here, is a nonviolent method of stopping children's misbehavior by not allowing it to continue. It should not be confused with hitting, spanking, or inflicting pain upon children.

Let's imagine a line that separates two types of misbehavior: 1. misbehavior that stops without the need for physical restraint, and 2. misbehavior that will only stop when you assert your physical control. How do you know when your children have crossed the line?

If your children are misbehaving and refuse to go to time-out, they have crossed the line. If they will not comply with your requests to stop behavior that is violent, destructive, or dangerous to themselves or others, they also have crossed the line. In these situations, children need our help to restore the lost control.

For example, if a child refuses to go to time-out, then we would carry or walk that child back to the time-out area. If a child is behaving violently, dangerously, or destructively, we would place our arms around that child for however long it takes to stop that behavior and help that child to get back under control. Let's look at how one parent used this technique.

Jill's mother arrived at my office very discouraged. For years, she had given in to her eight-year-old daughter's defiant and disrespectful behavior. She thought it was just a phase that would disappear with time, but the pattern continued to get worse. Their conflicts were coming closer and closer to what Jill's mother feared most — a physical confrontation.

Intuitively, Jill knew that her mom feared confrontation, and Jill used the threat to intimidate her mom. "You can't make me!" had become Jill's power card, and she played it with increasing frequency. It worked! Her younger brother also had begun to show defiance.

Jill's mother and I discussed the things that weren't working for her. She could see that her limits were soft and her consequences were late and ineffective. She was ready to try some new skills.

I showed her how to state clear messages and how to use the check-in procedure to avoid the old repeating and reminding routine. Next, Jill needed walls, so I introduced the time-out procedure and encouraged her to explain it to Jill.

One important step remained — getting prepared for the inevitable confrontation that would take place when Jill would respond to her mother's time-out with, "You can't make me!" We discussed physical restraint and how the method should be used. Jill's mother was ready to carry her daughter to her room if necessary.

The confrontation came the next day after school. Jill arrived home wearing a new outfit she had received as a gift from her grandparents. "I'm going outside to play," Jill announced.

"Not in those clothes, Jill. Change into your play clothes, please," said her mother.

"Come on, Mom," Jill contested.

Her mom remained firm. "You know the rules," she said. "Play clothes are for playing." Jill headed for the door. "Did you understand what I asked you to do?" said her mother as she blocked Jill's path. But Jill just stood there, her hands on her hips, and stared back defiantly.

"I hate you and your stupid rules," Jill exploded. "I'm not going to change, and you can't make me!" She struggled to get out the door. Her mother remained firm.

"It looks like you need some time to cool off by yourself," said her mother, matter-of-factly. "I'll set the timer for ten minutes." Jill continued her defiance.

"You can set it for two hours for all I care," Jill shouted. She dug in her heels. "I'm not going anywhere, and you can't make me!"

"That's up to you," said her mother, and, to Jill's astonishment, her mother picked her up and carried her to her room. Jill screamed and struggled the whole way.

When they arrived, her mother sat Jill down on the bed. Jill bolted for the door. Catching her by the arm, her mother said, "You can come out in ten minutes or as long as you need to get yourself under control." Jill screamed again defiantly.

Her mother left the room, but as soon as she closed the door Jill attempted once again to make a break for it. "I will hold the door shut for the full ten minutes or as long as it takes for you to get under control," said her mother.

Jill screamed insults and defiance for the next twenty minutes and checked the door intermittently to see if her mother was still holding it. She was. After five minutes of silence, Jill's mother opened the door to inform Jill she could come out.

Her mother fully expected to go through another round of confrontation over the dress. Instead, she was surprised to see that Jill had changed into her play clothes and was ready to go outside. Nothing more was said.

Jill and her mother had taken a big step toward ending their family dance and redefining the balance of power and authority in their relationship. They still had a ways to go. It took three more confrontations that first week before Jill realized that threats and defiance wouldn't work.

By the end of the week, she was going to time-out on her own and staying there the full time without leaving. Within five weeks, she showed less testing and more cooperation. None of this would have been possible if Jill's mother had not demonstrated her walls were solid.

Summary

Consequences are powerful tools in the teaching and learning process. They stop misbehavior. They provide clear and definitive messages about our rules and expectations, and they teach responsibility by holding children accountable for their choices and behavior.

The manner in which we apply consequences determines their effectiveness. Punitive or permissive consequences have limited training value. We can maximize the effectiveness of our consequences when we use them in a democratic manner and incorporate the six characteristics of immediacy, consistency, relatedness, acceptable role-modeling, time limits, and clean slates.

You learned four methods for applying consequences to support your rules: natural consequences, logical consequences, the time-out procedure, and physical restraint. Each of these methods will stop your children's misbehavior and teach your intended lessons without injuring feelings or bodies in the process.

PARENT STUDY GROUP QUESTIONS

1. Share your experiences using the various strategies for teaching problem-solving skills. How did your children respond? What worked best for you?

2. When Jamie, age six, turned on her favorite TV show one evening, her father walked over and turned it off. "Why did you do that?" Jamie asked.

   "Remember that you didn't come in for dinner last night when I called you," said her father. "See what happens when you don't cooperate?"

   Why is this consequence ineffective? What other consequences could Jamie's father use to get his message across?

3. Darrell, age twelve, discovered he left his new skateboard at the park. When he returned to look for it, it was gone. He arrived home very upset. What type of consequence is taking place here? Is there anything more his parents should do?

4. Meg, age six, is laying on the couch with her shoes on. Her mother asks her to put her feet down but Meg pretends not to hear. What kind of consequence should Meg's mother use? How could she set it up?

5. Discuss guidelines for using logical consequences. As a group, practice giving logical consequences for the following hypothetical situations.

   a. Twelve-year-old arrives home forty-five minutes after dinner was served.

   b. Sixteen-year-old borrows the family car without asking.

   c. Four-year-old refuses to pick up her toys in the hallway. (Set this up with limited choices.)

   d. Eleven-year-old procrastinates with her chores. (Set this up with limited choices.)

   e. Eight-year-old refuses to go to his room for a time-out. (Set this up with limited choices.)

6. Danny, age nine, was sent to his room for a time-out for talking disrespectfully to his mother. When the timer went off, Danny came out, but his father didn't think he looked remorseful, so he berated Danny and called him a "disrespectful little brat." What message did Danny really get? How did Danny's father sabotage the effectiveness of his time-out consequence?

7. Kelly, age twelve, was sent to her room for a ten-minute time-out because she refused to stop arguing with her father after she was asked to stop. Two minutes into the time-out, Kelly comes out and promises her father she won't argue anymore.

   "You better not," he says, and he lets her end the time-out early. By not supporting his rules with his stated consequence, what message is Kelly's father sending about his rules? What do you think Kelly will do next time her father tries to enforce his rules?

8. Nate, age ten, punches his sister in the arm for taking his headphone set without asking. Angered by his son's actions, Nate's dad gives Nate a punch in the arm to show him what it feels like.

   "How does that feel?" asks his father. "Now you know why your sister is crying." He sends Nate to his room for twenty minutes to emphasize his point. Did the time-out, in this case, have any value? What did Nate really learn?

9. Discuss situations for using time-out outside the home (such as at the mall, restaurants, supermarket, in the car). Share your experiences using this method. How did your children respond?

10. What does it mean when your child completes a time-out or experiences a logical consequence and comes out and does the same misbehavior all over again?

Practice Exercise. Note your children's reactions at home when you use logical consequences and the time-out procedure in a matter-of-fact manner. How does it feel when you shift responsibility for the problem away from yourself and onto your child where it belongs? Be prepared to share your observations next session.

Chapter

9

Setting Limits
with Teens

What happens when your child becomes a teenager? Do you need to learn an entirely new system of training? Certainly not. The basics still apply. Your teen will continue to need your firm limits, your encouragement, your guidance in problem solving, and your consistent consequences. This won't change. But you will need to adjust these steps to meet the needs of an older and more capable young person—an emerging adult. This chapter will show you how to do that.

Most teens want, and are often ready for, increased freedom, independence, and responsibility. They want to be more involved in the decision-making processes that affect them, and they want more control over their own lives. They're eager to negotiate and redefine the ground rules of early and middle childhood, which they feel they've outgrown.

Parents, on the other hand, often feel like they're caught in a balancing act. How much freedom is my teen ready for? How much responsibility? And how will I know? Should I give them as much freedom and responsibility as they are asking for? In this chapter, you will learn how to answer these questions and how to set limits with an age group that requires a lot of patience, communication, and understanding.

Understanding Your Teen

Adolescence has been described as a period of "normal craziness." "Normal" because all teens go through it. "Craziness" because their behavior can be so erratic and confusing. The one constant seems to be change, and change occurs at an accelerated pace. There are physical changes that come with sexual maturity, emotional changes that accompany the physical changes, and changes in thinking and behavior that come with the need for greater independence. The process can be very confusing to teens and parents alike.

Two developmental forces in particular have a major impact on the ways teens think and behave. The first involves a change in intellectual development — the ability to think and reason abstractly like adults. The second involves a striving for independence and separate identity, a process called individuation. Let's look briefly at each of these developmental processes.

Changes in Intellectual Development

Jean Piaget's research on children's intellectual development has shown that an important change occurs about the time of adolescence. Children acquire the ability to think and reason abstractly. They can consider logical possibilities in future time (the way things could be), and they can evaluate the pros and cons in hypothetical situations. Unlike younger children who deal largely with the present, adolescents are often concerned with the future. Their thinking is no longer limited to their concrete perceptions of immediate reality.

What does this mean in practical everyday terms? It means that teens are much better equipped intellectually to participate in decision making and problem solving. They are more aware of themselves and their behavior, and they are more capable of thinking and planning ahead into the future and exploring the consequences of possible choices or actions. Long-term consequences begin to make sense to them. In short, they can begin to test limits with their intellect as well as their behavior.

Individuation: A Self-Discovery Process

The second developmental process that has a major impact on the ways teens think and behave is individuation. Individuation is the primary task of adolescence. What is it? Developmental theorist Erik Erikson describes it as a search for identity as an emerging member of society. It's a time when teens begin to assert their independence from their parents and family in an attempt to discover who they are, what they believe, and who they want to become.

Experimentation is an integral part of the self-discovery process. Teens need to try out new roles, new values and beliefs, new relationships and commitments. They need to explore what it's like to be devoted to causes and beliefs and to have intimate relationships with boyfriends or girlfriends. Their commitments are usually brief. The exploration is the most important part. When something has been explored, they change course and try something new.

As crazy as this process sometimes seems, it's a normal part of adolescent self-discovery. In fact, it would be abnormal if teens didn't experiment. With each new experience, they collect a new piece of information about who they are, what they believe, and who they want to become. They discover a little bit more about themselves. Gradually, the pieces of the puzzle begin to come together.

How can we help teens through this necessary developmental process? We can help by understanding what they are going through and by supporting their self-discovery rather than resisting it. The process is temporary. Teens do not experiment and behave erratically forever. The way "they are" at a particular point in time is not the way "they will always be." They are more like movies than snapshots, and the movie is still in progress.

Teens need to explore the rules that go along with increased freedom and independence. They need to test our limits, bump up against our walls, and answer all those questions they struggled with in early and middle childhood: What's OK and not OK? Who's boss? Who's in control? How far can I go? What happens when I go too far? The answers provide more pieces of information to complete the puzzle about who they are.

When teens test, they need clear and direct answers to their questions, not soft limits or dances. We can't help them if we are stuck in a power struggle out on the dance floor. We can help by providing firm limits to guide their exploration, by helping them consider better choices for their behavior, and by allowing them to experience the consequences of their mistakes.

Recognizing When Limits Are Needed

Limits support the self-discovery process when they provide the walls teens need to guide their exploration. But limits can also be roadblocks to self-discovery when they are used for purposes of control or in situations where they are not needed.

To ensure that our limits have their intended effect, we need to ask ourselves some questions before we use them. What are we trying to achieve with our limits? Are they really necessary? Are we trying to guide exploration or suppress it? If our goal is to suppress exploration, the likely result will be a power struggle.

This is what happened with Stacey, a bright and capable thirteen-year-old who enjoyed wearing black. She and a group of her friends wore black outfits at school every day. Most of the time, it was black pants, black tennis shoes, and a black T-shirt. Their black outfits were their individual and collective statements of identity and independence.

At first, Stacey's parents went along with it. They didn't like it, but they didn't see any harm in it either. After all, she was doing well at school. She received good grades, belonged to many clubs, and her friends were generally polite and friendly. *What can it hurt?* they thought. *It's just a fad. It will pass.*

But a few months went by and Stacey continued to wear black, every day. Her parents were getting concerned. *What's going on?* they wondered. *I hope she isn't involved in some type of cult.* Comments began to slip out in the mornings like, "Stacey, you have so many pretty outfits. Why don't you wear the one you had on for your class picture."

"I'm happy the way I am," she would say with a smile, but the comments continued. As her parents became more concerned, the comments became more critical and sarcastic.

"Going to a funeral, Stacey?" her father chided one morning. Stacey felt she had taken enough.

"I don't tell you how to dress or make sarcastic comments about the way you look," she snapped. "Why do you have to do it to me? Why can't you just leave me alone?"

"If you dressed like a normal person, we would," said her father, "but you look ridiculous. I've had enough of this foolishness. You can wear your funeral attire once a week. The rest of the time, you're going to dress normal like everyone else." Stacey just gave him an angry look and stomped out of the room.

Stacey's father only succeeded in driving her underground. The next day, she brought two black outfits to school to keep in her locker. When she arrived at school, she changed into her black outfits. At the end of the day, she changed again before she went home. This went on for the next three weeks.

Her mother had a clue to what was going on when she noticed Stacey washing two of her black outfits with her gym clothes one weekend. "Are you wearing those outfits at school?" asked her mother.

"What would it matter if I was?" Stacey shot back defiantly.

"Your father and I said once a week was enough. Since you disobeyed us, all those outfits are going in the garbage," her mother said angrily. She put all of Stacey's black outfits in a trash bag and took them away.

For the next few weeks, Stacey did her best to avoid her parents. She seldom spoke at meals and spent most of her free time in her room. When they made comments about how nice she looked in the mornings, she just glared at them. Things were only getting worse. That's when Stacey's parents decided to call for an appointment, but Stacey was not included in the first visit.

Her parents filled me in on the events that had taken place over the black outfits. We discussed how experimentation was a normal part of the self-discovery process and how teens need to try out new roles and new ways of doing things.

"But this has gone on for months," said her concerned mother. "I'm really worried that something more is going on."

"I am, too," added her father. "She seems different now."

"What do you think might be going on?" I asked.

"I'm afraid she's involved in some type of cult, satanic group, or punk group," said her father.

"What did she say when you asked her what her black outfits meant?" I asked. Each parent just looked at the other. They had never asked. They were just guessing about what was going on in Stacey's world.

When Stacey joined us at the next session, I encouraged her father to share his concerns. When she heard him talk, Stacey rolled her eyes in disbelief.

"Oh sure, Dad!" she said. "Do I look like a punk rocker or a Satan worshipper to you? Get real."

"You've been acting very differently since you've been wearing those black outfits," he replied. "You've been sulking around and spending a lot of time by yourself."

"Do you think it might have anything to do with the fact that you're trying to run my life like I was a little girl?" Stacey responded. "I don't need anyone to tell me what I should wear to school." Her father didn't know what to say.

"Stacey, do you think it would help if you explained to your parents what those black outfits mean to you?" I suggested.

"That's just what we like to wear," she replied. "There are eight of us in our group. We're all in the drama club, and that's our thing now. We're not hurting anybody or doing anything wrong. We just like to hang out together."

The more her parents heard, the better they felt about what she was doing. They could see she was just experimenting the way teens are supposed to. They also could see that black outfits were not the problem. The problem was their fears about what those outfits represented.

Stacey's parents apologized for the way they treated her and offered to replace the clothes they had thrown out. She took them up on their offer, but the new outfits were not needed for long. In less than a month, Stacey and her group had given up wearing black and were on to something new.

Stacey's parents did not need limits to solve their problem. In fact, their limits were making matters worse. They were obstacles to Stacey's exploration and inspired her rebellion. The solution was really quite simple—a little communication and a better understanding of Stacey's world.

Adjusting Our Methods for Teens

Fortunately, teens are not so different that they require an entirely new system of training. The basics still apply. They still need our firm limits, our encouragement, our guidance in problem solving, and our instructive consequences. But we will need to adjust our methods in the following ways to meet the needs of older and more capable young people.

More Flexible Limit Setting

What do most teens want? When I ask this question during counseling, I usually hear: more fun, more freedom, more independence, more privileges, more privacy, and more input into decision making about the rules that affect them. In sum, they want more freedom and control over their own lives.

What do most parents want for their teens? When I ask this question in my workshops, most parents seem to agree that they want their teens to be happy, responsible, cooperative, trustworthy, well-adjusted, and to do their part at home and at school.

When we compare the two lists, we see that parents and teens want different things. Our different needs often bring us into conflict, but they are not incompatible. There is plenty of room for compromise.

How can people with such different needs live under the same roof in cooperation? By sharing a set of rules that are flexible enough to accommodate both — rules that are respectful to both parents and teens. The solution is flexible limit setting.

When I mention the term, flexible limits, some parents think I'm suggesting soft limits. I'm not. Teens need our firm limits as much as ever, but they also need more freedom within those limits to explore and experiment. How much freedom? The answer varies from teen to teen depending upon how much they can handle responsibly.

How do we know how much freedom they can handle responsibly? Often, we don't know, and neither do they. This is uncharted territory for both sides. We're both just feeling our way along. There is, however, a simple and effective way to find out. We can set it up as an experiment and test it out. Their behavior will tell us how much responsibility they are ready to handle.

For example, Kristy is a high school sophomore who just turned fifteen. She's excited because her parents agreed that at fifteen she could begin going out on dates with boys who drive. She's been asked out to a movie on Friday evening. First, her mom goes over the ground rules.

"Kristy, there's a few things we need to have happen so we can feel comfortable. First, we need to meet the person you're going out with before you leave. Second, we need to know where you're going in case we need to reach you. Third, we want you home by 11:15, and we expect a call if anything comes up that might affect that."

Kristy felt good about everything but the return time. "Eleven fifteen!" she exclaimed. "All my friends get to stay out until 12:00. Can't we make it 12:00?" Her mom held firm.

"Twelve is a realistic goal for us to aim for," her mom replied, "but we're going to start off with 11:15 for the first few months. If all goes well, we can revise it upwards. But if you don't handle 11:15 or follow the other ground rules, we can also revise it downward. Let's just see how it goes."

The experiment is set up. Both can get what they want, but Kristy is the one responsible for the outcome. Her behavior will answer the question about how much freedom she can handle. If she handles 11:15, then she knows she will have even more freedom a few months down the road. On the other hand, if she doesn't handle 11:15, she will probably be learning to handle 10:30. Either way, she and her mom will know how much freedom she is ready to handle responsibly.

Kristy's mom is showing flexibility in her limit setting. Her limits are firm, but she is also open to revising those limits based on the responsibility her daughter demonstrates. The terms are respectful to both sides.

Adjusting limits for teens is often a balancing act between freedom and responsibility. When teens demonstrate they can handle a certain amount of freedom responsibly, then they are probably ready for more. Limits can be adjusted upwards. When teens fail to handle their freedom responsibly, however, limits can be revised downward to find a level they can handle. Freedom is increased or decreased depending upon what teens demonstrate they can handle responsibly. Their behavior shows what they are ready for.

More Involvement in Decision Making

Most teens want to be more involved in decision making about the rules that affect them. Does this mean that they should be the ones making the decisions? No, but it does mean that they are ready to participate more actively in the process. This includes sharing their thoughts and feelings, discussing the reasons for your rules, and having their input considered seriously. It's a collaborative process in which parents and teens work together toward agreement, but parents retain the final decision-making power. Consider the following example.

Todd, fourteen years old, likes to have his friends over after school. They listen to music, play basketball in the driveway, or just hang out. They also get hungry, and, like most fourteen-year-olds, they eat large amounts of food and leave big messes.

Todd's parents are getting concerned. When they arrive home each evening, they find empty glasses, dirty plates, and messes scattered around the house. They also find very little in the refrigerator. One evening, Todd's parents sat down with him to discuss some ground rules for having friends over.

"Todd, we'd like you to be able to have your friends over after school when we're not home," said his dad, "but the messes that are being left and the amount of food that's being eaten have to stop."

"I guess part of it is my fault," said Todd. "I started offering them snacks when they came over, and after awhile they just started helping themselves. I didn't realize how much they ate."

211

"Now that you do, how do you think this should be handled?" asked his dad.

"I could tell them to have snacks at home before they come over," said Todd, "but I feel weird telling them that because I already said it was OK."

"There is a snack you can offer," his dad suggested. "They can have as much popcorn as they want as long as they are willing to clean up their messes. But sandwiches, sodas, chips, and everything else are off limits."

"What happens if I tell them that and they do it anyway?" Todd asked.

"Then they will have to learn the hard way," replied his dad. "They won't be allowed to come over when we're not here. Does that make sense to you?"

"I guess, but what happens if Tom and Greg go along with it and Sid doesn't?" Todd inquired. "Does that mean they all can't come over just because one person won't cooperate? That wouldn't be fair to Tom and Greg."

"That's something you're going to have to work out with your friends," replied his dad. "The ones that are allowed over are going to have to follow our rules."

"I'll let them know tomorrow," said Todd.

"Good," said his dad. "We'll give it a week and see what happens. If they cooperate, they are welcome, but if they don't, the house will be off limits to them until we are home."

Todd's dad could have solved this problem very easily by just declaring the house off limits to Todd's friends, but that wouldn't have provided much of a lesson in decision making or problem solving. Instead, he solicited Todd's views and helped him to sort through various options in the decision-making process. As it turned out, Todd got some firsthand training in decision making and discovered he was the one most responsible for the solution.

More Help Exploring Choices

Piaget's research shows that teens have the ability to plan into the future, but does this mean they will automatically begin thinking ahead and making better decisions? No. Having the ability and learning the skills are two separate things. There's still an important step that needs to happen. They need to be taught how to use their intellect to solve problems, and they need lots of opportunities to practice. Parents can help the learning process along by using the exploring choices technique we learned in Chapter Seven.

Exploring choices is an effective method for helping teens look ahead and discover what lies in their path — obstacles, choices, courses of action, and consequences associated with different choices. The parents' role is to serve as both a guide and a sounding board. They ask questions, provide feedback, and encourage further exploration. The purpose is to help the teen discover better choices for problem solving.

Wouldn't it be easier just to tell them what to do? Yes, it would, but that would lead to a different learning experience. Telling teens what to do, what choices they should make, and what lies in their path does not require much exploration, responsibility, or thinking ahead on their part. Why? Because parents do all the thinking, and parents do all the problem solving. Teens are passive participants in the process.

Exploring choices, on the other hand, involves teens more actively in their own problem-solving process. They are not simply given the answers. Instead, they are encouraged to use their own intellect to reach conclusions.

Exploring choices is most effective when carried out in an atmosphere of trust and open communication. This is not a time for lectures. Criticism, value judgments, or

213

strong emotion defeats the process and shuts down communication (for example, "That's a stupid way of looking at it!"). Let's take a look at how this technique was used to help one teen recognize that he had taken on too many commitments.

Allen's parents were surprised to receive an academic progress report in the mail notifying them that their fifteen-year-old was receiving Ds in social studies and math. His GPA had dropped below 2.0, the minimum for participation in school sports. There were only four weeks left in the semester. His athletic eligibility was in jeopardy.

Allen had always been responsible for his studies in the past. They knew how much sports meant to him. They also knew he had been distracted the last few months with a new girlfriend and a part-time job.

"Were you aware of how you were doing in those two classes?" they asked that evening.

"I knew I was a little behind, but I didn't think it was that bad," said Allen. "It's been hard to fit in study time with my job."

"I know your job is important to you," said his dad, "but do you think you might be taking on too much?"

"I can handle the job and get my grades up," Allen insisted, even though the evidence was suggesting otherwise.

"Have you thought about what might happen if you don't?" his dad asked.

"What do you mean?" Allen inquired.

His dad handed him the progress report. Allen read the section about losing his eligibility for spring baseball if his grades didn't come up above a 2.0 GPA. The seriousness of the situation was beginning to sink in.

"I forgot all about that," Allen said. He didn't think that rule would ever apply to him, but the rule was beginning to seem very real.

"There's another thing that's affected by all of this," added his dad. "What is our agreement about getting your driver's permit?"

Oh, no! Allen thought to himself. Now he was worried. He remembered their agreement, requiring a minimum of a C average at school and doing his part at home. *What am I going to do?*

"What do you think it will take to get those grades up?" his mom inquired.

"I can talk to each of my teachers and see if I can make up some of my missed work," he said. "I can also study hard for the final exams."

"That might help, but do you think your job commitment will leave you enough time to do that?" she asked. Allen thought about it for a minute. His priorities were becoming more clear.

"I'm going to have to quit," he announced. "I like the extra spending money, but I can't risk losing sports or my driver's permit."

Exploring choices helped Allen look ahead and make better decisions about his commitments and responsibilities. He had taken on a lot, and he had never considered the consequences of not being able to manage all of his commitments.

Allen's parents were probably tempted, like many of us would be, to tell their son what to do and save him the disappointment of learning from his mistakes. They also realized that if they continued to make his choices for him he wouldn't learn to be responsible for himself. They trusted in his ability to reason and reach conclusions. All he needed was some help exploring his choices.

Let's consider a different scenario to this story. Let's say that Allen decided to continue working and to try to pull up his grades at the same time. Would this decision have led to less of a learning experience? No. It might have decreased the likelihood that he would play sports and get his driver's permit, but, either way, he would have learned to be responsible for his choices.

Consequences of Longer Duration

The fact that teens are capable of thinking into the future also has implications for the way that consequences can be used. Consequences that extend into the future have instructional value. Teens can understand our intended object lessons when they experience loss of freedom or privileges for longer periods of time (such as weeks or even months).

For example, fifteen-year-old Dean knows he's not supposed to ride his father's dirt bike unless they go out together on weekends. But Dean really wants to show his friend that he knows how to ride. His parents aren't home. *Nobody is going to know,* he thinks to himself. *What's a little spin around the block going to hurt?* He tells his buddy to get on and off they go.

That evening, a neighbor comes over to borrow some sugar. She talks to Dean's parents briefly, and as she walks out the door she says, "I'll bet Dean is happy to finally get his license. He sure looked pleased to be riding off with his friend today." When she leaves, his father calls Dean downstairs.

"Dean, what's our rule about using the dirt bike when I'm not home?"

"I know, Dad," says Dean, "but I didn't think a little trip around the block would hurt anything."

"I'm not worried that you would do anything reckless," says his dad, "but that bike is not meant for the street. You're not licensed or insured. If anything happened, who would be responsible?"

"Yeah, I guess it wasn't such a good idea," Dean admits.

"I'm confident you'll think things through before

216

anything like this happens again, but the bike is off limits to you altogether for the next six weeks. May I have your key, please?"

Six weeks is a long time, but the consequence will certainly impress Dean with the seriousness of the rule he violated. Dean understands that the rule is intended to be followed. When he gets his key back, he will think carefully before deciding to go for any more quick spins around the block.

Redefining the Ground Rules

Setting limits and defining ground rules is a process we go through continually throughout our children's development. As children grow and mature, we are called upon to reexamine our limits and readjust our rules to meet their needs.

The process moves into high gear in adolescence. Teens are eager to renegotiate the ground rules of early and middle childhood, which they feel they've outgrown. How do they initiate this process? They begin pushing on our walls and testing our limits. Testing is their way of saying that we need to be more flexible with our ground rules.

Viewed one at a time, their requests don't seem very different from what they were asking for earlier — more freedom, more independence, more privileges, and more control over their own lives. But teens want these changes to happen all at once. There's a sense of urgency and impatience that wasn't there before.

The pressure for change can be overwhelming for parents. That's how it felt for Kerry's mom, a single parent. Kerry was fourteen and pushing for the walls. But each time she pushed, all she got was soft limits and drama — yelling, screaming, arguing, and angry lectures, but no answers.

So Kerry did what most kids do when confronted with soft limits. She kept on pushing. The more she pushed, the more her mom resisted, and the more stuck they became. Their dance was very dramatic. When I first met them, things had deteriorated into all-out rebellion.

Kerry had all the usual teenage complaints: "My mom treats me like a little kid. She won't let me do anything! Her rules are stupid. She won't let me go to my friends' houses after school, and now she says I can't have anybody over at our house. When I try to talk to her, she won't listen to my reasons. She tries to control everything I do. She won't even let me stay out past 10:00. What a joke! The games at my high school aren't even over before 10:00."

Translation: Kerry wanted most of the things other teenagers want — more freedom, more independence, more privileges, more input into decision making, less time at home, more time with her friends. She felt she was ready for a major overhaul in the ground rules at home, and she was probably right.

In the past, Kerry had always been responsible at home and at school. She did her chores, completed her homework, and was trusted to be on her own until her mom arrived home from work. Kerry was even permitted to have friends at the house when her mom wasn't home, a privilege that wasn't abused.

When Kerry turned fourteen, however, things began to change. She started spending more time with her friends and less time with her chores and homework. Her bedroom began to look like a disaster area. Household chores were often neglected, and her grades slipped from Bs to Cs. She was on the phone constantly.

But the most alarming thing to Kerry's mom was that Kerry was having friends over after school who were leaving messes. On several occasions, the house smelled like cigarettes. The house was declared off limits to Kerry's friends.

"I don't understand why she is doing this to me," said her mom. "She has never openly defied my rules before."

Kerry's mom and I spent several sessions discussing the process of adolescence. We discussed limit testing, the importance of firm limits, and how to use logical consequences to support her rules. It was reassuring for her to hear that the behavior she considered abnormal for Kerry was normal for teens.

We discussed her reluctance to provide more freedom when Kerry had always demonstrated responsibility in the past. Like many parents, she was aware of the dangers and disappointments teens faced growing up. She was afraid her daughter would make poor choices. She could also see, however, that trying to protect her daughter from the pain of poor choices was making matters worse.

Kerry would not learn to be more responsible until she had opportunities to make choices for herself and to experience the consequences of those choices. She needed room to explore. But she also needed solid walls to guide her exploration. It was time to revise their ground rules. They had a talk the next evening.

"Kerry, I can see now that I haven't been giving you very clear signals about what I expect," her mom began. "I think it's time we talked about changing some of the rules we've been fighting over." Kerry just about fell over when she heard it.

"Are you serious?" she asked in disbelief.

"I sure am," said her mom. "I'm done with all the yelling, screaming, arguing, and angry lectures. I've always trusted you before, and I think you're ready for more privileges and responsibility. But you are also going to have to do your part at home if you're going to keep those privileges. Let's just go down the list and see what we can work out. Would you like to begin with Friday and Saturday nights?"

"Can I stay out until 11:00?" asked Kerry.

"I'm ready to try that for school functions like dances and sports events as long as you ask several days in advance and parents do the driving. You also need to be home by 11:00 and no later. If anything comes up that might affect that, I expect a phone call so we can decide what to do. Can you agree to that?"

"Sure," Kerry said, pleased with her increased freedom.

"Good," said her mom. "We'll try it out for a few months and see how it goes. If you follow the ground rules, we'll stay with 11:00. If you don't, we'll be returning to 10:00 for a few weeks each time you arrive late. If you arrive late often, then we'll both know you're not ready for 11:00. We can try it again later on."

"Now, let's talk about doing your part at home," said her mom. "To me, that means doing your chores regularly, following my rules about having friends over, and limiting your time on the phone."

"Does that mean cleaning my room, too?" asked Kerry. "Aren't I old enough to keep my room the way I want it?"

"You are, but I have to look at that mess every time I walk by it," replied her mom. "It's not fair to me or others."

"What if I just keep the door shut so you don't have to look at it?" Kerry suggested.

"I can go along with that," said her mom, "but if you leave the door open, you're going to have to clean it up. Also, I'm not comfortable with you having friends in there when it's a mess, so there won't be any sleepovers unless it's cleaned up. If you can live with that, so can I." Kerry nodded her agreement.

"Can I start going over to my friends' houses and have them here again?" Kerry asked.

"Yes," said her mom, "if you're willing to follow the ground rules. You can go to your friends' houses after school if your chores are all done and if you call me at work and leave a message so I know where you are if I need to reach you. You also need to be home by 6 P.M. Can you agree to that?"

"Yeah, but what happens if I forget?" asked Kerry.

"Then you will lose that privilege for three days each time it happens, and we will try it again three days later. If you forget regularly, then we'll know you're not ready to handle that privilege, and we will stop it altogether. Understand?" Kerry nodded again.

"What about having my friends over?" Kerry asked. This issue was a real sore point with her mom because of the cigarette incidents. She was very reluctant to try it again.

"We can give it a two-week trial period and see how it goes," replied her mom. "If there are any messes or cigarette odors, then the house will be off limits to your friends when I'm not home. We can try it again a few months later. Can you live with those rules?"

"I can," replied Kerry, "but I don't know if my friends can."

"If they can't, then we'll know that they are not responsible enough to be here when I'm not home," said her mother.

"There's one more thing we need to talk about — the phone. We both like to use it, but most of our hassles happen because your conversations are very long. I need to have access to the phone too. Any suggestions?" asked her mom.

"I can't predict when my friends will call," said Kerry, "or how long they want to talk."

"But you do have control over when you call and how

long you talk," her mom replied. "You can also tell your friends the times you are available to receive calls."

"I like to have long conversations," said Kerry. "That's the best part about talking on the phone."

"Well, we could set aside two big chunks of time for long conversations that don't conflict with the times I need the phone," suggested her mom. "You can use it from 4:00 to 6:00 before I get home and from 8:00 to 9:00 in the evening. That should give you plenty of time for long conversations."

"What happens if my friends call outside those times?" Kerry inquired.

"You'll have to tell them you can't talk and have them call back when you can. You can tell them all at school the best hours to call. Can you agree to those ground rules?" asked her mom.

"I guess so," said Kerry reluctantly.

"If those rules aren't followed," said her mom, "then evening phone privileges will be suspended for a week each time."

"A week!" Kerry exclaimed. "Why so long?"

Two or three days probably would have achieved the intended purpose, but Kerry's mom thought less than a week would invite testing. She held firm. "You'll have another chance the following week if you need it," she said.

The negotiation session was over. Both sides had moved in the other's direction. Kerry was happy because she had an opportunity to get what she wanted, and she felt like she was being treated like an older person. Her mom was happy because the dancing was over. She was glad to be supporting her daughter rather than fighting with her. But Kerry still had to demonstrate that she could handle her freedom and privileges responsibly.

As expected, there were some problems in the beginning. Maybe she was testing or possibly she just forgot, but the first week that the rules went into effect Kerry did not arrive home from a friend's home until 6:30.

"I'm sorry, Mom," said Kerry, as soon as she walked in the door. She pleaded for a second chance, but her mom stuck to their agreement.

"You can try it again three days from now," said her mom.

Kerry was stuck at home for three days, but she decided to make the most of it. She invited her friends over each of the three days. Her mom was apprehensive, but Kerry kept to her agreement, and so did her friends. No messes. No cigarette odors. "She's really trying," her mom thought to herself.

Another issue came up the following week when Kerry was using the phone. "It's 9:00, Kerry. Time to get off," said her mom.

"I will," Kerry replied, but when her mom came back in the room thirty minutes later Kerry was still on the phone. When Kerry saw her mom, she hung up quickly, but it was too late.

"No calls after 6:00 for a week," said her mom matter-of-factly.

"That's not fair!" Kerry protested, but the rule was not negotiable. She knew she could use the phone as much as she wanted between 4:00 and 6:00. Besides, it was her own decision that lost her privileges.

Three months after their agreement, Kerry continued to live within the new ground rules. Like most teens, she tested from time to time, but when she did she experienced a consequence that helped her get back on track. She was demonstrating she could handle her freedom responsibly. Kerry was getting the guidance and support she needed through her mom's flexible limit setting.

Providing teens with too little freedom can lead to

conflicts and power struggles like Kerry and her mom experienced. But parents can err in the other direction as well. That's what happened to Brett's parents. They gave their son too much freedom, and he abused it.

Brett, age sixteen, had always been responsible at home and at school. He did his chores without reminders, maintained a B— average, earned his own money with a paper route, and hung around with friends who also seemed responsible. His parents trusted him, and, because they did, they extended many liberties.

He was allowed to have friends over when his parents weren't home. He didn't need to check in after school, and he wasn't required to tell his parents where he was going when he went out on weekends as long as he was in by 12:30. They even bought him a car when he turned sixteen with few ground rules attached.

But shortly after Brett turned sixteen, his parents noticed a change. He began spending more time with his friends away from home. He started showing up late for dinner, and on weekends he began arriving home well after his 12:30 deadline.

At first, his parents didn't think anything of it. *This is probably normal teenage behavior,* they thought. *He seems to be doing OK.* They didn't suspect that doing nothing was a tacit green light for more testing.

When they asked him how his schoolwork was going, he told them, "just fine." He said he liked doing his homework at the public library better than at home. It was quieter.

Brett's parents got their first clue that everything wasn't "just fine" a few weeks before the end of fall semester. They received a deficiency notice in the mail that said Brett's grades had dropped below a C average (1.4 GPA). His parents became concerned. When they asked him about it, he assured them that he had a few outstanding papers to complete and that his grades would be above a 2.0 by the end of the semester.

The next clue came on a weekend when Brett announced, "I'm taking Curt and Jon to a party tonight."

"Don't forget your 12:30 deadline," his father reminded.

"I won't," Brett replied as he headed out the door, but he didn't arrive home by 12:30 or 1:30 either. It was nearly 2:00 in the morning when Brett's car rolled up in front of the house. He fumbled with his key in the lock, and when his father came to investigate he could see that Brett was so drunk he could barely get his words out.

"We'll talk about this in the morning," said his father.

When Brett arrived for breakfast the next morning, he could see the anger and disappointment in his father's face. "I guess I really screwed up," Brett said.

"You sure did," replied his father. "How did Curt and Jon get home?"

"I drove them," said Brett.

"Do you realize the danger you put them and yourself in by driving that way?" asked his father. "What do you think would have happened if you had been pulled over or gotten into an accident?"

"I didn't think about it," said Brett contritely.

"Why didn't you call me or at least make some other arrangements to get home safely?" inquired his father.

"I knew I would get in trouble if you found out," said Brett. "Besides, I thought I could make it home all right, and I did."

"Yes, luckily you did," said his father, "but you were willing to risk your life, your friends' lives, and a drunk driving charge to pull it off. Unbelievable!" The seriousness of Brett's poor judgment was beginning to sink in.

"Where did you get the liquor?" asked his father.

"At the party," Brett replied.

"Were there any adults there?" his father inquired. Brett just shook his head.

"Look, Dad," said Brett. "I know I messed up, but I won't do it again. I promise."

"You're right about that," said his father angrily, "because you don't have a car any longer to drive around or any evening privileges to abuse. May I have your keys, please? All of your privileges are suspended until further notice. You can take the bus to and from school, but, other than that, you're grounded to the house."

As bad as things seemed, they got worse. A week later, Brett's grades arrived in the mail along with a letter from the high school attendance office. He finished his fall semester with a 1.4 GPA. But the letter from the attendance office was of greater concern. Brett had had six truancies during fall semester. Six excuse notes with his parents' forged signatures were attached to the letter.

"Is there anything more I should know about?" Brett's father asked that night after dinner.

"No, that's all," said Brett dejectedly.

"Where were you when you weren't in school?" asked his mom.

"We went to the park and downtown and just drove around," said Brett. "Sometimes we hung out at Jon's house while his parents were at work." His mom just shook her head in disappointment.

This is where things remained for the next eight weeks. Brett went to and from school, but, other than that, he was grounded to the house. No car. No trips to the library. No party or evening-out privileges. His friends were allowed to visit on weekends only.

Brett and his parents did their best to avoid one another. He didn't speak much to them, and they didn't speak much to him. Their house was a pretty gloomy place. The only bright spot was Brett's mid-semester progress report — mostly Bs and Cs. His grades were coming up again. That's when Brett's father decided to make an appointment.

"I don't really know what to do," his father admitted at the beginning of our session. "We've lost a lot of trust in Brett, but we can also see he's making an effort. His grades have improved. I don't feel comfortable about returning his privileges, but we can't keep him locked up in the house forever either. This isn't doing anybody any good. He's miserable and so are we." Brett's father filled me in on all the events that had taken place over the last two months.

Both parents recognized the need to revise their ground rules, but they didn't know how to begin. Their confidence had been shaken, and they were uncertain about how much freedom Brett was ready to handle.

Brett, on the other hand, was eager to have his privileges restored and another opportunity to show he was trustworthy. His mistakes had taught him some painful but important lessons. He discovered that trust was fragile. It couldn't be turned on and off like a faucet. He knew that regaining his parents' confidence would take time.

We spent several sessions discussing freedom, privileges, responsibility, and trust. We discussed limits, limit testing, and how to use logical consequences to support rules. By the time we were done, Brett's parents felt more comfortable about restoring some of his privileges. They were ready to give him another opportunity to show what he could handle. But this time, they were going to use firmer limits to guide his exploration.

"Brett, let's talk about getting some of your privileges back," his father announced one evening after dinner.

"Does that mean I can use my car again and go out on weekends?" Brett asked, in a hopeful tone.

"Yes," said his father, "if you're willing to live within

the ground rules and do your part. Your part means maintaining a C average in your studies, attending school regularly, and staying away from drugs and alcohol. If you're willing to follow those rules, you can use your car for going to and from school, to the library in the evenings, for errands, and to your friends' houses after school. We expect you home by 6:00 in time for dinner. We also expect you to keep us informed by note or phone when you go anywhere other than to and from school. Are the rules clear?"

"Yeah," said Brett, "but why are they so tight? I didn't have to leave notes or phone calls before."

"Those are the rules we need to feel comfortable for now," replied his father. "When we see you can handle those responsibilities consistently, we can discuss changing those rules later on." His parents wanted Brett to be accountable for being where he said he would be for awhile.

"What happens if I mess up or forget?" asked Brett.

"If your grades drop below a C average or if you have any unexcused absences, then your driving privileges will be suspended until your next report card that shows a C average and regular attendance. If there is any more drinking and driving, the car will be off limits for much longer than one quarter. If you neglect to keep us informed when you go anywhere other than school and back, then each time it happens the car will be off limits after school for one week," said his father.

"Can I start going to dances and parties again?" Brett asked. "And can I take my car?"

"Yes on both," said his father, "if you're willing to follow the ground rules. You'll have to be home by 12 P.M. If you're not, the next time we'll try 11:30 and see how that works out. If you come home drunk, dances and party privileges will be suspended for a month or longer each time it happens and you'll lose your driving privi-

228

leges altogether. But if everything works out fine, we can talk about increasing your deadline to 12:30 again. Does that sound reasonable?"

"I can understand the 12 P.M. time," said Brett, "and the consequences for not following the rules, but I don't understand why I have to phone or leave a note when I go somewhere after school. I didn't have to do that before. I'm going to feel real stupid doing that."

"That's what we need to feel comfortable for awhile," his father replied. "We can discuss changing it if everything goes well. We may seem strict to you right now, but we care about you very much. When we see that you're living within the ground rules we've agreed on, we'll be ready to drop that requirement. Can you go along with that arrangement for now?" Brett nodded reluctantly. Their new rules went into effect the next day.

I continued to meet with Brett and his parents twice monthly for the next six months. How did things go? As expected, there was testing and the usual ups and downs. Brett arrived home late on weekends many times during the first three months. Each time, his curfew was revised a half hour earlier. He complied for a few evenings, then he tested again. His parents became so frustrated at one point that they considered suspending his weekend privileges altogether for a month. Then things improved.

There were also many incidents of forgotten notes and phone calls during the first three months. Each time, Brett lost his car for afterschool use for one week. He complained, and on one occasion he decided to take it anyway, got caught, and lost it for two more weeks after school. When he finally realized there was no way around the rule, he started keeping his parents better informed.

But Brett didn't test the rules that mattered most to him. He kept his grades above a 2.0, attended school regularly, and there were no further incidents of arriving home intoxicated. He never lost his weekend privileges or

229

the privilege of using his car for trips to school. He was learning to live within the ground rules he and his parents had agreed on and to handle his freedom responsibly.

Teens Need Freedom Within Limits

The examples of Kerry and Brett illustrate that teens need freedom to experiment and explore, but they also need firm limits to guide their exploration and to teach them responsibility. There is a balance between freedom and responsibility that should be taken into consideration.

What happened when Kerry's mom provided too little freedom for her daughter? She inspired Kerry's rebellion. Her limits were so restrictive that Kerry had little opportunity to explore or to demonstrate that she could handle her freedom responsibly.

What happened when Brett's parents provided too much freedom for exploration? He tested for the walls. Their limits were so loose that Brett didn't know how far he could go until he went too far. There were no solid walls to guide his exploration.

Neither of these training approaches provided the guidance Kerry and Brett needed to learn to handle their freedom responsibly. Training models based on overcontrol (limits without freedom) or undercontrol (freedom without limits) do not achieve the needed balance between freedom and responsibility. Neither extreme provides the type of limits teens need to guide their exploration or to learn responsibility.

The democratic training model (freedom within limits) is ideally suited for teens. It provides them with opportunities to experiment and explore within clear boundaries, but it also teaches them responsibility because they are held accountable for their choices and behavior. They receive as much freedom as they can handle

230

responsibly. When Kerry and Brett's parents began using this approach, they started meeting their teen's needs and teaching the lessons they intended.

Becoming Better Problem Solvers

By now, you probably accept that teens need to experiment and test limits, but can you accept the logic of teaching them to test limits more effectively? We can help them do this, and we should. Why? Because teens are ready to begin testing limits with their intellect rather than just their behavior, but they are not likely to do this on their own. Most will need further guidance and training.

How can parents help? We can teach teens to become more proficient limit testers by guiding them through the problem-solving process. We can help them clarify their choices and explore possible consequences for not following rules. We can also support their learning process by not interfering when they choose to learn by their mistakes. Consider the following example.

Carly's mom received a call from her daughter's high school guidance counselor. Carly, a fourteen-year-old freshman, had been suspended from her history class for the third time for being disrespectful. If it happened again, she would be dropped from the class and given an incomplete. It was too late in the semester to consider a transfer, so she would have to make the credits up during summer session. Carly's mom said she would discuss the matter with her daughter when she got home.

"I got a call from your guidance counselor today," said her mom when Carly arrived home.

"I thought you probably would," said Carly. "I got suspended again from Mr. Becker's class. He's such a jerk! I really want out of his class."

"Your counselor said that would happen if you are suspended one more time," stated her mom.

"Good!" said Carly. "I'm tempted to tell him to take a leap tomorrow. I can't stand him."

"I know he makes you angry, but what do you think will happen if you are dropped from his class?" asked her mom.

"I'll just transfer to another history class," replied Carly. "The best part is that I'll be rid of him."

"Your counselor said it's too late to transfer. There are only four weeks left in the semester. You have a solid B in the class now. What would happen to your credits if you got an incomplete?" inquired her mom.

"I guess I would lose them," Carly responded, "but it would be worth it."

"It might seem like it now, but when would you have to make them up?" asked her mom.

"Summer school?" replied Carly, a little less enthused.

"Right, for six weeks. Didn't you have other plans?" asked her mom. She knew Carly was planning on visiting her aunt in Philadelphia for three weeks. That trip would have to be cancelled. Carly realized it too.

"What am I going to do?" asked Carly.

"What do you think your best choices are?" replied her mom.

"Well, I guess I could keep my mouth shut for four weeks and follow his stupid rules," said Carly, "but it would be torture. I'm not even sure I could do it."

"That's one choice," replied her mom. "What's another?"

"I could tell him to go jump," said Carly with a big smile. "It would feel great, but I would miss Philadelphia and spend the summer making up lost credits." The sensible choice was clear.

"So what's the decision?" asked her mom.

"I'm not going to let him ruin my summer, too," Carly replied. "I'll try to hang on for four more weeks."

Carly may not realize it but she just received some valuable instruction in testing limits with her intellect. With her mom's assistance, Carly was guided down the path that stood in front of her. She looked at the rules and the consequences for violating them. She explored her choices, the consequences of her choices, and reached her own conclusions about the best thing to do. Best of all, Carly got her answers without having to test things out with her behavior.

Consequences for Teens

Consequences can be the walls that guide exploration and help teens stay on the path toward responsible independence. Or they can be the source of continual conflicts, power struggles, and family dances. This all depends upon how they are applied.

If your consequences are punitive or permissive, you will probably find yourself spending a lot of time on the dance floor in power struggles over your rules. Your dances will fuel your teen's rebellion and sabotage the lessons you're trying to teach. Responsibility will be lost in the shuffle.

If your consequences are democratic, however, you will be taking the battles out of your training. In their place, you will be providing valuable opportunities for teens to learn from their mistakes. You will be teaching responsibility because they will be held accountable for their choices and behavior. They will find the walls they need to answer their questions and guide their exploration.

What kind of consequences will you need? The natural and logical consequences you learned in Chapter Eight will address most of the problems you're likely to encounter — problems with chores or homework, abuse of freedom or privileges.

233

As you recall, a natural consequence occurs when someone violates a natural order of events. For example, you agree to wash all the laundry that is placed in the downstairs hamper on Saturdays, and your teen forgets to bring his dirty clothes downstairs. What would be the natural consequence? Of course, his clothes wouldn't get washed. Unwashed clothes are the natural result of not doing his part.

Logical consequences, on the other hand, are arranged by the parent for a violation of some social rule. They give a matter-of-fact message about unacceptable behavior. Kerry and Brett's parents supported all of their revised ground rules with logical consequences.

A logical consequence for abusing a privilege is temporary loss or reduction of that privilege. For example, Kerry's mom revised her daughter's curfew to 11:00 on the condition that Kerry followed the ground rules and arrived home by the agreed-upon time. The logical consequence for abusing that privilege was a return to the 10:00 curfew for the following two weeks. An 11:00 curfew was very important to Kerry. This wasn't a rule she chose to test.

The basic guidelines for applying consequences (discussed in Chapter Eight) apply to teens as well as to younger children with one important exception. Teens often require consequences of longer duration. Consequences of longer duration make sense to them and have instructional value.

Does this mean all your logical consequences should be long-term? Certainly not. The longer the consequence, the fewer the opportunities for teaching and learning. Briefer is generally better because it permits more time for training, but your consequences need to be long enough in duration to be instructive.

How long is that? There are no guidelines here. You're going to have to make a lot of judgment calls like

234

Kerry's and Brett's parents did when they decided to use logical consequences to support their rules.

If you've tended to be punitive in the past, you're more likely to err in the too long direction like Kerry's mom did with her consequences for abusing phone privileges. Three days would probably have accomplished her purpose more effectively than one week.

If you've tended to be permissive in the past, you're more likely to err in the too short direction like Brett's parents did with their consequence for arriving home late on weekends. Moving his curfew back a half hour each time did not make a great deal of difference to him. He didn't take that consequence seriously until his parents considered withholding this privilege altogether.

Expect Testing

What can you expect when you first begin using logical consequences to support your rules? You can expect your consequences to be tested. How else will teens know that your rules are really rules and that the walls are really there? It may seem like they spend a good portion of their time learning the hard way, from their mistakes, but they are learning. If you continue to follow through with instructive consequences and use the other techniques you've learned in this chapter, you will get your message across.

Don't assume that your logical consequences are ineffective because your rules are frequently tested or violated. More likely, your teen just has a lot of learning to do. Give teens the time they need to get it right. They may need to crash up against your walls many times before they realize that there is no way around them.

This is what Brett needed to do when he confronted his parents' rule about keeping them informed of his afterschool travels, a privilege he often abused. His parents wanted Brett to be accountable for being where he said he would be and for arriving home in time for dinner. They requested that he notify them by note or phone if he went anywhere after school.

Brett's parents supported their rule with a logical consequence. Since Brett used his car for most of his afterschool travel, his parents decided that withholding his afterschool driving privileges temporarily was an appropriate logical consequence for not keeping them informed or honoring his deadlines.

Brett balked and complained and tested on many occasions, but each time he did he found the consequence that supported his parents' rule. No angry lectures. No long discussions and no additional punitive consequences. The responsibility belonged to Brett alone. He was held accountable for his own choices and his own behavior. It took time for Brett to realize that his parents' rule was firm, but when he did he began keeping them better informed. He eventually learned the lesson they were trying to teach.

Brett's parents (and Kerry's mom, too) were effective because they let their training tools do the work for them. They established clear rules and boundaries to guide exploration, and they supported their rules with logical consequences. Then, they stayed off the dance floor and let their teens do the learning. The teaching and learning process went much smoother when these parents started controlling the limits, not their teens.

Summary

Self-discovery is the primary task of adolescence. Teens need the freedom to experiment with new roles, new values and beliefs, new relationships and commitments. Each new experience brings them a step closer to fulfilling their task and discovering who they are.

Teens are better equipped intellectually to handle their developmental task. They are capable of looking ahead and considering hypothetical situations. They have the tools to test limits with their intellect before they act. This change in intellectual development has implications for our guidance methods.

Teens still need our firm limits, our encouragement, and our instructive consequences, but they also need more flexibility in our limit setting, more involvement in decision making, and more help exploring choices with their intellect. They need more freedom to explore, but they also need firm limits to guide their exploration. Too much or too little freedom can both be damaging to exploration and self-discovery. Parents can adjust their limits to achieve a balance between freedom and responsibility.

Consequences will continue to play an important role in the teaching and learning process. They will be the walls that support your rules, answer your teen's questions, and guide his or her exploration. They will teach responsibility by holding your teen accountable.

PARENT STUDY GROUP QUESTIONS

1. What is the primary developmental task of adolescence? Describe some of the things your teen is doing to accomplish this necessary task.

2. What type of limits have you been using with your teen? Firm or soft? Is your teen learning the lessons you're trying to get across? Can you understand why? Share your experiences with other group members.

3. What does flexible limit setting mean? How are you using flexible limit setting with your teen? Share your experiences with other group members.

4. How are you involving your teen in decision making? How is your teen responding?

5. Exploring choices is an effective technique for teaching teens to be more responsible and better problem solvers. How does your teen respond to this guidance technique?

6. Why are consequences of longer duration more effective with teens than with younger children? What considerations should you keep in mind when adjusting the length of your consequences?

7. Why is the democratic approach ideally suited for guiding teens?

8. How can we help teens test and explore their limits more effectively? How does your teen respond when you use this guidance method?

9. What kind of consequences have you been using with your teen to support your rules? Have your conse-

quences been working for you? Are your consequences teaching the lessons you intended?

10. Sharon, age fourteen, told her parents she was going to a friend's house for the afternoon and went to hang out with some friends at the mall instead. When her parents found out, they took away all of her privileges for two weeks and grounded her to the house. How might Sharon's parents have handled this situation differently? What would have been a more effective consequence or set of consequences?

11. Terry, age sixteen, got permission to drive the family car to school. He picked up several friends on his way, but he never made it to school. He and his friends went to a popular hiking trail instead. When his parents found out, they gave him a lecture about responsibility and expressed their disappointment. No further consequences were used. Do you think Terry is likely to regard his parents' rule about using the car for trips to school very seriously? How might they have supported their rule more effectively?

12. Sabina, age fifteen, got her own phone in her room. During the first month she had it, she ran up $80 worth of charges calling one of her best friends who had moved to another state. Sabina's parents gave her a choice. She could pay off the charges by doing extra chores for the next two months or they would remove the phone from her room and recover the $80 through savings of the monthly service charge. Sabina decided to pay off the charges by doing extra chores. Discuss the methods Sabina's parents used. Did those methods hold Sabina accountable for her behavior? Will she learn to be more responsible for her phone?

Discussion Exercise. Share specific concerns you're having now with your teen. Describe the methods you've used to handle those concerns. Ask other group members for suggestions regarding strategies you might use to guide your teen more effectively.

▼

Chapter

10

Handling Chores

Chores are an excellent method for teaching children responsibility and for helping them feel like useful and valued members of the family. In many families, however, chores also can be the source of ongoing conflicts and power struggles. If the latter has been your experience, then help is on the way. This chapter will show you how to use firm limits, encouragement, and logical consequences to make chores an exercise in responsibility rather than one of coercion.

Getting Started Early

Like many parents, I've read a number of books extolling the benefits of chores for children. Chores teach children responsibility, independence, and self-reliance, they said. Children who get started early with chores develop a greater sense of usefulness and belonging. These ideas made a lot of sense.

Then I had children of my own, and suddenly things were different. I found that putting the ideas into practice was not as easy as it sounded. There were questions I hadn't anticipated. What kinds of chores should they be doing? How early should they get started? And how would I know when they were ready? Someone needed to fill me in on the details. Fortunately, that someone was a preschool my two sons attended.

At this particular preschool, chores were an integral part of the program. All the kids had jobs. Some jobs were rotated, but they did them every day. They passed out snacks, put away their personal items in their cubbies (such as sweatshirts, jackets, shoes, and completed crafts), and when they were finished with a play item they were expected to put it away on the shelf where they got it.

I was able to observe these preschoolers in action several days a week when I picked up my boys after work. I usually arrived around 5 P.M. As I entered the classroom, I was greeted with a hug. Then something amazing would happen. My boys would return to their play area, pick up their play items, and put them away neatly on the shelf! Then they'd collect their sweatshirts and lunchboxes from their cubbies and off we'd go.

I wasn't the only parent who watched this event in awe. On several occasions, I heard other parents comment, "I wish I could get my child to do that at home." But all the children did it, and they did it every day!

It was clear from the proud look on the kids' faces that there was something intrinsically rewarding about doing their part. They felt useful and capable, and they were learning responsibility just like the books said they would. All they needed was a little guidance and direction. The staff provided this by making their expectations clear and by using generous amounts of encouragement.

When we arrived home, my boys returned to their normal behavior. They threw their sweatshirts on the floor, dropped their lunchboxes wherever they fell, and headed off to the kitchen for a snack. And who picked up

242

the sweatshirts and the lunchboxes and cleaned up the messes they left at the table just like always? That's right. Mom and dad. Each night, after the boys went to bed, Jeanne and I spent the next twenty minutes cleaning up their messes. We were beginning to get annoyed.

One day, after surveying the litter of sweatshirts and lunchboxes, I decided I had had enough. "What's going on, guys?" I asked. "You don't leave messes on the floor at school."

"Of course not, Dad," replied my oldest son, Scott. "They won't let us."

I wanted to say, "We don't allow you to leave messes at home either!" But I knew it wasn't true. When it came to doing chores, I could see that their preschool was doing something we were not — setting firm limits and making expectations clear. I was beginning to understand why my sons saw their messes as my responsibility.

Like many parents, Jeanne and I had fallen into the habit of doing things for our kids that they were capable of doing for themselves. We did it for all the usual reasons: We weren't sure they were old enough, or capable, and sometimes it was just quicker and easier to do the jobs ourselves. But we weren't doing them or ourselves any favors.

That night, when the kids were in bed, I shared Scott's comment with Jeanne. It was time we stopped being their personal clean-up service, we agreed. The boys were ready to take responsibility for looking after their own belongings and for cleaning up their own messes.

Jeanne suggested that I move their toy chest downstairs and that I build some shelves into the entryway closet so they could have their own set of cubbies like school. Good idea. I built the shelves, and when the cubbies were done, we had a family meeting.

"Guys, Mom and I want to talk to you about some

new rules," I announced. "We're going to start doing some things just like school. We made some cubbies in the closet for you. When you get home from school, it's your job to put your sweatshirts and lunchboxes there. We also moved your toy chest into the family room. That's where your toys should go when you're done playing with them. Finally, when you're done with your snacks, the cups and plates should be placed on the counter, and the garbage goes in the wastebasket. Any questions?"

"What happens if we forget to put our stuff away?" asked Scott.

"That shouldn't be a problem," said Jeanne. "You guys remember things just fine at school, but, if you do forget, we'll let you know, and there won't be any playing until things are picked up to help you remember."

"What happens if we don't put our toys away before we go to bed?" asked Ian.

"That's what the Saturday basket is for," I said.

"Saturday basket?" they said, surprised.

"Yes. The toys that don't get put away go in the Saturday basket. You can have them back on Saturday," I said.

I wish I could claim originality for this idea, but I learned the technique from a parent in one of my workshops. Saturday baskets are a wonderful way to teach children responsibility for their toys and to discover which toys they do and do not value. Unimportant toys seem to end up in the basket with greater frequency.

Our new rules went into effect the next day. I expected testing, but when we arrived home Scott hung up his sweatshirt, put his lunchbox on the shelf, and headed for a snack that he cleaned up himself. Ian followed his lead. "Thanks, guys," I said, surprised at how easy things went. The rest of the week followed the same pattern.

The testing didn't come until the following week when the novelty wore off or perhaps they really did forget as Scott said they might. Whatever happened, all we needed to say each time was, "Is that where your sweat-shirt goes?" or "No playing until things are put away," and the boys picked up their things as expected. The plan was working.

Thanks to the preschool, our boys got off to an early start, and now the habit of doing chores is well-established. We still get tested from time to time, and occasionally logical consequences are needed to support our rules, but the boys have accepted the fact that it's their responsibility to clean up their own messes.

Getting Started Late

It wasn't difficult to get our boys started with chores. They were young, and the patterns of dependency on mom and dad were not well established. But what happens when parents continue to do their children's jobs until they are eight, ten, or even older? Is it too late to get them started and teach the lesson of responsibility?

In most cases, it's not too late, just more difficult. You'll need to rely more heavily on your firm limits and logical consequences to support your new rules. You also should expect a lot of testing, but if you stick with your plan, the rewards will follow. Getting started late is certainly preferable to not getting started at all.

Patty, age ten, was a typical late starter. For as long as she could remember, her mom had been making her bed, cleaning up her room in the morning, and picking up all her dirty clothes. Then her mom attended one of my workshops and decided it was time for Patty to start taking responsibility for herself. She presented the plan one night after dinner and tried to explain that it was best for both of them.

"No way," said Patty when she heard what her mom

had in mind. "I'm not doing those things. Those are your jobs."

"Not any longer," said her mom. "I'm turning them over to you. I've got enough to do."

"Well, I'm not doing them," Patty said defiantly, "and you can't make me!"

"You're right," said her mom, avoiding the pointless power struggle. "Doing your jobs is up to you, not me. I'm not going to force you to do them, but if you don't make your bed, clean up your room, or put your dirty clothes in the hamper each morning, then there won't be any TV or playing time with your friends in the afternoon until those jobs are done. It's up to you."

Patty mounted a formidable resistance. She didn't lift a finger to do any of the things her mom requested during the first two weeks. As a result, she slept in an unmade bed in a messy room as her dirty clothes piled up all around her. She also spent a lot of time alone in the house in the afternoons without TV or friends.

"It doesn't bother me," Patty said to her mother whenever they crossed paths. "I can live like this a long time."

"That's up to you," said her mom, doing her best not to say more.

In the bus line, Patty got a "reality check" from her friends when they asked why she couldn't play after school. "My mom is trying to make me do chores," Patty said. "She says I have to clean up my room, make my bed, and pick up all my dirty clothes every day or I can't go out and play."

"I have to do that," said Beth.

"So do I," said Annie. "It's no big deal. It only takes a few minutes, and then you can do what you want."

But it was a big deal to Patty. Somehow, it just didn't seem fair. Her mom had been doing those jobs for years without complaint, and Patty had come to depend on it.

Why did things have to change? she wondered. She continued her resistance.

Midway through the third week, I got a call from Patty's mother. She was feeling desperate and about to give in. "The plan isn't working," she said. "It's been nearly four weeks and Patty hasn't done a thing. I've done my part. I've been firm, encouraging, and I've followed through with the consequences, but all she does is glare at me and sulk and tell me how mean and unfair I am for doing this to her. I feel terrible."

"That's probably how she wants you to feel," I said. "It sounds like she's trying her best to wear you down and get you to cave in."

"If she is, then I think she's succeeding," said Patty's mother. "I don't think I can last much longer." I encouraged her to stick to her plan and hold on awhile longer.

A few days after the call, Patty stumbled upon a natural consequence. She ran out of clothes. "I don't have anything clean to wear," she complained at breakfast.

"I'd be happy to wash them as soon as you put them in the hamper," replied her mom.

Patty didn't say a word, but after she left for school her mom noticed that all her clothes had been picked up and put away in the hamper. Not only that, her room was clean, and her bed had been stripped and readied for fresh linen. "Maybe she's coming around," her mom thought to herself.

When Patty got home that afternoon, she found a stack of clean clothes on her freshly made bed. It felt good to be in a clean room again. She headed out to play.

But the next day, the testing continued. Patty left her bed unmade and her dirty clothes were on the floor. "I'm going over to Annie's," she announced.

"Is your bed made and your room picked up?" her mom asked, hopeful that the job had been done.

"Well, mostly," said Patty.

"Let's take a look," replied her mom, but when she went to inspect she could see that only a few items had been put away. "You got a good start on it," said her mom, "but you can't go out and play until the full job is done."

"I hate you!" Patty exploded. "Why did you have to turn into such a tyrant?" She sat in her room and cried for the next half hour. When the tears were over, she finally realized what her mom had been saying. There was no way out of it.

Reluctantly, Patty cleaned up her room and announced a second time that she was going to Annie's. Her mom did a quick inspection. "Good job," was all she said as Patty headed out the door.

A few weeks later, I received a second call from Patty's mother. "I think we've turned the corner," she said. "Patty has done her chores for two weeks now with only occasional testing and complaints. It worked!"

"Congratulations!" I said. "I know you've worked hard to get to this point." I encouraged her to continue to keep her limits firm and be ready to step in with logical consequences if she encountered further testing. The hardest part was behind her, but it would probably take several more months of consistency before Patty was convinced that things had really changed.

Chores: Mandatory or Optional?

Whether your children get started early or late, your rules about chores are only as firm as the limits you use to support them. You can expect to be tested if your limits are soft. Firm limits are the key to teaching children responsibility for doing their chores.

Each day after school, eleven-year-old Melissa is supposed to empty the dishwasher and set the table for dinner before going out to play. Sometimes she does, too, particularly when her mother is around to remind her before she makes it out the door.

"Are your chores done?" her mother asks. "If not, go back and finish up before you go out."

Rats! Melissa thinks to herself. *Caught again!* and off she goes to finish up.

Most often, however, Melissa makes it out the door before the unfinished chores are ever noticed. When they are discovered, her mother usually throws her hands up in frustration and does the job herself. Melissa may get an angry lecture when she gets home, but that's usually as far as it goes.

Melissa's mother may believe her daughter's chores are mandatory, but, in actuality, they are optional. Melissa understands this better than anyone. She knows that if she can make it out the door without getting caught the likelihood is good that she won't have to do them at all.

What's the worse thing that might happen if she does get caught? She'll have to do the chores anyway and endure her mother's lectures. Melissa can live with that. As things are, she has little incentive to change.

Seventeen-year-old Chris discovered another effective way to avoid chores—arguing and bargaining. Chris's chores each week include taking care of the front and back yards—mowing lawns, weeding, and raking leaves in the fall. These jobs are supposed to be done on weekends, but each weekend something seems to get in the way. Chris always has a good excuse.

"The yards need some attention, Chris," said his dad one Friday evening. "I hope you're planning on taking care of them this weekend."

"I will," said Chris.

"When?" asked his dad.

"Probably on Sunday," said Chris.

"What's wrong with Saturday?" asked his dad.

249

"I'm going to Kevin's on Saturday and then to the ball game. Kevin's dad got us tickets. The game starts at one. I probably won't be home until dark."

"You could do the yards in the morning before you go," suggested his dad.

"Come on, Dad," said Chris, with a tone of annoyance in his voice. "What's the big deal? I'll do it on Sunday."

"Just be sure you do," said his dad.

On Sunday, Chris slept in until nearly 11:00. By the time he finished breakfast and got going, it was noon. Then some of his buddies showed up and wanted him to go with them to the mall where a sports celebrity was signing autographs.

"I'm going to the mall," Chris announced.

"Not so fast," said his dad. "I thought we agreed that you would do your jobs today."

"Come on, Dad," Chris pleaded, "He's only going to be there until 4:00."

"Then I suggest you get started on your jobs quickly so you can make it," said his father.

"Be serious," said Chris. "I may not have another opportunity like this again. Are you saying you want me to miss out just because the lawns need to be mowed? You can at least let me do the front lawn now and the backyard when I get back."

"OK," said his dad reluctantly, "but I expect you to finish the job as soon as you return."

"I will; I promise," said Chris. He mowed the front lawn and left.

But Chris didn't return until 5:30, just as it was getting dark. His dad was waiting. "Well, Chris. I see you managed to weasel out of doing your jobs again."

"I couldn't help it, Dad," said Chris. "The lines were really long. By the time we got to the front, it was nearly 4:00."

250

"But it's 5:30 now. Where did the extra hour and half go?" asked his father.

"Kevin dropped off Pete and Ryan first. They had to be home early," said Chris. "I'll mow the backyard first thing next Saturday. I promise."

What did Chris learn from all of this? He learned a lesson he already knew — that his chores could wait as long as he could find a way to avoid them. He probably felt a little guilty about disappointing his dad, but he knew that everything would be forgotten after awhile.

Chris's and Melissa's parents are using soft limits to support their rules about doing chores. Their words say, "Do your jobs," but their actions say, "You really don't have to." Compliance is optional, not required. The kids know this, so they do only as much as they have to.

Setting Firm Limits on Chores

What's the solution for Chris's and Melissa's parents? They need to put some accountability back into their system. They can do this by stating their expectations clearly and firmly and by supporting their words with effective action (consequences).

Let's begin with Melissa. If Melissa is going to learn the rules her mother intends, then her mother will need to stop all the reminding and lecturing and start being more consistent about enforcing them. Her new message might sound something like this: "Melissa, it's your job to empty the dishwasher and to set the table each day before you go out to play [firm limit]. You can do it before or after your snack, whichever you choose [limited choices], but it must be done before you go out to play. If you choose to leave the house without doing it, then I'll be bringing you back to do it anyway, and you'll lose your play privileges for the rest of that afternoon [logical consequence]."

Now her mother's rules about doing chores have some accountability. Her rules and the consequences for violating them are clear. Whether Melissa chooses to co-operate or test, either way she cannot avoid learning responsibility for her choices. All her mother needs to do now is encourage her daughter's cooperation and follow through.

The solution for Chris's dad is much the same. He was using unclear directions, another form of soft limits, when he requested Chris to do the yards "this weekend." What does "this weekend" mean to someone who doesn't want to do chores? On Saturday? On Sunday? Before lunch? After lunch? The last possible moment? And who decides? If you recall, Chris and his dad spent a lot of their time negotiating and bargaining over these terms, which were unclear.

If Chris's dad really expects the yards to be done each weekend and wants to teach responsibility in the process, then he needs to support his words with effective action. His new instructions might sound something like this: "Chris, the yards need to be started on Saturday mornings [firm limit]. You can do them first thing in the morning or just before lunch if you choose [limited choices], but you won't be going anywhere or doing anything else with your friends until your jobs are done [logical consequence]."

The way things are set up now, Chris has little wiggle room to plan his escape. He either does his jobs on time or he doesn't. Either way, he can't avoid learning responsibility if his dad stops bargaining and follows through with the stated consequences.

Let's add a new wrinkle to the picture now. Let's say, for the sake of argument, that Melissa does her chores like many kids do, in a hurried and careless manner. She unloads only the top shelf of the dishwasher and neglects to put any silverware or cups at each place setting. The job is not acceptable.

What should her mother do? Should she let it go and just be thankful that at least Melissa did part of her chores? If she does, what's the message? Isn't she really saying that a partially completed job is acceptable? And what do you think Melissa is likely to do next time? Sure, more of the same. If her mother is willing to settle for less, Melissa probably won't have any problems doing less.

Specifying an acceptable job also is part of the limit-setting process. How do you do it? There are probably lots of ways, but I prefer the method we discussed in Chapter Seven: role-modeling acceptable behavior. The parent takes a few minutes and goes over the details of the job with the child in a very step-by-step manner. Here's how Melissa's mother might use this approach.

"Melissa, let's go through your chores together so we can be clear about what I expect. Clearing the dishwasher means emptying both the top and bottom shelves and putting everything away in the proper cabinets. Setting the table means putting plates, silverware, cups, and napkins at each place setting like this [role-modeling the job]. When both jobs are done, this is what it should look like. Any questions?"

Now, her mother's expectations are clear, and there can be no doubt about what is really expected. If Melissa decides to test those limits by doing less than an acceptable job, then it's time to move on to logical consequences.

Work Before Play

Sometimes, problems with chores can be remedied by simply rearranging the times in which they occur. My youngest son, Ian, taught me this lesson when he was nearly four.

About 6:30 each morning, Ian would arrive at the kitchen hungry and ready for breakfast. Breakfast was one of his favorite times of the day, and he usually tried to stretch the meal out as long as possible. About 7:00 or a little after, I would announce, "Breakfast is over." Then it was time for him to begin doing his chores.

Ian's chores each morning consisted of helping to feed our two dogs (he scooped the chow into their bowls), brushing his teeth, and getting dressed. Jeanne would lay his clothes out on the sofa in the family room, and Ian would handle everything but putting on his shoes and socks. At least, that was the way it was supposed to go.

What really happened most mornings was that Ian would eat breakfast, brush his teeth, feed the dogs, then he would wander over to his clothes. He'd take maybe five minutes to put on his underwear, then he'd dawdle with his shirt and pants for awhile as Jeanne and I prodded and reminded him that time was running out. It was quite a dance. Somehow, he always managed to complete the task just as we were getting out the door.

Ian knew he was capable of getting himself dressed on time. Scott knew it. All of Ian's friends at the preschool knew it too. The issue was not about getting dressed. It was about attention, and Ian's dressing routine was getting far more of it than it deserved. In fact, it was the big event of the morning.

After a few months of this, Jeanne suggested that we do something about it. "We," in this case, meant me. *OK,* I thought. *I'm the behavior specialist in the family. I'm up to the task.*

The next morning when Ian came down for breakfast, I was prepared to show him all my best moves — firm limits, the timer, limited choices, logical consequences, whatever it took. We had pancakes that morning, Ian's favorite, and he stretched the meal out to 7:00. Then he brushed his teeth, helped feed the dogs, and headed to the sofa for his clothes.

"Ian, you can get dressed downstairs or upstairs. What would you like to do, pal?" I asked.

"I'll do it downstairs," he said, with a suspicious look in his eyes.

"OK," I said, "I'll set the timer. You have ten minutes to get it done or you can finish the job upstairs."

Ian didn't really know how long ten minutes was, but he did know that he was expected to get dressed faster than usual. I expected him to test. He did.

Five minutes after I set the timer, Ian only had his underwear on and was dawdling just like always. Jeanne and I both wanted to say, "Come on, Ian. Hurry up!" and I could see that was what he was waiting for, but it didn't happen. The buzzer went off while he was still in his underwear.

"OK, Ian," I said, matter-of-factly. "Take your clothes and head upstairs to finish dressing in your room." I handed him his clothes and watched him trail off at a snail's pace.

I expected the final act in this drama to end upstairs in Ian's bedroom with Jeanne or I announcing that it was time to leave for school and Ian scrambling to finish dressing at the last possible moment. It didn't happen. After a few minutes, Ian arrived downstairs dressed and ready to go. "Good job," I said.

This pattern continued for the next three weeks. Each morning, I gave Ian his limited choices, set the timer, and sent him upstairs to finish up when he tested. He tested most of the time. The methods were working. We managed to reduce his dressing time from a half hour to a little more than ten minutes, but it was still receiving more attention than it deserved.

Then, one morning, the simple solution occurred to

me. Why not rearrange the order of events? If Ian can't wait to get to breakfast, why not lay out his clothes in his room each night and have him get dressed before he comes downstairs for breakfast. We introduced the plan that evening and laid out his clothes. The next morning, he arrived for breakfast fully dressed and on time. What a simple solution! We had no further problems with Ian's morning dressing routine.

The basic principle — chores before pleasure — that worked with Ian can be applied to children of all ages with a wide variety of chores: bath times, making beds, cleaning rooms, picking up toys, doing dishes, setting the table, mowing lawns, to name just a few. The parent's job is to specify when chores should be done and schedule this to occur before other more rewarding activities (such as play time, TV, etc.). The consequence is now in place to hold your child accountable. Let's see how Mattie's parents used this principle to stop her dawdling at bedtime.

Five-year-old Mattie has a 7:30 bedtime but usually manages to stretch it out another fifteen minutes by dawdling with her last chore of the day — brushing her teeth. "I don't believe it," said her frustrated father. "It takes her two minutes to put on her pajamas and fifteen minutes to brush her teeth!"

Mattie's bedtime routine begins a little after 7:00 each evening when one of her parents announces, "time for pajamas." On cue, Mattie hurries to her room, puts on her pajamas, and reemerges a short time later ready to go. Story time is one of her favorite times. She loves to snuggle up close, inspect the pictures, and turn the pages when mom or dad pause.

At 7:30, the book is put away and Mattie hears her cue to begin dawdling: "Time to brush your teeth."

"OK," says Mattie reluctantly as she selects the right stuffed animal to accompany her on the long journey to the bathroom. With the animal tucked securely under her arm, she sets off at an extra-slow pace. Five minutes go by.

"Mattie, aren't you done yet?" one of her parents usually asks.

"Almost," says Mattie, but in reality she hasn't even put the toothpaste on her brush. Another five minutes go by, and more inquiries are made.

Finally, about fifteen minutes after she got started, one of her parents enters the bathroom and escorts Mattie back to her bedroom. And that's the way it goes night after night.

The solution is a simple reordering of events. If Mattie was required to brush her teeth before story time, the task would probably require less time than putting on pajamas. But let's say, for the sake of argument, that Mattie still decides to dawdle. What happens then? She would only lose valuable story time, and she still would experience going to bed at 7:30. Mattie will catch on quickly to that. Brushing teeth will not continue to be a problem.

Allowances for Chores

Let's look at another topic that frequently comes up in discussions about chores for children—allowances. Offering an allowance for chores is a common practice in many homes, but does this practice really teach children responsibility? Tony's parents thought it did until something unexpected happened to change their minds.

Ten-year-old Tony was at the age where earning money was becoming important. His parents thought an allowance would be a good idea. "An allowance will teach him to save and to be more responsible for doing his chores," they thought. After agreeing on the amount, they introduced the plan to Tony.

"Your mom and I have decided that it's time to start

257

giving you an allowance for doing your chores," said his dad. "We'll start you off with $2.50 a week, but we can increase this as you add more chores to your list. You need to save half, but the other half is yours to spend."

"Great!" said Tony. He liked the idea of having a weekly allowance and not having to ask mom and dad each time he needed money.

Everybody seemed happy with the new arrangement. Tony did his chores each week as expected, and on Sundays he collected his $2.50. He saved half, spent the rest, and appeared to be learning responsibility for managing money. Things seemed to be going well for several months, then something unexpected happened. Tony's dad noticed one week that many of his son's chores had not been completed.

"Tony, there won't be any allowance this weekend until your chores are done," said his dad.

"That's OK, Dad," said Tony. "I don't need any allowance this week. I've saved up plenty."

Wait a second, thought his dad. *This isn't what I was trying to teach! What happened?*

Tony's dad confronted a dilemma many parents face when they rely too heavily on allowances to teach the lesson of responsibility. Allowances can be effective incentives as long as children are motivated to pursue them, but what happens when they lose interest as Tony did? What holds them accountable for doing their part? That was the problem. Their system lacked accountability.

Tony's parents can repair their training system by clarifying their expectations and by supporting their rules with logical consequences other than the loss of an allowance Tony doesn't care about. Let's back up a little now and give Tony's dad another chance to respond to his son's statement about not doing chores because he didn't need the money. His dad's new message might sound like this:

"Tony, there seems to be some confusion about what we expect. When we offered you an allowance, we were trying to reward you for doing good work and teach you to save some money. We didn't mean that you only need to do your chores when you want the money. We still expect you to do them whether you get paid or not, and there won't be any afterschool TV or play privileges each day until they're done."

Now Tony's parents are in a position to teach both their intended lessons. If Tony does his part, he gets rewarded with an allowance or the portion of that allowance he earned. If Tony chooses not to do his part, then he is held accountable by experiencing the consequences of that choice. Either way, he cannot avoid being responsible and learning the lessons his parents intend.

Getting Organized with Chores

Homes are busy places, and, even with the best of intentions, chores sometimes get lost in the shuffle of other competing priorities (such as music lessons, soccer practice, and dentist appointments). You and your children may need some help staying on top of things. A chore chart might be the answer.

Chore charts have many advantages. For children, they serve as a visual reminder of what needs to be done when placed strategically on a bathroom mirror, kitchen cabinet, or refrigerator door. For parents, chore charts provide a method for monitoring what needs to be done and a way to acknowledge their children's contributions.

There are many excellent types of chore charts available on the market. You can usually find them in children's catalogs or at stationery stores. You may even wish to get creative and make your own.

For preschoolers and nonreaders, I prefer picture-

chore charts. For older children and teens, the
tility model should work fine. Whatever type you
select, be sure it includes adequate space to write in additional chores and the corresponding days of the week.

Chores for Children of Different Ages

The following list of chores for children ages two to twelve has been adapted from a list compiled by the Counseling and Guidance Department of the University of Arizona. The list is by no means complete, and the suggested ages are only reference points. Your child may be able to complete tasks above or below the ages suggested. The list is intended to be a starting point for parents who want to use chores to teach the lesson of responsibility.

CHORES FOR TWO- AND THREE-YEAR-OLDS

1. Pick up toys and put them in their proper place.
2. Put books and magazines in a rack.
3. Sweep the floor.
4. Place napkins, plates, and silverware on the table but not necessarily in the correct positions.
5. Clean up their messes after eating.
6. Learn to make simple decisions by being given a choice of two foods for breakfast.
7. Clear their place at the table after meals. Put their dishes on the counter.
8. Cooperate with toilet training.
9. Undress and dress with assistance.
10. Help put away groceries on lower shelves.

11. Pick up the newspaper.
12. Help with simple meal planning.
13. Assist with feeding pets.
14. Put recycling items in their containers.
15. Hang up coats and sweatshirts on low hooks.

CHORES FOR FOUR-YEAR-OLDS
1. Set the table.
2. Put groceries away.
3. Help make up a grocery list and assist with shopping by taking items off the shelf.
4. Feed pets on a regular basis.
5. Help with garden and yard work.
6. Help with vacuuming, sweeping, dusting.
7. Help fill the dishwasher.
8. Spread butter or peanut butter on sandwiches.
9. Prepare cold cereal.
10. Hold the hand mixer when making cakes or mashed potatoes.
11. Get the mail.
12. Tell parents his or her whereabouts when playing.
13. Hang up coat or backpack on a low hook in the closet.
14. Bring milk in from front porch if delivered.
15. Put away toys or belongings after using them.

CHORES FOR FIVE-YEAR-OLDS
1. Assist with meal planning and grocery shopping.
2. Make a simple breakfast or sandwich.
3. Clean up messes after eating.

4. Set the dinner table with items in correct positions.

5. Make beds and clean rooms.

6. Choose their own outfits with guidance and dress on their own.

7. Put dirty clothes in a hamper.

8. Put clean clothes away in a drawer.

9. Answer the telephone appropriately.

10. Help wash the car.

11. Take out the garbage.

12. Feed pets.

13. Learn to tie shoes.

14. Participate in self-grooming (comb and brush hair).

15. Empty dishwasher and stack items on counter.

CHORES FOR SIX-YEAR-OLDS

1. Choose own clothing for the day according to weather or special events.

2. Water plants and flowers.

3. Peel vegetables.

4. Cook simple foods with supervision (such as popcorn, hot dogs, toast, eggs).

5. Prepare their own school lunch.

6. Hang up their own clothing in closet.

7. Carry wood to the fireplace.

8. Take pet out for a walk.

9. Tie own shoes.

10. Rake leaves or pull weeds.

CHORES FOR SEVEN-YEAR-OLDS

1. Take phone messages and write them down.

2. Run simple errands for parents.

3. Sweep and wash patio or garage areas.

4. Do minor maintenance and repairs on their own bike.

5. Water yards or flower beds.

6. Wash pets.

7. Train pets.

8. Carry in groceries from the car.

9. Get self up in the morning with an alarm clock.

10. Manage lunch money dependably.

CHORES FOR EIGHT- AND NINE-YEAR-OLDS

1. Fold napkins and set table correctly.

2. Mop floors.

3. Manage bathing routines without assistance.

4. Keep closets and drawers clean and organized.

5. Assist in shopping for clothing with parents.

6. Change school clothes without prompts.

7. Do homework regularly without prompts.

8. Fold blankets.

9. Put away laundry.

10. Clean up animal messes in the yard.

11. Read simple recipes and assist with simple cooking.

12. Pick fruit from trees.

13. Help make fires in the fireplace.

14. Assist with painting and home repair projects.

15. Write thank-you notes.

16. Feed the baby.

17. Assist with bathing of younger brother or sister.

18. Carry dirty clothes to wash area.
19. Operate small electrical appliances without assistance (such as the blender, can opener, or popcorn popper).
20. Put recycling bins on the curb for pickup.

CHORES FOR TEN-YEAR-OLDS

1. Change sheets on their bed.
2. Operate the washer or dryer.
3. Measure detergents.
4. Load and run the dishwasher without assistance.
5. Buy groceries from a list.
6. Keep track of their own appointments (such as dentist or sports team practices).
7. Prepare simple pastries from box mixes.
8. Receive and answer their own mail.
9. Wait on guests.
10. Plan their own birthday parties or special events.
11. Handle minor first aid (small cuts and scrapes).
12. Do chores for neighbors on regular basis.
13. Carry out chores without prompts.
14. Save money and plan for long-term purchases.
15. Wash the family car.

CHORES FOR ELEVEN- AND TWELVE-YEAR-OLDS

1. Earn money by babysitting, yard jobs, etc.
2. Handle themselves alone at home for several hours at a time.
3. Take city transportation independently (bus, subway).

4. Use proper conduct in public places (libraries, stores, theaters).

5. Be responsible for their own hobbies.

6. Join outside organizations (Scouts, youth groups).

7. Assist with dressing siblings and putting them to bed.

8. Clean pool and pool area.

9. Respect other people's property.

10. Run own errands.

11. Mow lawns with power equipment.

12. Help parents with home repair projects.

13. Clean oven and stove.

14. Manage own homework schedule independently.

15. Manage a paper route independently.

Parent Study Group Questions
(Optional Session)

1. Share with other group members the chores you expect your children to do on a regular basis. Do you think you might be expecting too much or too little of your children? If you are unsure, are you doing chores for them that they are capable of doing for themselves? What do you believe should be a reasonable set of expectations for chores? Discuss your beliefs with other members.

2. Are your children's chores mandatory or optional? If you are unsure, what type of limits are you using to get the message across? How are your children responding? Do you understand why? Share your experiences with other group members.

3. Are your expectations about your children's chores consistent with those of your spouse or others who assist you with child care? If not, what is your plan for developing better consistency?

4. Are your children held accountable when they choose not to do their part at home? What type of consequences are you using? Are the consequences effective? If not, what can you do differently? Share your experiences and ask for suggestions from other group members.

5. What is your plan for improving the way chores are handled at home? Do you anticipate resistance? How will you handle it? Share your plan with other group members.

Chapter
11

The Homework Dance

One of the most familiar dances I see in my counseling work is the dance parents and children do over homework. That's right. The *homework dance*. The one where the parents remind, cajole, threaten, and reprimand, and the kids avoid, make excuses, resist, dawdle, or procrastinate. Like most dances, there's a punitive version that's a little louder and a permissive version that's more drawn out. Some parents do a little of both.

Call it homework battles, nightly coercion routines, or whatever term you want. One thing is for sure — there are a lot of parents out there doing it. Most can't say how they got started or what keeps it going, but once it does get started, no one seems to know how to stop. This chapter will show you how to do that and how to put the responsibility for doing homework back on your child's shoulders where it belongs.

Many parents don't realize that homework takes place in a system involving three participants: parents, teacher, and the child. Each has his or her own set of jobs or responsibilities to carry out if the homework system is to operate smoothly and remain in balance. The system can break down, and often does, when its members do less than or more than their own part.

In this chapter, you'll learn how the homework system works, why it breaks down, and how to fix it without returning to the nightly coercion routine. You'll see that the key to a successful homework system is learning to do your own part, and only your part, without taking responsibility away from your child or the teacher. In so doing, you will be allowing homework to teach the lessons it was intended to teach.

The Dance

Darren, a fourth-grader, and his parents were referred by Darren's school. The problem: Darren wouldn't do his homework. His grades were falling, and he was failing two subjects.

Darren's teacher had tried everything — deadline extensions, extra credit and makeup opportunities, stickers, contracts, success charts, pep talks, even a daily note system between school and home. Nothing worked.

Yes, homework sounded like the problem, but was it really? Each year, I see a few kids like Darren where homework appears to be the problem, but it's only a symptom of something larger going on (such as a lack of skills or ability, a learning disability, a behavior problem, an emotional or relationship problem, or a problem with drugs or alcohol). I needed to check this out. Together, we completed a child history questionnaire and a structured interview.

From the interview, Darren sure sounded like a normal well-adjusted kid. He spent his free time with friends, skateboards, and bicycles, and, other than the power struggles over homework, he enjoyed good relationships with his parents and others. I needed to be sure, however, that Darren was really capable of doing his work.

"Is there any chance that the assignments might be too difficult for him?" I asked.

His parents were prepared for the question. Darren's mother handed me an envelope with copies of past report cards and test scores. I glanced them over briefly. Mostly Bs. Strong test scores. OK, I was convinced. Darren was capable. Back to homework matters.

Darren's parents had all the familiar complaints: "He tells us he doesn't have any homework, then we find out later that he does. He knows he's supposed to write down his assignments, but half the time he doesn't do it. When we ask to see them, he says he forgot or lost them or that he doesn't have any that night. So, we get on the phone and call around and find out what's going on. Some nights, it takes us forty-five minutes just to figure out what his assignments are! Fortunately, that's changed. Now the teacher calls me every Monday and gives me all his homework assignments for the week in advance."

"Has that helped?" I directed the question to Darren's mother, who was telling most of the story.

"Well, at least now we know what he's supposed to be doing," she said. "But getting him to actually do it hasn't gotten any easier. We still go through the same old routine.

"Each night about 7:00, when dinner is finished and he's enjoyed a half hour of television, we sit down together at the dining room table and go over his assignments. I read the directions, and sometimes I do the first problem with him to make sure he understands how to do it. But he just sits there!

"So I begin to prod. 'Come on, get going!' I say, 'Let's get it done tonight before 8:00 for a change.' He may do a problem or two, but then I glance over and he's just sitting there again. So I prod some more, and he does a few more. This is how it goes until bath time. If we're lucky, we may be half done.

"After the bath, it's more of the same. Sometimes, I get so frustrated I start yelling which usually brings my husband in, and he starts to yell too. Then Darren gets upset. So I console him, and my husband blames me for being too soft. It's crazy! I usually end up lecturing both of them, while Darren sneaks off to watch TV. The homework never gets done.

"His teacher tells us that homework should take about thirty to forty minutes a night. In our house, it can drag on for hours! He won't do it unless we stand over him and make him do it."

And so it goes, Monday through Thursday, week after week, with his parents devoting a good portion of their evening pushing and prodding, threatening and lecturing, as Darren dawdles and works as slowly as possible. Does homework really deserve this much attention? Is the act of "getting it done" really what's most important?

What's the Purpose of Homework?

Sometimes, we become so caught up in the task of "getting it done" that we lose sight of what homework is all about. So, let's take a moment to consider why children are asked to do homework in the first place.

Homework teaches children two sets of lessons — one that is immediately apparent and one that requires us to look a little deeper. The most apparent reason for assigning homework is to provide children with opportunities to practice and improve their skills. Practice is essential to skill mastery. A regular homework routine helps children sharpen their skills and get better grades. This is what Darren's parents were most concerned about. Let's call this Lesson 1.

But homework also teaches other, more important,

lessons that can't be measured with letter grades—responsibility, self-discipline, independence, perseverance, and time management. In the long run, these skills have a much greater influence on your child's future success, not only in the classroom, but on the job and in life. These lessons are what Darren's parents and his teacher were overlooking. Let's call this Lesson 2.

How do children learn this second set of lessons? By being allowed opportunities to stand on their own and do their part without interference from parents and teachers. The act alone conveys a powerful set of behavioral messages: "I believe you're capable." "I trust you to do this on your own."

A System Out of Balance

When we look at all the steps the school and Darren's parents had taken to get him to do his homework, one question looms rather prominently: Whose homework was it really? Darren's? But who keeps track of his assignments? Mom and the teacher. And who does part of the work? Mom and dad. And who makes sure it gets turned in on time? Mom. And who experiences the consequences for the homework not getting done? Mom, dad, and the school. If the homework really belonged to Darren, then why was everyone else doing his jobs for him?

What Darren's parents and teacher didn't realize was that they all were playing "hot potato" with responsibility, and guess who ended up holding the potato? Not Darren. The way things were, he had no incentive for changing his behavior. He knew, from experience, that he could count on his teacher and parents to do his part for him.

Darren's parents and the school had fallen into a trap. They had been compensating for Darren's lack of responsibility by doing more of his jobs themselves. The

271

more they compensated, the less Darren did, and the more out of balance their homework system became. Without realizing it, they were actually enabling him to behave the way he was.

Sure, all their dancing was getting a little homework done, but at whose initiative? And what about Lesson 2? Things were not going to get any better until they all got back to doing their rightful jobs.

"I think it's time we took a closer look at your homework system," I suggested to Darren's parents.

"Homework system?" inquired Darren's father, looking a little puzzled. "I don't think we have one, at least not one I'm aware of."

His response was not unusual. Most parents who are stuck in homework dances are not aware of the roles they play or that they are operating within a system.

"Almost every parent has one," I said. "Yours just hasn't been working very well for you." I handed each of them a diagram (Figure 11A) and gave them a few minutes to look it over.

"Look familiar?" I asked. Both parents nodded. "This is what the homework system looks like when parents and teachers end up doing their children's jobs." We reviewed each list.

"How do things get this way?" Darren's father asked.

Some families just start off this way, with their system out of balance. The jobs are not clear from the beginning. There's too much parent involvement. The parents think they are helping, but as time passes and patterns become established they notice that they are doing more and more while their children are doing less and less.

Other parents get sucked into the trap by getting too involved when the work gets difficult and their children start to struggle. Again, the parents want to help, but over time all the rescuing and involvement results in a gradual shifting of jobs.

272

Figure 11A. A homework system out of balance

Parent's Jobs	Child's Jobs	Teacher's Jobs
Make frequent inquiries about assignments.	Provide excuses about assignments (such as, "It was lost, stolen; none was assigned; dog ate it").	Lecture, persuade, or coerce child to do the work.
Remind them to do their lessons.	Wait until the last moment to get started.	Give frequent reminders to do the lessons.
Ask if the work is done.		Provide deadline extensions and extra
Make extra trips to school to pick up books or assignments.	Listen to reminders, lectures, reprimands from parents and teachers.	credit and makeup opportunities.
Help out by doing some of the work.	Do the work in a busy place where it attracts maximum attention.	Make the work easier in hopes more will get done.
Lecture or punish for not doing the work.	Pretend not to understand so parents will get involved.	Ask parents to become more involved.
Feel responsible for child's failures.	Rush through or do it carelessly to get it over with.	Provide special rewards for completed work.
	Blame parents and teacher for poor grades.	Feel responsible for child's failures.

The problem is gradual and insidious. In many cases, it may go unnoticed until children stop doing their homework altogether like in Darren's home. By the time parents realize something is wrong, patterns have already become well-established, and a great deal of compensating has been going on.

Darren's mother was looking confused. "Wait a second!" she said, pointing to the list of parent jobs. "I thought I was supposed to be doing all these things. Are you saying that I shouldn't help Darren keep track of his assignments each day or remind him to turn in his homework?"

"Exactly right," I replied. "Not if you want to put your system back in balance and have Darren learn responsibility. That's not likely to happen until you stop doing Darren's jobs for him and do only the jobs that are rightfully yours. What incentive will he have for doing his part if he can count on someone else to step in and bail him out?"

"But I know my son," she countered. "If I don't do those jobs, he won't either."

"I think you're right," I agreed. "He probably won't until you build some consequences into your homework system that hold him accountable. As it is now, all Darren has to do is endure the prodding and lectures and he's home free."

I could appreciate her confusion. Earlier in the year, the school had advised her that the solution was to get more involved with Darren's homework, not less. When they offered no specific plan for going about it, Darren's mother thought this meant that she was supposed to do more of what she was already doing. More dancing.

"How do we get off this treadmill?" asked Darren's father.

"You're right," I said. "It's time we started talking

about handing the hot potato back to Darren and how to begin putting your system back in balance."

Putting Your System Back in Balance

I handed each of them a second diagram (Figure 11B). "This is what the homework system looks like when it's in balance," I said. "Notice the distribution of responsibility between the three participants." I gave them a few minutes to look it over, then we reviewed each list of jobs.

In a balanced system, parents and teachers limit their involvement and operate like a facilitator, someone who supports and promotes the homework process but plays only a brief role. The key word here is *brief*. They set limits on the jobs to be done, and they make sure children have everything they need to carry out their tasks, but that's where their job ends. The rest is up to the child. The child is the one who does the work.

"According to the chart, we should establish a regular time and a regular place for homework," said Darren's mother. "How is that different from what we've been doing?"

"Good question," I replied. "Let's look at some guidelines for establishing times and places for homework in a balanced system."

A Time for Homework. When selecting a suitable time for homework, keep three considerations in mind. First, select a time that can be used regularly. Homework should be a habit, a routine, something your child can learn to do on a regular basis. When you select a consistent and stable time, you will be helping your child develop good homework habits.

Secondly, choose a time that is earlier in the day

Figure 11B. A homework system in balance

Parent's Jobs	Child's Jobs	Teacher's Jobs
Establish a regular time for homework.	Keep track of books and assignments.	Provide instruction.
Establish a regular place for homework.	Start on time and allow time to finish work.	Provide materials.
Provide necessary materials and supplies.	Do his or her own work with only limited assistance.	Provide time deadlines.
Provide limited instruction and assistance.		Provide encouragement.
Establish logical consequences for noncompliance and follow through.	Turn the work in on time.	Provide feedback regarding work returned.
	Accept responsibility for grades or other consequences.	

rather than later. Why? Because children are generally fresher and more alert in the late afternoon or early evening than they are later on. They also will be more motivated to complete their jobs so they can get on to the "good stuff" (such as playing, friends, or TV that awaits them when they're done).

There is an accountability issue to consider here. When homework is the last act before bed, what consequences are available to you if your child chooses noncompliance? None. The accountability system breaks down. Late homework schedules eliminate opportunities to teach Lesson 2 with logical consequences. There is more than a little wisdom to the old axiom work before play.

Finally, homework sessions should have a beginning and an end. That is, a time when parents are available to assist and a time when they are not (for example, "I'll be available to help between 4:30 and 5:30, but not after that time."). This is one of the surest ways to keep the hot potato on your child's lap and to define how much time you're willing to devote to homework.

An upper time limit has other advantages too. It teaches children to plan and manage their time wisely, and it provides parents and children with time to enjoy each other's company without the intrusion of homework.

Sure, you can be flexible and extend these deadlines when big exams and special projects occur, but otherwise designate a regular homework period and do your best to stick to it. If you don't, you may be setting yourself up for situations where homework can drag on for hours and where it can be used as a device for negative attention, power, and control over other family members. Again, homework is not worth this much attention.

How much time should you set aside each day (Monday through Thursday) for homework? The guidelines I generally hear from teachers are 30 – 45 minutes a night for primary-level children (grades 1 and 2), 30 – 60 minutes a night for intermediate levels (grades 3 – 6), and 60 – 90 minutes a night and sometimes longer for secondary levels (grades 7 – 12). Also, homework on weekends is not unusual for secondary-level students. I recommend that you consult with your child's teacher or counselor before deciding.

What if your child finishes up in less than the allotted time? Terrific! If the work was completed and good efforts were made to do it accurately, then there is no point in making your child stay there until the end of the session. Even if some of the items are wrong? Yes, unless your child specifically asks you to check all of the items for accuracy. The emphasis should be on *effort* not *outcome*, *process* not *product*. If your child puts forth a good effort and does the work, that's enough. It doesn't have to be perfect to fulfill Lessons 1 and 2.

A Place for Homework. Where should homework be done? The best location is a separate, quiet place away from parents and other family members. A balanced system is not possible if homework is permitted to occupy center stage in the house. When we allow children to do it at the kitchen table or other busy family areas, we are risking that homework will receive more attention and parent involvement than it deserves. That's another invitation to dance.

If not the kitchen or dining room, then where? The best place for children to do homework is in their room, but a den or study or other quiet room with a desk should work just fine. The room should be available on a regular basis, away from traffic and distractions (TV or other family activities), and provisioned with all the right equipment and materials (such as desk, comfortable chair,

278

lamp, paper, pencils, pens, a dictionary, ruler, tape, paper clips, and maybe a tray or two to keep things organized).

"How do we get this new system going?" Darren's mother asked, relieved at the prospect that help was on the horizon.

Three Steps to a Balanced System

The good news for any parent who wants to end the dance and pass the hot potato back to the child is that the remedy requires less time, energy, and involvement than you're already putting out. Here are the three steps you'll need to follow: 1. clarify the jobs; 2. build in accountability; and 3. stay off the dance floor.

Step 1. Clarify the Jobs

First, you will need to set firm limits on the various jobs to be done. I recommend that you sit down with your child and explain that there will be some changes in the way homework is done at home. Review each list of jobs in a balanced system (the parent's jobs, teacher's jobs, and child's jobs), and be very specific about the details (the how, when, and where) of your child's jobs. Some parents prefer to post the jobs and time schedules on the refrigerator so their children can refer to them if needed.

"OK," said Darren's father, "the system sounds good so far, but what happens when Darren chooses not to do his jobs?"

"This is where your accountability measures will come in," I replied. "In a balanced system, children are held accountable for their poor choices because they experience regular and consistent consequences for not doing their part. This is what was missing in the system you've been using and why you've been stuck. Consequences provide additional incentive and motivation for making good choices."

Step 2. Build in Accountability

If your children have found a way to avoid doing homework on a regular basis without experiencing consequences, then your system lacks accountability. They are not likely to change their behavior until you build some accountability back into your system. You do this with a system for monitoring your child's assignments and with logical consequences when your children choose to do less than their part.

Let's begin with methods for monitoring assignments. I am sure there are many creative ways to go about this, but I prefer two methods in particular because they are brief, simple, and require as little of your involvement as possible.

The monitoring system for elementary school children consists of having one assignment sheet for the entire week (Figure 11C) that goes home with the child on Mondays. The teacher writes down the assignments and indicates any outstanding assignments in the space at the bottom of the sheet. It's the child's responsibility for getting the assignment sheet home. Consequences go into effect if that doesn't happen (such as loss of that day's privileges).

The monitoring system for teens is a little more complicated because more teachers are usually involved. In this case, it's the teen's responsibility to write down all of his or her assignments each day on a single daily assignment sheet (Figure 11D). At the end of each class, the teen presents the assignment sheet to the teacher who initials it

Figure 11C. Sample assignment sheet for elementary students

HOMEWORK FOR WEEK
February 24–28

MONDAY

Read Chapter One in *Explorers* (pages 10–22).
Answer five study questions at end of chapter.

TUESDAY

Review spelling list.
Write each word in a complete sentence.
Bring materials for science experiment: jar with lid, candle.

WEDNESDAY

Complete 25 division problems on page 119 in math book.
Answer five work problems on page 120.

THURSDAY

Read Chapter Two in *Explorers* (pages 23–31).
Answer five study questions at end of chapter.
Study map on page 24 for quiz on Friday.

for accuracy and indicates any outstanding assignments in the space provided at the bottom. If no new assignments are given for that day, the teen simply writes "no new assignments" and the teacher initials it.

It is the teen's responsibility to write down all assignments, get them initialed, and bring the sheet home each

Figure 11D. Sample assignment sheet for secondary students

Date _____

Class: _____   Assignment due: _____

Assignment:

Teacher's
initials:_____

Class: _____   Assignment due: _____

Assignment:

Teacher's
initials:_____

Class: _____   Assignment due: _____

Assignment:

Teacher's
initials:_____

Class: _____   Assignment due: _____

Assignment:

Teacher's
initials:_____

Class: _____   Assignment due: _____

Assignment:

Teacher's
initials:_____

day. Again, consequences go into effect if that doesn't happen (such as loss of some or all of that evening's privileges depending upon what happened). At the end of each daily homework session, the parent simply compares work assigned to work completed and allocates privileges earned.

"Doesn't this monitoring system take away some of Darren's responsibility?" his father asked.

"Yes, it does, a little," I replied, "but very little in comparison to the amount of responsibility it places on him for doing the rest of his jobs. Monitoring simply removes the gray area about what jobs need to be done and provides you with a basis for evaluating if assigned work was completed and if further consequences are needed."

Let's look at the second part of your accountability system — your consequences. Logical consequences, when applied consistently, help children learn responsibility (Lesson 2) by holding them accountable for their unacceptable choices. All parents need to do to ensure the lesson is learned is follow through and enforce the consequence without dancing. No lectures, no threats, no reminders, no angry displays. Just let your children hold the hot potato and learn from their mistakes.

The logical consequence for not doing homework is temporary loss of the privileges or pleasurable activities your child would normally enjoy after school each day. The system is really very simple. Privileges are based on performance. If your child chooses to bring home all of his or her assignments and completes all assigned work during the designated time, then he or she receives full afterschool play privileges for that day. If all homework assignments are completed for the entire week, then full weekend privileges are earned.

If, on the other hand, your child chooses not to bring home assignments or not to do the work altogether that day, then you simply withhold his or her privileges for that afternoon or evening. Just call it "a quiet time in the house" and take it one day at a time. Left over or incomplete work can be made up during a designated time on Saturday or Sunday (but not both). Each school day your child is earning privileges not only for that day but for the weekend as well.

CONSEQUENCES FOR ELEMENTARY SCHOOL CHILDREN

No afterschool play privileges

No friends over

No TV or video games

Stay in the house and do quiet activities (such as reading or drawing)

CONSEQUENCES FOR TEENS

No afterschool free-time privileges

No friends over

No telephone privileges

No TV privileges

Stay in the house and do quiet activities

Revised limits on curfew, dating, car use, or evening-out privileges, based on level of compliance

Step 3. Stay off the Dance Floor

Once you've clarified the jobs to be done and put your accountability measures in place, then you're ready to back off and let your system teach its lessons. The hot potato is now in your child's lap, and your primary goal should be to see that it stays there. How do you do that? By limiting your involvement to doing only your jobs and by letting your accountability system do the rest.

"When we put this new system into effect, how long will it take to get things back in balance?" asked Darren's father.

What You Should Expect

Every parent wants to hear the good news — that things are going to get better quickly. But some problems, like homework dances, don't lend themselves to the quick fix. Changing old habits takes time. I had confidence Darren's parents would be successful because they were motivated to do what was needed. I wanted to be sure, however, that they left my office with a realistic set of expectations.

I tried to put things in perspective. "The time it takes to put things back in balance usually depends upon how long things have been broken down," I said. "If this were a recent development, then just clarifying the jobs and following through with your consequences would probably do the trick in a few weeks.

"But your homework dances have been going on for some time," I observed. "Things will probably get worse before they get better. That is, Darren will need to experience repeatedly the consequences of his poor choices before the full impact of Lesson 2 sinks in. This takes time, perhaps three to six weeks or more. But when it does happen, and it should, you will also begin to see a lot more of Lesson 1."

During the transition period, parents should expect testing — lots of it. Your children will probably continue to do all the things they were doing before — making excuses about lost or forgotten assignments, dawdling, procrastinating, or displaying confusion or helplessness. They may even intensify their routines in a desperate attempt to get you to rescue, lecture, punish, or do more than just your part.

As tempting as the bait may be, don't give in. Keep your limits firm and follow through with the three-step plan. The testing won't last forever. It's just a normal, but very stressful, part of the change process.

That evening, Darren and his parents reviewed all the jobs once again and put their new system into effect. A homework schedule was set for 4:00 with an upper limit of 5:00. Neither parent would be available for help after 5:00 unless arrangements were made in advance.

The schedule gave Darren plenty of time for a snack after school and time to play with his friends or watch TV if he got everything done. Best of all, it left the rest of the evening for activities other than homework.

The new place for homework was Darren's room upstairs. His dad set up a desk and provisioned it with all the necessary stuff and relocated Darren's TV and Nintendo downstairs. If Darren needed help, it was his job to go downstairs and ask for it, then return to his room to do the work.

For accountability, Darren's parents decided to switch over to the monitoring system I recommended. It would be Darren's responsibility to bring the assignment sheet home on Mondays. If that didn't happen, after-school play privileges were suspended each day until it did. No excuses were accepted.

In short, Darren's afterschool play privileges were based on his job performance. If he completed all his jobs each day (brought assignments home and did his own work within the allotted time), then he received his full complement of privileges. He could have friends over, go outside and play, watch TV, and enjoy his evenings without restrictions.

If, on the other hand, Darren chose not to do his jobs, then he lost his privileges for that day, spent the hour before dinner (5:00 – 6:00) in his room, and after dinner he just had a quiet time in the house without friends, TV, or Nintendo. Incomplete or leftover work had to be made up on Saturdays before any playing.

Two weeks later, Darren's parents returned for their first follow-up appointment. "How did everything go?" I asked.

"Well, we didn't see much homework completed until very recently," said Darren's father, "but we also didn't hear much fighting."

"He's right," agreed Darren's mother. "For the first time in months, my stomach hasn't been in knots before dinner. Our home has been a much quieter and more peaceful place to live."

"Did Darren do much testing?" I inquired.

"As predicted," said his mother. "He didn't bring his assignment sheet home until Wednesday of the first week, but each time we followed through with the consequences — no play privileges.

"When he finally did bring it home, he informed us that he wasn't going to do it. 'That's up to you,' I said. But when 4:00 rolled around each day, I made sure he was in his room. Then, I left saying, 'I'll be here until 5:00 if you need help.' He never asked.

"In fact, he didn't do any homework that first week," she continued. "He just sat there. So, we followed through — no play privileges. After each homework session, he spent the hour before dinner in his room, and, after dinner, it was quiet time. On Saturday, he made no efforts to do the work, so again he was restricted to the house. When his friends came by, we just informed them that he couldn't play."

"How did he handle all that?" I inquired.

"At first, he said he didn't care," said Darren's father, "but later he started crying and telling us that we were mean and unfair. This past week, he's been scowling and glaring at us a lot in the evenings."

"You mentioned that he did complete some work during the end of this two-week period," I inquired.

"Yes, on Thursday, he just went up to his room and did it!" said his mother. "I thought he was up there pouting, so you can imagine how surprised I was at 5:00 when he passed it over and headed out to play. The strange thing was, it was no big deal to him. That evening, we all watched a program together, and he acted like nothing had happened.

"On Saturday, he surprised us again because he had accumulated a fair amount of leftover homework during the week. We were anticipating another day of moping and scowling and turning friends away at the door. But after breakfast, Darren headed up to his room and had all of it done by 10:30. Three days worth! Then, off he went. No big deal."

Their homework system was having its intended effect. For two weeks, Darren held the hot potato by himself with no one to pass it to. He tried avoidance, then defiance, then waited for the rescue that never came. Lesson 2 was beginning to sink in, and Lesson 1 wasn't far behind.

Darren and his parents were well on their way to a successful outcome. They just needed more time for their system to do its work. I agreed to meet with them every two weeks until they were ready to solo.

The improvement continued. By the end of week four, Darren was completing more homework than he was leaving unfinished and doing the mop-up work very quickly on Saturdays. The pattern continued into week six. His grades were coming up. During week eight, all homework assignments were completed on time. A milestone! Saturday wasn't needed.

By week ten, Darren was showing initiative and independence by heading off to his room before his usual prompt, "Time for homework." His parents decided to reduce their involvement to only random spot-checks of completed work. Darren was so eager to get out to play each day he didn't even notice. By week twelve, they stopped checking altogether. Their system was in balance.

When they came in for their final follow-up session, Darren's parents were pleased, and with good reason. The homework battles that had dominated their house for so long had been gone for many weeks. Darren was now doing his part independently, and his grades showed it. Things seemed to be fixed. But were they really?

Change can be fragile, particularly in the early stages when things seem to be going smoothly. Relapses sometimes occur, and they can happen to parents just as easily as children. It begins with a missed assignment here and a reminder there, more missed assignments, more reminders, maybe a lecture or two, and before you know it, you're dancing again!

Keeping a system in balance requires vigilance on the parents' part. I encouraged Darren's parents to be on guard for lapses and relapses and to be prepared to use their monitoring system again if needed. They had worked hard to put things back in balance and they left with the tools to see that they stayed that way.

When Professional Help Is Needed

The three-step system works great for children like Darren when homework really is the problem and not just a symptom of something larger that is going on. But this is not always an easy thing to determine. What should you do if you've implemented the recommended steps and your child doesn't respond as expected after four to six weeks?

If this is the case, then it's time to consider that something else might be going on that keeps you stuck. You may need assistance from a qualified professional to sort it out.

If you recall, I began my work with Darren and his parents by conducting an evaluation. A number of factors were considered: learning problems (a lack of skills or ability), behavior problems, emotional or relationship problems, or even problems with drugs or alcohol. After reviewing the necessary background information and Darren's past school records, I felt comfortable that homework was the primary concern.

You may need the same type of evaluation for your child. A licensed child psychologist or an educational psychologist can help you collect the information you need and determine the type of help that is needed. Ask your child's school, pediatrician, or your family physician for recommendations.

After other issues have been addressed, you should be able to implement the three-step homework system with better success.

Questions about Homework

1. *How do you start children off with good homework habits?*

Answer: The best way is to begin with your system in balance — parents and children doing their own jobs at regular times and in regular places. Homework should be a habit, a routine. By keeping your limits firm and establishing consistency early, you're much less likely to need monitoring or consequences later on.

2. *When is it time to implement the three-step homework system?*

Answer: If your child has been avoiding his or her homework responsibilities on a regular basis, then it's time to implement the three-step system.

3. *My child has been doing all of his homework regularly for years, but he has been doing it last thing in the evening at the dining room table. Should I make him change?*

Answer: As you know, I don't recommend late homework schedules or that children be permitted to do their homework in busy family areas, but these habits do not always lead to problems either. If your system isn't broken, don't fix it. The most important thing is that Lessons 1 and 2 are taking place, and this seems to be the case.

4. *Do younger children need more help getting started with their homework?*

Answer: Yes, and this is a major reason why many parents get overinvolved early on. Younger children usually do require more assistance getting started on time and assistance with directions and instructions once they do get started. If you keep your prompts and assistance brief ("Time for homework" or "What happens at 4:00?"), you'll be sending the right messages.

5. *My child goes into a dawdling mode just before it's time to get started. How do I avoid getting hooked into the old repeating and reminding routine?*

Answer: Use your kitchen timer and limited choices. When homework time approaches, set your timer for five minutes and inform your child, "You can start your homework now or when the timer goes off. What would you like to do?" Then, follow through.

6. *What should I do if my child's teacher asks me to initial completed homework assignments or to get more involved with my child's homework?*

Answer: Teachers are human like the rest of us. The gesture is probably well-intended, but, unfortunately, not very helpful. Both sides might benefit if you choose to share the steps you're taking to keep your homework system in balance.

7. *If I've been implementing the three-step system and getting good results, how long should I wait before discontinuing the monitoring?*

Answer: Generally, I recommend that parents taper off gradually rather than drop the monitoring all at once. After two or three weeks of full compliance, try moving on to random spot-checks for another two to three weeks. If full compliance continues, then you're probably ready to discontinue the monitoring altogether. Be ready to reinstate it if needed.

8. *Do relapses on my child's part indicate that the system doesn't work?*

Answer: No. Relapses indicate that your child still has more learning to do. Lesson 2 is not complete. It's time to resume the three-step system.

9. *I've been using the three-step system for three weeks. My child goes off to her room without protest, but after what seems a very short time she announces that she's done. When I check the work over, I find that most of it was done hurriedly and carelessly just to get it over with. What should I do?*

Answer: This is probably a form of limit testing. If your daughter's work doesn't satisfy your definition of a "good effort," then you should let her know ("This doesn't look like a complete effort to me.") and send

292

her back to finish up. Don't waste your time getting sucked into pointless arguments or debates about your standards for quality. If your child truly needs more help figuring out what you mean, he or she can ask for it.

10. *Do you recommend giving prizes or special rewards to children when they complete their homework on time?*

Answer: No. This sends the wrong message. Special rewards are usually reserved for special accomplishments. You're not asking your child to do anything that would not be expected of any other child.

PARENT STUDY GROUP QUESTIONS (OPTIONAL SESSION)

1. How is homework handled in your home? Is your homework system in balance with everyone doing their own jobs? If not, has this become a problem yet? Share your experiences with other group members.

2. Is your current homework system teaching both Lesson 1 and Lesson 2? Discuss with other group members why you think this is the case.

3. If your homework system is out of balance, can you identify the specific problem areas? Are the various jobs clear to all? Are your children held accountable when they fail to do their part?

4. If accountability is a problem area, what logical consequences do you plan to use to hold your children more accountable?

5. What is your overall plan for improving the homework system in your home? Can you describe the specific steps you need to take? Share your plan with other group members. Ask them if they think you are doing enough.

6. What are your expectations for change? Do you expect it to happen quickly? If so, is this realistic? Discuss your expectations with other group members and ask if they believe you are being realistic.

7. Do you expect to encounter resistance when you put your new plan into effect? If so, are you prepared to respond without returning to the old dance? Share with other group members what you plan to do when you encounter resistance.

8. Do you know where to go for assistance if professional help is needed? Ask other group members and your group leader for information regarding available resources in your area.

▼
Chapter
12

Preparing for Change

Learning the methods in this book will be the easiest part of your training. Most are fairly straightforward and easy to carry out. The hardest part will be coping with the resistance you are likely to encounter from many sources — from your children, from other family members, and, most of all, from yourself.

You may recognize intellectually that the methods you've learned will lead to the type of change you desire, but the methods may not feel comfortable to you or your children in the beginning. Your children will probably resist, and you will probably be tempted to give in to your compelling desire to revert back to old bad habits and do things the way you always have. Overcoming old habits is not an easy process.

This chapter will prepare you for the changes that lie ahead. You will gain a better understanding of the change process, learn to cope with resistance, develop realistic expectations, and identify your need for support systems to keep you on track.

What You Can Expect

When you first begin using the methods in this book, you will likely encounter an initial increase in testing and resistance from your children. Don't be alarmed. This is temporary, and it's a very normal part of the learning and retraining process.

After all, your children's beliefs about how you are supposed to behave are based, in many cases, upon years of experience. They are not likely to change these well-established beliefs overnight just because you said things are going to be different. They will need more than your words to be convinced.

Imagine how you would react if someone you knew for many years suddenly told you that he was going to behave differently. Let's say this person had been very critical and judgmental in the past, and now he was going to be more tolerant and accepting. Wouldn't you want to see the change for yourself over time before you believed it? Most of us would. Children are much the same way.

Telling children that you've changed or that you are going to change is often not enough to change their beliefs. They will need to experience this change for themselves before they are likely to revise their beliefs and accept the fact that you are different. You will have to show them with your consistent behavior.

In the meantime, you should expect them to test your new methods and do everything they can to get you to behave "the way you are supposed to." If you've been dancing with them in the past, they will likely continue to ignore you, tune you out, challenge and question your requests, and dangle some very tempting baits to get you back out on the dance floor. You will probably be relying heavily upon the methods you learned in Chapter Five to interrupt your dance before it gets started (the check-in procedure, the cool down, and the cut-off technique).

Consequences also will play an important role for you during the initial retraining period. You will probably need to use them frequently to support your rules, to stop misbehavior, and to hold your children accountable for their unacceptable choices. The more hours of consistency you achieve between your verbal and action messages, the quicker your children will learn to tune back in to your words, reduce their testing, and cooperate without the need for consequences.

How long will this take? This depends on several factors—the age of your child, your consistency, and how much history you both need to overcome. Most parents who apply the methods consistently report a significant reduction in limit testing during the first eight weeks. Younger children (three to seven years) have less history to overcome and generally respond more quickly, some within the first two to three weeks.

Older children and teens, on the other hand, have more history to overcome and usually require more time and consistent exposure to your methods before they begin to tune back in, reduce their testing, and accept that your rules have changed. Most will show a reduction in testing between four and eight weeks. Some require longer. Your consistency will accelerate the learning process for children of all ages.

The idea of a quick fix is very appealing. We all want our children's behavior to improve as quickly as possible, but we also need to recognize that these patterns did not develop overnight. Retraining takes time. Expectations of a quick fix will only set you and your children up for unnecessary disappointment.

You should expect to encounter persistent limit testing during the initial retraining period. This does not mean your methods don't work. In most cases, it means that your children's retraining is incomplete. Their beliefs about your rules will have to change before their

299

testing will. Allow the teaching and learning process the time it needs to do its part.

Actually, your children's testing is a blessing in disguise because it gives you more opportunities to practice the methods and improve your skills. The more you practice, the more skilled you become. If their behavior improved too quickly, you wouldn't have enough opportunities to practice and improve your skills. You might slip back into old patterns more easily.

Understanding the Change Process

Family therapists and many other helping professionals recognize that families try to maintain a state of balance or equilibrium in the way they communicate, solve problems, and relate with one another. This balance defines a *comfort range* for acceptable behavior — the family's normal way of doing things.

Punitive and permissive parenting styles and family dances are often part of this comfort range. They are familiar and accepted patterns that most family members are reluctant to give up. When these patterns are disrupted, family members often respond with resistance and attempt to restore the balance that has been disrupted. Resistance is a normal and expected reaction to change.

The methods you've learned in this book will interrupt your family dance, but they may also upset your family equilibrium for awhile. You should expect resistance from your children. They will likely do everything they can to get you to revert back to your old ways and "behave the way you're supposed to." At times, you will probably be tempted to give in to their pressure.

But if you persist with your new methods, you will see that their heavy testing is a temporary phase in the learning process. After awhile, they will begin to accept that your rules have really changed. They will do less testing and more cooperating. When this occurs, the change process will begin to shift into another gear.

Behavior change in families usually comes in two forms. Family therapists refer to the first form as *first order change.* This change usually involves a superficial adjustment in the behavior of family members without any lasting impact on their beliefs about family rules. When this change is discontinued, old patterns of behavior usually return.

For example, if you used the methods in this book for two weeks, then decided to stop, you would likely stop your children's misbehavior, but you would have little influence on their beliefs about your rules. They would probably resume their old patterns of misbehavior as soon as you discontinued using the methods.

This book will help you move beyond superficial change and on to *second order change,* or an enduring change that becomes a new part of your family's normal way of doing things. This involves a change in beliefs about your rules that all family members come to accept and follow. Second order change requires consistent application of your methods over time.

You should be heading down the path toward second order change after the first eight weeks of this program. When your children begin to reduce their testing, you will know they are beginning to accept your new rules, but your mission will not yet be complete. Change is fragile at this point. If you begin to slip and revert back, you will likely encounter renewed testing.

If you remain consistent with your methods, however, you and your children should begin to reach a new level of comfort and acceptance in the weeks and months to come. Most parents report reaching a new comfort range within four to six months.

Coping with Resistance

As anyone knows who has attempted to give up a bad habit, change is certainly possible, but it's rarely easy. It requires motivation, persistence, and, most of all, realistic expectations to help us overcome our discouragement when we encounter setbacks and obstacles along our way.

When you begin implementing this program, you are likely to encounter more resistance than support. Resistance may come from a variety of sources — from your children, from your spouse, from friends and other family members, and from within yourself.

What can you expect from your children? When you use the methods effectively, you're not likely to hear: "Gee Mom, you handled that well," or "Good job, Dad! I really appreciate it!" Instead, you will probably hear comments like: "You're not fair!" or "You're mean!" The positive feedback you may want and need to feel effective is not likely to come from your children.

You may also encounter resistance from your spouse when you try to change your methods. This is what happened to Heather. She attended several of my workshops looking for more effective ways to handle her four-year-old's tantrums. She tried calming him, reasoning with him, bargaining, pleading, cajoling, but nothing was working. Giving in only made matters worse. Justin's tantrums were becoming more frequent.

Heather encouraged her husband to join her in the workshops, but he didn't see any problem. "All four-year-olds do that," he insisted. "It's just a stage he's going through. We don't need any parenting classes to tell us that."

"Maybe we can learn some better ways to handle his behavior," Heather suggested.

"Then you go," said her husband. "I think we're handling things just fine."

So Heather attended the workshops. In a short time, she became very skillful at handling Justin's tantrums. She gave him limited choices when he started fussing and complaining, and she followed through with time-outs when he decided to have a tantrum. Two weeks after she started, Justin's tantrums had nearly disappeared during the day.

But his tantrums still continued during the evenings, and Heather could see why. Her husband was the one who usually handled them. He continued to reason, cajole, and give in whenever Justin became upset or started crying. Heather was beginning to get discouraged.

"Maybe he'll learn by my example," Heather thought to herself one evening. She suggested that her husband take a break from discipline for a few nights. He was more than happy to cooperate.

After dinner that evening, Justin made a pitch for a second helping of dessert. "Can I have another bowl of ice cream?" he asked.

"One is all we get tonight," Heather replied matter-of-factly. But Justin wasn't about to accept no for an answer with his father in the room. He started to fuss and complain, very loudly.

"Justin, you can stop the fussing or you can spend the next five minutes in your room to get yourself back under control. What would you like to do?" Heather asked. This still sounded like a no to Justin, so he increased the volume. He lay down on the floor kicking and screaming.

Calmly, his mother reached down, picked him up, and carried him to his room. "You can come out in five minutes if you're done fussing," she said as she left the room.

When Heather returned to the family room, she couldn't help but notice the look on her husband's face. He didn't say anything, but he was clearly impressed. He was even more impressed when Justin reappeared five minutes later calmed down and under control. No more fussing about ice cream!

Heather handled several more tantrums during the next few evenings. Each time, the same result. She didn't give in, and Justin ended up in his room only to reemerge later under control. On one occasion, he even decided to stop his fussing without the need for time-out. None of this was missed by Heather's husband.

The next evening, Heather attended her last workshop. Her husband stayed home with Justin.

"How did it go?" asked Heather when she returned home.

"Justin did all his usual stuff," replied her husband, "but he didn't get away with it."

"What did you do?" she inquired.

"I gave him a time-out," said her husband with a big smile. "You're right; it really works!"

If your partner is a reluctant supporter, you may not win him or her over as quickly as Heather did. You may have to demonstrate your effectiveness for some time before your spouse is convinced, but your role-modeling will be a powerful tool of persuasion. Give him or her some time to see you in action.

Sometimes, other family members really do want to support us, but they don't believe their support should include changing their methods too. This was the dilemma Barbara faced. She was a single parent with two children, ages four and seven. She was dependent upon her mother and her ex-husband for part of her children's care.

Barbara became inspired when she attended one of my workshops. She had been operating from the permissive approach for years, and for the first time she could understand why she spent so much of her time arguing and debating with her children. She recognized her permissive approach, her drawn-out family dances, and her "lecturing style" of soft limits. She couldn't wait to get started.

In a short time, Barbara was stopping misbehavior she couldn't stop before and feeling very good about it. But what she hadn't counted on were the influences of her mother who stayed with her children after school each day, and her ex-husband who had them every other weekend. Both disciplined permissively, and neither was willing to do anything different. The children always did more testing after their visits. When Barbara realized that change was going to take longer than she had anticipated, she began to get discouraged.

You may also encounter the conflicting influences of other family members when you begin using your new methods. Some of these influences will be beyond your control, and, like Barbara, you may become discouraged. Hang in there. There is plenty of reason for optimism. You can work around those who won't support you. The resistance may slow you down, but it shouldn't prevent you from achieving your long-term goals. Your persistence will be rewarded.

Friends, neighbors, and colleagues at work also can be sources of resistance. Their influence is sometimes insidious. Some may hold strong beliefs about the way children should be raised. Others may disagree with your methods and offer unsolicited advice like: "If he were my child, I'd give him a good swat!" or "What she really needs is a good talking to." These comments may be easy to pass off as someone else's opinion but they add up to pressure, and they don't validate or support what you're trying to do. They can be sources of discouragement.

The biggest obstacle to change for most of us, however, will not be our friends, or relatives, or even our resistant children. The biggest obstacle will come from within ourselves as we struggle against our compelling desire to revert back to old habits and do things the way we always have. You may recognize intellectually that the methods in this book will lead to the type of change you desire, but the methods may not feel comfortable to you for awhile.

If you've been permissive in the past, the methods may seem too strict to you. When your children complain or protest your firm limits, you will probably continue to feel guilty or unfair and want to give second chances or compromise your position. Your challenge will be to resist your temptation to give in and to follow through consistently.

If you've been using punishment in the past, you will probably continue to have problems with the notion that your methods don't have to hurt to be effective. The methods in this book will probably seem too lenient to you. Your challenge will be to resist your temptation to do more than is needed.

I recall one parent I spoke with when I followed up on the progress of their time-out system. "How are the time-outs going?" I asked. "Have you noticed any reduction in his testing?"

"No, he's still testing," replied the father, "and he still seems as defiant as ever."

That's curious, I thought to myself. Three weeks had passed since they first implemented the procedure. I expected a decrease in his testing. "Have you been carrying out the procedure as we discussed?" I asked.

"Well, we were for the first few days," his father replied, "but it didn't seem to be working. Dale didn't appear the least bit upset or remorseful when they were over. So we started having him write 100 times "I will not sass my parents" each time we sent him to his room."

I could see why Dale was still defiant. His father could not resist the temptation to do more, and doing more was sabotaging the effectiveness of the procedure. Dale's father was having a difficult time understanding that effective learning could take place in the absence of visible pain or upset. When he later dropped the punitive addition to his time-outs, he began to see a reduction in Dale's testing and defiance.

Ten Myths about the Change Process

Some of the resistance parents experience is created by their unrealistic expectations about the change process. There are ten myths in particular that can be a source of great disappointment and discouragement. Let's look briefly at each of these myths.

1. Things are supposed to get better, not worse, when I first begin using my new methods.

   Reality: You will be able to stop misbehavior effectively when it occurs, but an initial increase in testing is normal and should be expected.

2. Children should change their behavior quickly.

   Reality: There are many things that lend themselves to the quick fix, but changing well-established patterns of misbehavior is not one of them. Second order change takes time. When your children's beliefs about your rules begin to change, so will their limit-testing behavior.

3. My children should change even if I don't.

   Reality: Your children will adjust their behavior to changes in your behavior. It is unrealistic to expect children to change if you are unwilling to do so yourself.

4. If my children continue to test and violate my rules, then my methods are not effective.

Reality: More likely, repeated testing and violation of your rules indicates that your children's learning is incomplete. They need more consistent exposure to your methods over time to realize that your rules have really changed.

5. Child guidance should be easy.

Reality: Correcting old mistakes by being consistent with your methods is just plain hard work. It requires motivation, constant awareness, and persistence to overcome the resistance you are likely to encounter.

6. Only fathers can set firm limits.

Reality: This is a belief I sometimes encounter from moms who grew up with firm fathers and permissive mothers. Both parents are equally capable of setting firm limits.

7. If my methods don't hurt, they can't be effective.

Reality: Nonpunitive methods like the ones in this book will teach all your intended lessons and help you accomplish all your training goals with less time and energy and without injuring feelings or bodies in the process.

8. My methods can't be effective if my child is unhappy with me when I use them.

Reality: Few people, adults or children, are happy when they don't get their own way. Feeling unhappy or dissatisfied in these situations is the normal way to feel. Don't expect them to like it.

9. I should not make mistakes with my methods.

Reality: Mistakes are a normal part of learning for parents and children. You should expect to make mistakes. When you do, catch yourself, refocus on your goals, and try harder next time. Aim for improvement, not perfection. Parents need clean slates just like children do.

10. I should be able to quickly overcome the old scripts and dances I learned in my family of origin.

Reality: If we were robots, then changing old scripts and dances would be a simple matter. We would simply remove one program for our behavior and replace it with another. But real human beings don't work that way. Our scripts and dances were learned over years. It usually takes time and conscious effort on our part to learn to do things differently and to feel comfortable with the changes.

Developing Support Systems

You're probably convinced by now that resistance is a normal part of change. You should expect to encounter some resistance along the way, and you should also expect to feel discouraged, like most of us do, when resistance slows you down. If the resistance becomes too great, you may need some additional support to stay on track.

What kind of support will you need? You will probably need one or both of two kinds of support: 1. support for your program; and 2. support for yourself in coping with the resistance.

Support for your program involves developing consistency between your methods and those of other important adults in your children's lives (such as teachers, child care providers, and relatives). The more consistency you can establish, the quicker and easier the change process will be for all. Children learn more rapidly when the primary teachers in their lives are teaching the same lesson.

Share the book and your methods with the other important adults in your child's life. Tell them what you're trying to accomplish, and show them the methods that are working for you. You will probably find that most will be happy to use methods that are effective and to support you in your goals.

Mark's parents received a lot of support from their son's preschool teachers, and that support helped Mark to get off to a successful start in kindergarten. Mark was only four years old when I first met him, but he had already been expelled from two preschools for his defiance and violent and aggressive behavior. He was attending two part-time programs because no one program was willing to take him for a full day.

Mark's parents were desperate for solutions. Their son was scheduled to begin kindergarten the following fall, but they couldn't imagine how that would be possible given his volatile behavior. They were eager to learn some new methods, but first we had to identify the methods they were using.

Mark's parents discovered they used a mixed approach. They started off permissively with lots of repeating and reminding, but when Mark resisted, and he usually did, they became angry and ended up yelling and spanking. They had a very angry dance.

In a few brief sessions, Mark's parents learned how to interrupt their dance, how to set firm limits, and how to use logical consequences and time-out rather than spankings. I asked them to keep track of the number of time-outs Mark received each day so I could monitor and chart improvements in his behavior.

Next, we needed to establish consistency between home and school. Mark's teachers were more than happy to cooperate. Mark's parents showed them how to give the same type of verbal directions they were using at home and how to use logical consequences and time-out for noncompliance. His teachers agreed to record the number of time-outs he received daily so I could monitor his progress.

As expected, Mark tested a lot during the first few weeks. Then he began to show gradual and steady improvement. Four months after we initiated the program, Mark showed nearly a 70 percent reduction in his defiant and aggressive behavior at school and even better progress at home. His behavior continued to improve in the months that followed. Mark's parents and teachers began to feel more comfortable about his impending kindergarten placement.

Mark's teachers proved to be a valuable support system for his parents. The consistency his teachers helped to achieve between home and school had a lot to do with the improvement Mark was able to make. Although your child's behavior may not be as volatile as Mark's, and you may not be as desperate for change as Mark's parents, involving the important adults in your child's life may also prove to be a valuable way to support the change you're trying to accomplish.

Support for your program can be very helpful, but sometimes parents need more. Sometimes they need support for themselves as they attempt to cope with the resistance they encounter. How do you know if you need this level of support? A number of factors should be considered: 1. the supportiveness of your spouse and others, 2. your motivation and commitment to change, 3. the amount of resistance you are encountering from your children and others, 4. the amount of history you and your children have to overcome, and 5. how stuck you've become in your dance. The first two factors fall under the category of support. The last three make up the category of resistance.

Parents who are high in support and low in resistance often find that they are able to interrupt their dance and apply the methods in this book without the need for any additional personal support. They have the support they need to overcome their occasional setbacks and discouragement and stay on track.

Parents who are high in support but also high in resistance find that additional personal support is helpful and sometimes necessary for them to overcome their obstacles and stay on track. Mark's parents were in this group. When Mark's behavior got worse during the first few weeks, they felt validated and encouraged to hear that this was normal. The feedback helped them overcome their discouragement and persist with their methods.

Later on, when Mark's behavior began to improve significantly, his parents had fewer opportunities to practice and improve their skills. They began to slip back into old patterns of repeating and reminding, their old familiar dance. The personal support and feedback they received helped them stay on track.

Parents who are low in support and high in resistance are the most likely of all to become discouraged and give up. For them, personal support is not only helpful, it's essential. They need this level of support to overcome their many obstacles and to stay on track.

Where do parents find the personal support they need? Most communities have a variety of parent support resources to select from. These include: parent support groups; parenting workshops; and other services for parents offered through your church, nursery school, public schools, hospitals, or community mental health agency, among others. You can contact your community services office or local mental health agency for information about resources in your community.

Where do you stand on the support and resistance scale? If you are just finishing this book for the first time, you may need another month or so before you can answer this question. You will have to put your new methods into practice before you will know. If you discover that you are in a high resistance mode, don't lose heart. Your goals are certainly attainable, but you may need some additional personal support in reaching them.

Enjoying the Rewards

If this book has fulfilled its mission, then you should have the tools and information you'll need to correct your old mistakes and begin setting limits more effectively. You've discovered many of the obstacles to effective teaching and learning—punitive and permissive training styles, soft limits, discouraging messages, and the family dances many parents use to try to get their children to cooperate.

You've also learned a variety of effective methods to help you reach your goals. You know how to prevent dances by giving clear messages, how to inspire cooperation with encouragement, how to teach responsible problem solving, and how to support your rules with consequences that don't injure feelings or bodies. You've learned how to adjust your methods for teens, and how to use your methods to handle problems with chores and homework.

You've even looked down the road at the change process that awaits you. You've anticipated many of the obstacles in your path, and you know what to do to overcome them. Your preparation is complete. The next step is to put your skills into practice and begin enjoying the many rewards of your efforts.

The immediate rewards will be stopping misbehavior quickly and effectively, getting better cooperation, and eliminating all those stressful dances that wear you down and leave you feeling so frustrated and discouraged. Soon, you'll be hassling less and enjoying your children more. You will also have the satisfaction of knowing that

you are teaching your intended lessons about cooperation, responsibility, independence, and self-control.

The long-term rewards of your efforts should be the
most satisfying of all because your methods will be laying a
foundation for cooperative and satisfying relationships
with your children for the years to come. By your example, you will be teaching a process of communication and
problem solving your children will need to be successful
out in the world — at school, in the community and work-
place, and eventually in their own homes with their own
children. The skills you teach are the ones your children
will carry forward.

PARENT STUDY GROUP QUESTIONS

1. Why should you expect increased testing during the first four to eight weeks after implementing this program? Discuss why it takes time for children to revise their beliefs and accept that your rules have really changed.

2. Discuss first order change and second order change. Can you see why second order change requires more perseverance and commitment?

3. Are you having difficulty overcoming your old beliefs about disciplining children? If you were permissive in the past, do you sometimes think you are being unfair and feel like giving in? If you used punishment in the past, do you feel like you are being too lenient now and that you should be doing more? Share your experiences with other group members.

4. How much resistance are you encountering? Is the resistance coming from your children? From your spouse? From other family members? From friends and neighbors? From within yourself? From a combination of these sources? Share your experiences with other group members. Is the resistance greater than you expected?

5. Do you find yourself holding on to some of the myths about the change process? Did you think change would be easier than it really is?

6. How realistic are your expectations now? Are they too high? If so, do you think you might be setting yourself up for disappointment? Share your expectations for change with other group members. Ask others if they think you are being realistic.

7. How comfortable do you feel with the new methods you're using? Did you expect you would feel more comfortable than you do? Is this discouraging to you? Share with others what it feels like to use the new methods you're learning.

8. Where are you on the support vs. resistance scale?

9. If you need more ongoing support, what steps are you going to take to get it? What is your plan?

10. Will it be important for you to enlist support from your children's teachers or care providers to establish consistency between your methods and theirs? How are you going to approach them? What is your plan?

SUGGESTIONS FOR GETTING STARTED

I recommend starting off with the following skills for children of different ages. I've also included a suggested schedule for adding new skills as you move along. These suggestions are based on my experiences with my clients and parents in my workshops. You may prefer to add new skills to your repertoire at a faster or slower rate.

Whatever you choose, I encourage you to go at a pace that is comfortable to you. This may mean adding one or two new skills each week for some of you or adding one new skill every two or three weeks for others. There is no one correct way, but I caution against trying to learn too much too quickly.

Expect to make mistakes when you begin using the new methods. That's OK. The more you practice, the more proficient you will become. If you are having particular difficulty with any one method, refer back to the pertinent chapter for assistance. Note the specific language used to set up each technique in the examples.

GETTING STARTED WITH TWO-YEAR-OLDS
Week 1

Clear verbal messages	Chapter Four
Encouraging messages	Chapter Six
Role-modeling	Chapter Seven
Logical consequences	Chapter Eight

Week 2

Add try it again	Chapter Seven

Week 3

Add limited choices	Chapter Seven
(If child has sufficient language to understand your choices)	

GETTING STARTED WITH THREE- TO SEVEN-YEAR-OLDS

Week 1

Clear verbal messages	Chapter Four
Check-in, cut-off, cool down	Chapter Five
(Select methods needed)	
Encouraging messages	Chapter Six
Logical consequences	Chapter Eight
Time-out procedure	Chapter Eight

Week 2

Add try it again	Chapter Seven

Week 3

Add natural consequences	Chapter Eight
Add role-modeling	Chapter Seven

Week 4

Add limited choices	Chapter Seven

GETTING STARTED WITH EIGHT- TO TWELVE-YEAR-OLDS

Week 1

Clear verbal messages	Chapter Four
Check-in, cut-off, cool-down	Chapter Five
(Select methods needed)	
Encouraging messages	Chapter Six
Logical consequences	Chapter Eight
Time-out procedure	Chapter Eight

Week 2

Add try it again	Chapter Seven
Add role-modeling	Chapter Seven

Week 3

Add limited choices	Chapter Seven

Week 4

Adding exploring choices	Chapter Seven
(For 10- to 12-year-olds)	
Add natural consequences	Chapter Eight

GETTING STARTED WITH TEENS
Week 1

Clear verbal messages	Chapter Four
Check-in, cut-off, cool-down	Chapter Five
(Select the methods needed)	
Encouraging messages	Chapter Six
Exploring choices	Chapter Seven
Logical consequences	Chapter Eight

Week 2

Add limited choices	Chapter Seven

Week 3

Add time-out procedure	Chapter Eight
(For disrespectful behavior)	

Week 4

Add natural consequences	Chapter Eight

Appendix

Starting a Parent Study Group

Purpose of the Group

1. To help group participants practice and improve their skills.

2. To provide support during the critical first eight weeks of the program.

Suggested Length

The recommended length for the group is seven weeks with an optional session in the eighth week to cover problems with chores and homework (Chapters Ten and Eleven). Most parents find this optional session extremely helpful.

Separate Groups for Children (Ages Two to Twelve) and Teens

The basic methods in this book apply to all children, preschoolers to teens, but we need to make some adjustments in how the methods are used with teens. For this reason, I recommend offering separate study groups for parents of teens and of younger children (ages two to twelve). Separate treatment will minimize confusion and allow participants to focus on only the methods they need to learn.

Preparation for Study Groups

I recommend that all group participants read the entire book prior to becoming involved in a group. This preparation will lead to a much richer workshop experience.

Study Group Leaders

Ideally, a parent study group leader should have a solid working command of the material in the book as well as some formal training in child development, learning theory, and group dynamics. Teachers, guidance counselors, social workers, psychologists, and a variety of other helping professionals are good candidates for study group leaders.

Study Group Questions and Exercises

Study questions and practice exercises that cover major themes and methods are provided at the end of each Chapter. The questions and exercises are intended to get participants more involved with the material and to give them opportunities to practice the methods in a supportive setting.

Don't feel limited by the questions and exercises I've provided. These are only suggested items for practice and discussion. Feel free to add additional questions or practice exercises that might help participants become better acquainted with the material. I also recommend setting aside the last thirty minutes of each session for a question and answer period.

Overview of Study Sessions

Week 1
Objective: Parents will develop a better understanding of the teaching and learning process.
Preparation: Review Chapters One and Two.
Discussion questions.
Practice exercises.

Week 2
Objective: Parents will learn to recognize their family dance.

Preparation: Review Chapter Three.
Discussion questions.
Practice exercises.

Week 3
Objectives: Parents will learn to identify the type of limits they've used in the past, learn new skills for giving clear messages, and learn three highly effective methods for stopping their family dances.
Preparation: Review Chapters Four and Five.
Discussion questions.
Practice exercises.

Week 4
Objective: Parents will learn how to use encouraging messages to inspire their children's cooperation.
Preparation: Review Chapter Six.
Discussion questions.
Practice exercises.

Week 5
Objective: Parents will learn four highly effective techniques for teaching children decision-making and problem-solving skills.
Preparation: Review Chapter Seven (Chapter Nine for teens).
Discussion questions (adapt for teens).
Practice exercises (adapt for teens).

Week 6
Objective: Parents will learn how to stop misbehavior and support their rules with effective consequences.
Preparation: Review Chapter Eight (Chapter Nine for teens).
Discussion questions (adapt for teens from Chapter Nine).
Practice exercises (adapt for teens from Chapter Nine).

Week 7
Objective: Parents will discuss specific steps they can take to prepare and support themselves for the changes they will experience.
Preparation: Review Chapter Twelve.
Discussion questions.
Practice exercises.

Week 8 (optional session)
Objective: Parents will learn to apply the methods they've learned to handle problems with chores or homework.
Preparation: Review Chapters Ten and Eleven.
Discussion: Use a question and answer format.

Suggested Reading

Adler, A. *What Life Should Mean to You.* New York: Capricorn Books, 1958.

Adler, A. *Superiority and Social Interest.* Illinois: Northwestern University Press, 1964.

Ansbacher, H., and Ansbacher, R. *The Individual Psychology of Alfred Adler.* New York: Harper Touchbooks, 1964.

Bandura, A. *Social Learning Theory.* Englewood Cliffs, N.J.: Prentice-Hall, 1977.

Dinkmeyer, D., and Dreikurs, R. *Encouraging Children to Learn: The Encouragement Process.* Englewood Cliffs, N.J.: Prentice-Hall, 1963.

Dinkmeyer, D., and McKay, G. *Raising a Responsible Child.* New York: Simon & Schuster, 1973.

Dreikurs, R., and Grey, L. *A New Approach to Discipline: Logical Consequences.* New York: Hawthorne Books, Inc., 1968.

Dreikurs, R., and Soltz, V. *Children: The Challenge.* New York: Hawthorne Books, Inc., 1964.

Elkind, D. *Children and Adolescents: Interpretive Essays on Jean Piaget.* New York: Basic Books, Inc., 1981.

Erikson, E. *Childhood and Society* (2nd ed.). New York: Norton & Company, 1963.

Fisch, R.; Weakland, J. H.; and Segal, L. *The Tactics of Change: Doing Therapy Briefly.* San Francisco: Jossey-Bass, 1982.

Glasser, W. *Control Theory.* New York: HarperCollins, 1984.

Goldenberg, I., and Goldenberg, H. *Family Therapy: An Overview.* Monterey: Brooks/Cole Publishing, 1985.

Jackson, D. D. "Family Rules: Marital Quid Pro Quo." *Archives of General Psychiatry* 12 (1965): 589–594.

Jackson, D. D. "The Study of the Family." *Family Process* 4 (1965): 1–20.

Kohlberg, L. "The Development of Children's Orientations Toward a Moral Order: I. Sequence in the Development of Moral Thought." *Vita Humana* 6 (1963): 11–33.

Kohlberg, L. "Stage and Sequence: The Cognitive-Developmental Approach to Socialization. In D. A. Goslin (ed.), *Handbook of Socialization Theory and Research.* (347–480). Chicago: Rand McNally, 1966.

Losoncy, L. *Turning People On: How to Be an Encouraging Person.* Englewood Cliffs, N.J.: Prentice-Hall, 1977.

Minuchin, S. *Families and Family Therapy.* Cambridge, Mass.: Harvard University Press, 1974.

Piaget, J., and Inhelder, B. *The Psychology of the Child.* New York: Basic Books, Inc., 1969.

Wadsworth, B. J. *Piaget's Theory of Cognitive and Affective Development* (4th ed.). New York: Longman Publishing, 1989.

Index

Accountability. *See also* Consequences; Firm limits
for homework, 280–283
Action messages. *See also* Encouraging messages; Mixed messages; Verbal messages
discouraging messages and, 126–127
firm limits and, 97–98
permissive training and, 50–51
punitive training and, 62–65, 67
soft limits and, 92–93
and teaching rules, 35–38, 43, 96
Adlerian psychology, 170
Adolescents. *See* Teenagers
Ages of children
chores for different, 260–265
retraining with different, 317–319
Aggressive behavior, 186–187
Allowances, for chores, 257–259
Anger. *See* Cool-down technique; Tantrums
Antagonism, 185–186
Arguing, 88–89
Assignments. *See* Homework
Authority
limits and, 78
limit-testing behavior and, 80
Autocratic training. *See* Punitive training
Automobiles, time-out procedure in, 191

Bargaining, 87–88
Bribes, 89–91

Carelessness, 167
Cars, time-out procedure in, 191
Changing training techniques. *See* Retraining
Check-in procedure, 107–110. *See also* Techniques
Choices. *See* Exploring choices; Limited choices
Chores, 241–266
allowances for, 257–259
for children of different ages, 260–265
chore charts, 259–260
firm limits and, 251–253
play and, 253–257
soft limits and, 248–251
starting with older children, 245–248
starting with young children, 241–245
Clean slate
consequences and, 165
time-out procedure and, 183–184
Comfort range, 300
Communications skills. *See* Action messages; Discouraging messages; Encouraging messages; Mixed messages; Verbal messages
Consequences, 157–200. *See also* Logical consequences; Natural consequences; Techniques; Time-out procedure
clean slate and, 165
consistency of, 161–162
in democratic training, 24
effective, 160–166, 176–177
firm limits and, 96

Consequences *(continued)*
homework and, 277, 279–
280, 283–284
immediacy of, 161
importance of, 158–160
limit-testing behavior and,
158–160
overview of, 157–158, 197
parent study-group questions
about, 198–200
in permissive training, 16
physical control and, 194–197
in punitive training, 7–8
relatedness of, 162–163
retraining and, 299
role modeling and, 163–164
for teenagers, 216–217,
233–235, 284
time limits and, 164–165
Consistency
of consequences, 161–162
soft limits and, 91
Cool-down technique, 113–
117. *See also* Techniques
Cooperation. *See also* Democratic training
discouraging messages and,
121–122
encouraging, 121–122, 127–
130, 133
permissive training and, 17
Corrective behavior
encouraging, 131–132
teaching, 142–144
Cut-off technique, 110–113.
See also Techniques

Dances. *See* Family dance
Dawdling
consequences and, 173–174
homework and, 291–292
Debating, 88–89
Decision-making skills. *See* Problem-solving skills; Tech-
niques
Defiance, 185–186

Democratic training, 20–29. *See
also* Permissive training;
Punitive training
diagram of, 21–23
examples of, 2–4, 21–22,
24–25, 27–29
overview of, 21
strengths of, 20–21
teaching rules via, 33–35,
41–43
teenagers and, 230–231
Destructive behavior, 175–176
Directions, unclear, 86–87
Discipline. *See* Consequences;
Democratic training; Per-
missive training; Punitive
training; Techniques
Discouraging messages, 121–
127, 136–138. *See also* Encouraging messages; Mixed
messages; Verbal messages
action messages and, 126–127
cooperation and, 121–122
versus encouraging messages,
121–122, 136
family dance and, 122–125
parent study-group questions
about, 137–138
verbal messages and, 125–126
Disrespect, 185
Dreikurs, R., 170

Encouraging messages, 121–
122, 127–138. *See also* Discouraging messages; Mixed
messages; Verbal messages
for acceptable actions, 131–
132
for better choices, 130–131
consequences and, 165
cooperation and, 121–122,
127–130, 133
versus discouraging messages,
121–122, 136
for improvement, 134–136
for independence, 133–134

parent study-group questions about, 137–138
role modeling and, 142–144
Erikson, E., 203
Exercises. *See* Parent study-group questions
Experimentation, self-discovery and, 203–204
Exploring choices. *See also* Limited choices; Techniques
encouraging messages and, 130–131
teaching problem solving via, 146–148
with teenagers, 213–216

Family dance, 47–75. *See also* Techniques
anger and, 114–115
comfort range and, 300
defined, xiv, 47–48
discouraging messages and, 122–125
family history and, 52–53, 56–57, 65–66, 69–70
homework and, 267–270
parent study-group questions about, 73–75
permissive, 48–59
punitive, 59–71
stopping, 57–59, 71–72, 105–107
Family members, retraining and, 302–307
Firm limits, 93–98. *See also* Limits; Rules; Soft limits
action messages and, 97–98
chores and, 251–253
defined, 93–94, 98–99
encouraging messages and, 121–122
guidelines for, 94–98
myths about, 308
parent study-group questions about, 103
questions about, 100–102

versus soft limits, 98–99
verbal messages and, 97
Flexible limits, 208–211. *See also* Limits; Teenagers
Follow-through, ineffective, 91–92
Forgetfulness, 167–168
Freedom, teenagers and, 209–211, 230–231

Grandparents, family dance and, 52–53, 56–57, 65–66, 69–70
Ground rules. *See* Rules
Group leaders, 323

Homework, 267–295
adapting to balanced system for, 285–289
choosing time for, 275–278
consequences and, 277, 279–280, 283–284
creating a place for, 278–279
dawdling and, 291–292
evaluating problems with, 289–290
family dance and, 267–270
imbalanced system for, 271–275
limit-testing behavior and, 285–286
monitoring system for, 280–283
parent study-group questions about, 294–295
parents' role in, 267–268, 271–275, 279
purpose of, 270–271
questions about, 290–293
rewards and, 293
teachers' role in, 267–268, 273, 279
three steps for balanced system, 279–285
Hopes, soft limits and, 83–84

Ignoring misbehavior, 85–86
Immediacy of consequences, 161
Improvement, encouraging,
    134–136
Inconsistency
    consequences and, 161–162
    soft limits and, 91
Independence
    encouraging, 133–134
    homework and, 270–271
Individuation. *See* Self-discovery
Instruction. *See* Problem-solving
    skills; Rules; Techniques
Intellectual development, in
    teenagers, 202–203
Irresponsibility. *See* Responsibil-
    ity

Jail, versus time-out procedure,
    179–181
Jobs. *See* Chores

Language. *See* Discouraging
    messages; Encouraging
    messages; Mixed messages;
    Verbal messages
Leaders, study-group, 323
Learning rules. *See* Rules; Tech-
    niques
Lectures, 84–85
Limited choices. *See also* Explor-
    ing choices; Techniques
    chores and, 251–253
    examples of, 151–154
    guidelines for, 149–150
    logical consequences and,
        171–172
    questions about, 150–151
    teaching problem solving via,
        148–149
    time-out procedure and,
        182–183
    "Try it again" technique and,
        145

Limits, 77–103. *See also* Conse-
    quences; Firm limits; Rules;
    Soft limits; Teenagers
    flexible, 204–208
    importance of, 78
    overview of, 77–78, 98–99
    parent study-group questions
        about, 103
    questions about, 100–102
Limit-testing behavior
    consequences and, 158–160
    cut-off technique and, 110–
        113
    homework and, 285–286
    limit setting and, 78–81
    myths about, 308
    retraining and, 299–300
    in teenagers, 204, 217–230,
        231–233, 235–236
    time-out procedure and,
        182–183, 184–185
Logical consequences, 169–
    178. *See also* Consequences
    chores and, 251–253
    guidelines for, 170–174
    ineffective, 176–177
    overview of, 169–170
    questions about, 177–178
    teenagers and, 233–234,
        235–236
    "Try it again" technique and,
        145
    when to use, 174–176

Messages. *See* Action messages;
    Discouraging messages; En-
    couraging messages; Mixed
    messages; Verbal messages
Messiness, 175, 211–212, 217–
    223. *See also* Chores
Mistakes, myths about, 308–309
Misusing possessions
    logical consequences for,
        174–175
    natural consequences for, 167
Mixed messages, 35–38

Mixed training, 25–27
Monitoring system, for homework, 280–283
Myths, about change, 307–309

Natural consequences. *See also* Consequences
overview of, 166–167
teenagers and, 233–234
using, 167–169
Negative reinforcement. *See* Discouraging messages

Parent study-group questions. *See also* Questions
chores, 266
consequences, 198–200
encouragement, 137–138
family dance, 73–75
homework, 294–295
limits, 103
problem-solving skills, 155–156
purpose of, 323
retraining, 315–316
rules, 46
stopping family dance, 118–119
teenagers, 238–240
training methods, 30–32
Parent study-groups, starting, 322–325
Parents
family dance and, 52–53, 56–57, 65–66, 69–70
homework and, 267–268, 271–275, 279
support systems for, 309, 311–313
Partners, retraining and, 302–307
Permissive training, 11–20. *See also* Democratic training; Punitive training
comfort range and, 300
diagram of, 15

examples of, 2–4, 12–13, 17–20
family dance and, 48–59
limitations of, 14–17, 18–20
mixed with punitive training, 25–27
overview of, 19
retraining and, 306
teaching rules via, 33–34, 39–41
time-out procedure and, 180
Physical control, 194–197
Piaget, J., 35, 202, 213
Play, chores and, 253–257
Positive reinforcement. *See* Encouraging messages
Power
limits and, 78
limit-testing behavior and, 80
Practice exercises. *See* Parent study-group questions
Privileges, consequences and, 176
Problem-solving skills, 139–156. *See also* Exploring choices; Limited choices; Techniques
parent study-group questions about, 155–156
role modeling and, 140–144
teenagers and, 203, 211–212, 231–233
"Try it again" technique and, 144–146
Procrastination, 173–174
Punishment. *See* Consequences; Firm limits; Punitive training; Techniques
Punitive training, 5–11. *See also* Democratic training; Permissive training
comfort range and, 300
diagram of, 6–8
examples of, 2–4, 5–6, 9–11
family dance and, 59–71
limitations of, 8–9

Punitive training *(continued)*
  mixed with permissive train-
    ing, 25–27
  overview of, 11
  retraining and, 306
  teaching rules via, 33–34,
    38–39
  time-out procedure and,
    179–180
Questions. *See also* Parent study-
    group questions
  about homework, 290–293
  about limited choices, 150–
    154
  about limits, 100–102
  about logical consequences,
    177–178
  about rules, 44–45
  about time-out procedure,
    191–194

Rages. *See* Tantrums
Relatedness, of consequences,
    162–163
Reminding, soft limits and, 84
Resistance
  coping with, 302–307
  discouraging messages and,
    121–125
  to retraining, 302–307
  support systems and, 309–313
Responsibility
  homework and, 271–275
  natural consequences and, 167
  Saturday basket and, 244
  teenagers and, 209–211
Restaurants, time-out procedure
    at, 190–191
Retraining, 297–319
  myths about, 307–309
  parent study-group questions
    about, 315–316
  programs for children by age,
    317–319
  resistance to, 302–307
  rewards of, 313–314

support systems for, 309–313
  understanding process of,
    300–302
  what to expect in, 298–300
Rewards
  homework and, 293
  of retraining, 313–314
  soft limits and, 89–91
Role-modeling. *See also* Tech-
    niques
  chores and, 253
  consequences and, 163–164
  ineffective, 87
  teaching problem solving via,
    140–144
Rules, 33–46. *See also* Conse-
    quences; Firm limits;
    Limits; Soft limits
  action messages and teaching,
    35–38, 43, 96
  democratic training and, 33–
    35, 41–43
  how children learn, 33–35
  parent study-group questions
    about, 46
  permissive training and, 33–
    34, 39–41
  punitive training and, 33–34,
    38–39
  questions about, 44–45
  redefining for teenagers,
    217–230
  teaching effectively, 41–43
  teaching ineffectively, 35–38
  time-out procedure and, 183
  verbal messages and teaching,
    35–38, 43, 96

Saturday basket, 244
Self-discovery
  limit setting and, 204–208
  in teenagers, 203–204
Sermons, 84–85
Sharing, 169–170
Shopping, time-out procedure
    when, 188–190

Shoulds, soft limits and, 83–84
Soft limits, 81–93. *See also* Firm
     limits; Limits; Rules
   action messages and, 92–93
   arguing and debating and,
     88–89
   bargaining and, 87–88
   bribes and, 89–91
   chores and, 248–251
   defined, xiii, 81–83, 98–99
   discouraging language and,
     121
   versus firm limits, 98–99
   follow-through and, 91–92
   ignoring misbehavior and,
     85–86
   parent study-group questions
     about, 103
   parental inconsistency and, 91
   questions about, 100–102
   repeating and reminding and,
     84
   rewards and, 89–91
   role modeling and, 87
   speeches, lectures, and ser-
     mons and, 84–85
   teenagers and, 217–218
   unclear directions and, 86–87
   wishes, hopes, and shoulds
     and, 83–84
Speech. *See* Discouraging mes-
     sages; Encouraging mes-
     sages; Mixed messages; Ver-
     bal messages
Speeches, 84–85
Spouses, retraining and, 302–
     307
Study-group leaders, 323

Tantrums
   retraining and, 302–304
   time-out procedure and,
     183–184, 187–188
Teachers, homework and, 267–
     268, 273, 279

Teaching rules. *See* Rules; Tech-
     niques
Techniques. *See also* Conse-
     quences; Encouraging
     messages; Exploring
     choices; Limited choices;
     Problem-solving skills;
     Role-modeling; Time-out
     procedure
   check-in procedure, 107–110
   cool-down technique, 113–
     117
   cut-off technique, 110–113
   "Try it again" technique,
     143–146
Teenagers, 201–240
   consequences for, 216–217,
     233–235, 284
   decision making and, 211–
     212
   democratic training and,
     230–231
   exploring choices with, 213–
     216
   flexible limits for, 204–208
   intellectual development in,
     202–203
   limit setting for, 208–211
   limit-testing behavior in, 204,
     231–233, 235–236
   overview of, 201–202, 236–
     237
   parent study-group questions
     about, 238–240
   problem solving and, 203,
     211–212, 231–233
   redefining ground rules for,
     217–230
   retraining program for, 319
   self-discovery in, 203–204
   starting parent study-groups
     for, 322
Testing behavior. *See* Limit-test-
     ing behavior
Time limits, consequences and,
     164–165

Time-out procedure, 178–194.
    See also Techniques
  guidelines for, 181–184
  versus jail, 179–181
  outside the home, 188–191
  overview of, 178–181
  questions about, 191–194
  when to use, 184–188
Timers, use of, 173–174, 182
Training models. *See* Demo-
    cratic training; Mixed train-
    ing; Permissive training;
    Punitive training; Retrain-
    ing
"Try it again" technique, 143–
    146. *See also* Techniques

Unclear directions, 86–87

Verbal messages. *See also* Action
    messages; Encouraging
    messages; Firm limits; Soft
    limits
  discouraging messages and,
    125–126
  firm limits and, 97
  guidelines for, 94–98
  mixed, 35–38
  permissive training and, 50–
    51
  punitive training and, 62–65,
    67
  and teaching rules, 35–38,
    43, 96
Violent behavior, 186–187

Wishes, soft limits and, 83–84
Work. *See* Chores

A TRIO OF BOOKS ON PARENTING

Best-selling parenting expert Jane Nelsen, Ed.D., and co-authors offer real solutions to parenting problems.

Positive Discipline A-Z:
1001 Solutions to Everyday Parenting Problems
by Jane Nelsen, Ed.D., H. Stephen Glenn, and
Lynn Lott, M.A., M.F.C.C. $14.95

Using her nationally acclaimed positive discipline approach, Jane Nelsen and co-authors H. Stephen Glenn and Lynn Lott offer short, practical, "what to do" solutions to parenting dilemmas in an alphabetized, A to Z format. This book not only helps you solve problem behavior but also helps your children feel good about themselves, gain self-confidence and self-discipline, learn responsibility, and develop problem-solving skills.

Positive Discipline for Single Parents
by Jane Nelsen, Ed.D., Cheryl Erwin, and
Carol Delzer, J.D., M.A. $12.95

Jane Nelsen has teamed up with two single mothers to emphasize ways that single parents can make clear, focused discipline decisions while maintaining positive levels of interaction with their children. Single parents can learn how to turn what is often thought to be a disadvantage into an empowering and victorious experience.

Raising Self-Reliant Children in a Self-Indulgent World
H. Stephen Glenn and Jane Nelsen, Ed.D. $12.95

Those who think in terms of leniency versus strictness will be disappointed. This book goes beyond these issues to teach children to be responsible and self-reliant—not through fear and intimidation, which are outer-directed concerns (what happens when the disciplinarian is on vacation or asleep?), but through feeling accountable to one's commitments (inner-directed behavior).

FILL IN AND MAIL TODAY

PRIMA PUBLISHING
P.O. BOX 1260BK
ROCKLIN, CA 95677

USE YOUR VISA/MC AND ORDER BY PHONE:
(916) 632-4400 (M-F 9:00-4:00 PST)

Please send me the following titles:

Quantity	Title	Amount
_____	_____	_____
_____	_____	_____
_____	_____	_____
_____	_____	_____
_____	_____	_____

Subtotal $_____

Postage & Handling
($4.00 for the first book
plus $1.00 each additional book) $ _____

Sales Tax
7.25% Sales Tax (California only)
8.25% Sales Tax (Tennessee only)
5.00% Sales Tax (Maryland only)
7.00% General Service Tax (Canada) $_____

TOTAL *(U.S. funds only)* $_____

❏ Check enclosed for $_____(payable to Prima Publishing)

Charge my   ❏ Master Card   ❏ Visa

Account No. _____Exp. Date _____

Signature _____

Your Name _____

Address _____

City/State/Zip _____

Daytime Telephone _____

Satisfaction is guaranteed— or your money back!
Please allow three to four weeks for delivery.
THANK YOU FOR YOUR ORDER